GOVERNORS STATE UNIVERSITY LIBRARY

W9-ALV-775

3 1611 00123 1718

QUALITY OF LIFE FOR HANDICAPPED PEOPLE

The 'Rehabilitation Education' series examines developments and innovations in research and practice concerning the education and welfare of handicapped people. The scope of the series extends well beyond the classroom, hospital or institution.

Volume 3 in this series discusses the very important and timely topic of 'quality of life'. This issue is now seen as of central importance to a client-centred approach by teachers and health and welfare personnel. The book should therefore be of great interest to all academics, professionals and service providers concerned with handicapped children and adults.

Edited by Roy I. Brown, Director of Rehabilitation Studies, University of Calgary

REHABILITATION EDUCATION: A SERIES IN
DEVELOPMENTAL HANDICAP

Edited by Roy I. Brown, University of Calgary

Quality of Life for Handicapped People

Edited by
ROY I. BROWN

WITHDRAWN

UNIVERSITY LIBRARY
GOVERNORS STATE UNIVERSITY
UNIVERSITY PARK, IL 60466

CROOM HELM
London • New York • Sydney

HV 1568 .Q92x 1988

228804

Quality of life for
handicapped people

© 1988 Roy I. Brown
Croom Helm Ltd, Provident House, Burrell Row,
Beckenham, Kent, BR3 1AT

Croom Helm Australia, 44-50 Waterloo Road,
North Ryde, 2113, New South Wales

Published in the USA by
Croom Helm
in association with Methuen, Inc.
29 West 35th Street
New York, NY 10001

British Library Cataloguing in Publication Data

Quality of life for handicapped people. —
   (Rehabilitation education; V.3).
   1. Rehabilitation
   I. Brown, Roy I. II. Series
   362.4'048   HV1568

   ISBN 0-7099-3992-2

Library of Congress Cataloging-in-Publication Data
ISBN 0-7099-3992-2

Printed and bound in Great Britain
by Billing & Sons Limited, Worcester.

CONTENTS

GOVERNORS STATE UNIVERSITY
UNIVERSITY PARK
IL 60466

GOVERNORS STATE UNIVERSITY
UNIVERSITY PARK
IL 60466

GOVERNORS STATE UNIVERSITY
UNIVERSITY PARK
IL 60466

PREFACE

This book is the third in a series on Rehabilitation Education. The volume is particularly
concerned with issues relating to quality of life.
It is timely to discuss what is meant by quality
of life and the types of measures and systems
which will be required to measure the variables
involved. The area is new and therefore many
issues remain unresolved. The development of this
concept and its application is likely to play a
major role in the development of and changes to
the delivery of services in the coming decade.
Probably the most critical aspect will be the
direct role that clients and sponsors play in this
process. It is becoming recognized that they must
be given or seize the opportunity to play a more
dominant role in designing and selecting the types
of services that they require, and the people who
will be responsible for delivering the services to
them.
     Rehabilitation Education, which in these
volumes portrays the involvement and interaction
of psychological, social, educational and allied
processes underlines the pivotal issue concerning
how the individual feels about him or herself, and
the ways in which the individual perceives
services enhancing his or her development and
overall rehabilitation. Unless the individual
becomes personally committed to this process, it
is unlikely that any of the changes that are made
will have major or lasting impact on the
individual.
     An attempt has been made to ensure that a
range of disabilities are included in the various
chapters in this book. In other volumes it has
been argued that there are underlying principles

GOVERNORS STATE UNIVERSITY
UNIVERSITY PARK
IL. 60466

of Rehabilitation Education which apply across all disability areas and this theme is still underlined. Chapters are concerned with environment and the improvement of environment for disabled individuals. There is some examination of programmes in areas of poverty and crowding, including their cost evaluation. There is a look at a variety of vocational and social programmes both from the individual client's perspective and from that of service delivery. It is felt appropriate that the area of fine arts and religion should be discussed.

The material is directed towards a wide range of professionals in the areas that have been mentioned, but it is also felt that the book will be particularly helpful to practitioners, administrators, and a variety of research workers. It is anticipated that some of the material may be very relevant to students in both college and university systems where there is increasing attention to rehabilitation as defined in this book.

Little has been mentioned about government services, and yet it is the personnel in these services which need to look closely at quality of life issues for disabled persons. Some will argue that disabled persons do not make up a very large portion of the population, and yet increasingly we come to recognize that most of us at some time in our lives are likely to have need of services which are critically influenced by the views of administrators and practitioners concerning quality of life of the people they serve.

R.I.B.

ACKNOWLEDGEMENT

I wish to thank a number of people for helping in the preparation of this book. The various chapter authors dealt with various concerns and suggestions in a timely manner which was much appreciated. Thanks are due to UNICEF, the National Institute of Public Cooperation and Child Development, India, and the Ministry of Human Resource Development, India, for permission to produce figures and tables in the chapter by Tehal Kohli. It is appropriate to thank the three colleagues - Dr. Trevor Parmenter, Mr. Barry Gray, and Mrs. Anna Lou Pickett - who wrote country sections in Aileen Wight Felske's chapter on practitioner training. I would also like to thank Dr. Ed Whelan, University of Manchester, for his helpful suggestions on the chapter by Patrick McGinley. Finally I would like to thank Linda Culshaw who, as in the previous two volumes, carried out the typing and preparation on word processor. She has not only committed the authors' words to print, but has carefully checked through material making certain that omissions and errors are minimized. Finally I am grateful to Mr. Tim Hardwick of Croom Helm for his advice and usual encouragement to ensure that this series of volumes remains on time.

R.I.B.

Chapter One

QUALITY OF LIFE AND REHABILITATION: AN INTRODUCTION

Roy I. Brown

Quality of life is a concept which has major
implications for the field of rehabilitation, but
it is a complex term and ill-defined. In one
sense quality of life is a logical extension of
the concept of normalization. It has relevance to
national guidelines on standards of service and
living conditions. It is directed to an examination of our awareness of needs and standards and
leads naturally to evaluation procedures (Bonano
et al., 1982). Perhaps of more importance, the
measurement of quality of life relates to both
subjective and objective criteria and includes
aspects of external behaviour, personal perception and descriptors of the environment. It will
be apparent from reading the following chapters
that quality of life expresses itself idiosyn-
cratically, although there are common elements
from individual to individual. It is this
uniqueness that links quality of life to
individual programme planning. Quality of life
relates to improvement and is affected negatively
by deterioration in skill or performance. But
over a lifespan compensations can be made.
Individuals have different wishes and different
perceptions of personal fulfilment. Quality of
life is partly concerned with internal processes,
which are not readily measured by the traditional
techniques accepted by psychologists. The views
that the individual has about him or herself, the
enjoyment that an individual experiences, and the
problems that he or she faces help to make up this
quality. It is, in essence, a phenomenon which
recognizes, regardless of level of disability, the
personal needs and perceptions of each individual
which necessarily lead to changes in service

1

Introduction

directions and the way that rehabilitation
personnel are trained (see later Wight Felske).
Blunden (see later) notes the use of diaries
and interviews to chart changes in people's
location, activity and contact. Such methods as
diaries and cassette tape recordings have been
used by Brown et al. (1986) to allow people to
report their personal opinions about quality of
life and experience. The soft systems analysis
described by Checkland (1981) which allows for
some qualitative assessment of variables which may
not be easily subject to mathematical expression
at this point in time is of particular interest.
Various authors in these chapters on quality of
life appear to have used comparable techniques
quite independently of one another.
It is recognized that strategies and aspects
of failure, sadness and depression may not
necessarily be associated with negative qualities
of life. Thus quality of life is a global concept
and not just something happening at one point in
time. It is an integrated and flexible process.
The following chapters are intended to
examine some aspects of quality of life, and
relate to various types of disabling conditions.
Some of the chapters represent studies in the
field of mental handicap, and others relate more
clearly to the physical disabilities, but, as
argued in previous volumes, it is believed that
the major principles and issues involved may have
application across age and disability groups.
Therefore this book is not directed towards one
particular disability group, and it is suggested
that research workers and practitioners may wish
to look at a wide range of perceptions and
measures from various disability areas including
developmental handicap, mental health, criminality
and aging in coming to a personal view on quality
of life. The object of this book is to attempt to
make the reader more aware of some aspects of
quality of life which may be important in
improving the standard of living and experiences
of persons with disabilities.
Quality of life relates to different communities and different settings, and an attempt has
been made to introduce aspects of quality of life
from developing countries as well as more
advantageous settings. It is recognized that
economy, local attitudes, political climate and
professional skill may all be relevant variables.
That quality of life can be improved in a cost

effective manner at a community level is demonstrated in Kohli's chapter. Quality of life is
not simply associated with professional services,
competence and knowledge, for it is the people who
surround an individual, the situations in which
individuals live, and their future prospects for
continued life or increasing standard of living
which may be perceived as important. However,
perhaps more than many other areas in applied
science, the actions of the professional should be
partly determined by the expressed views of the
individual and the individual's representatives,
such as guardian or advocate, and are also
affected by what local community, friends,
neighbours and relatives do and say.

Quality of life puts the accent not just on
employment, and therefore vocational training, but
on educational, social, interpersonal and leisure
activities which require a broad range of integrated training. Quality of life accents all
aspects of the individual's behaviour and his or
her integration with the environment, including
particular prosthetic devices and strategies to
overcome handicap.

Certain aspects of quality of life are more
likely to be associated with one particular age
group than another. The ability to improve and to
control one's environment are recognized as
important aspects of quality of life.

Quality of life as an holistic concept
precipitates a number of issues which, although
coming to the fore in legal arguments and in
professional practice, are most clearly
exemplified in the study of day-to-day living.
Quality of life involves talking about an
individual's perception of his or her life. What
an individual feels and thinks represent important
quality of life statements, and may have little to
do with the nature of a disability. Therefore,
without a knowledge of the disabled person's
thoughts and feelings, we may be able to say
little about quality of life. Where handicap is
very great, or when the individual is very young,
and perhaps when he or she is very old, other
individuals need to become responsible for
ensuring that quality life experience is present.
A personal and detailed knowledge of the
individual concerned is still critical.

A number of ethical questions are raised. At
what point are we in a position to say that an
individual has no say, or a limited say, in his or

3

her quality of life? For example, if an individual shows certain behavioural characteristics, should he or she be deprived of freedom or should the individual be given an opportunity within an environment which provides support? For example, an individual who has committed a range of negative behaviour or misdemeanours, including aggressive outbursts, may be seen by some as requiring institutionalization, not just for his or her own good, but for the protection of society. Others may believe the person can survive in society, provided certain supporting structures are present, but the availability of structures may be few and far between within the society concerned. The legal system may not reflect the changing knowledge base in relation to rehabilitation, thus may not support the necessary structures for improvement in quality of life, or may at times produce rulings which make rehabilitation and improvement in quality of life a near impossibility.

Individuals with disabilities may have a different perspective, believing that they must learn to cope, but at times find they are out of control and unable to show appropriate social behaviour. A parent, though the person may be a young adult, may feel that the individual should not be away from home or away from professional supervision, yet the parent may have no status in the eyes of the law in terms of parenting. The laws of guardianship or dependency may not be present or adequate, or may be applied for reasons of expediency rather than on a basis of knowledge of rehabilitation education.

This book does not deal with the legal aspects of rehabilitation, although these are extremely important in relation to quality of life, but it does try to tease out some of the variables which are important in developing and delineating quality of life. In a number of countries it is becoming increasingly common for systems of brokerage and contracting to be carried out between an individual client, or his or her representative, and a professional group. Thus, in theory, an individual, or the guardian or sponsor in law, is able to contract professional workers and the type of support or attention deemed advisable. Such systems at best provide for and recognize that a) the individual is not a patient in the traditional sense of the word, b) integration in programming across life domains is

important, and c) the individuals or their representatives may dismiss their professional support
if they perceive performance as inadequate or
undesirable. These characteristics are at
variance with the policies of most formal
agencies. Such a system recognizes that involvement may not be agency bound, but involve local
community and personal constraints and interests.
But there is a price to pay, for individuals may
not be able to recognize easily when they are
unable to make judgments effectively. This is a
very different statement from saying that their
judgment is correct or incorrect. Many of us, and
all of us from time to time, disagree with the
judgments or procedures adopted by our colleagues
or friends, yet we have a right to such judgments
and procedures under most circumstances,
particularly if they concern our quality of life.
Therefore, part of the judgment process required
in the application of a professional service is
not simply whether it is in the best interests of
the individual, but whether the individual is in a
position to make a consciously reasoned judgment
about particular situations.

Many people do not live in surroundings
conducive to their education or to their social
wellbeing. Yet they maintain they are content and
happy in such circumstances. The question arises
whether we have a right to interfere, or at what
point should society demand that intervention
occurs. The argument here is that although major
issues may be involved, and a government or a
service is required to intervene, the process must
involve consultation with the individuals
concerned.

In much of the field of rehabilitation we
have not sufficiently taken into account the
judgments of sponsors (largely parents) or of
individuals themselves, nor have we balanced the
views of parents and the individual with the
competing needs of services. Frequently service
personnel believe 'they know best'. Further,
parents may also feel they know what is best for
the individual. But the individual may disagree.
Individuals with disabilities have perceptions
which should be heard, and an attempt should be
made to come to a practical balance in providing
effective services. Yet many services do not have
a wide range of programmes or practices to offer.
Now is the time to ensure that a wide range of
options are available, and that philosophy and

practice are clearly enunciated for all parties to view, consider and evaluate. But effective choice is made through experience and this makes for nice dilemmas in the provision of services in the field of disability.

REFERENCES

Bonano, R., Gibbs, E. F., & Twardzicki, N. (1982) *Quality of Life Index*, Wrentham State School and Children's Hospital, Boston, at Wrentham, MA, USA.

Brown, R. I., Bayer, M. B., & MacFarlane, C. (1986) *Rehabilitation Programmes Study*, Report to Health and Welfare Canada, Project No. 4558-29-4.

Checkland, P. (1981) *Systems Thinking, Systems Practice*, John Wiley & Sons, Chichester and New York.

Chapter Two

AN ANALYSIS OF THE DIMENSIONS OF QUALITY OF LIFE
FOR PEOPLE WITH PHYSICAL DISABILITIES

Trevor R. Parmenter

INTRODUCTION

This chapter seeks to provide the groundwork for
the development of a model of quality of life
(QOL) which may be used to generate valid outcome
measures for people with disabilities who are
undergoing independent or community living
programmes. Firstly, a number of the current
shortcomings in evaluative research will be
explored. In order to arrive at a deeper understanding of quality of life and to establish a
sound theoretical base, the issue of disability
will be addressed from a sociological perspective.
In particular, it will be argued that symbolic
interaction theory is a useful framework in which
to formulate a quality of life model. Next, the
development of the independent living model
devised by De Jong will be critically analyzed.
The utility of Halpern's model of Community
Adjustment for people with intellectual disabilities will also be assessed. Finally, the
components of a QOL model for people with physical
disabilities will be proposed.

EVALUATION OF COMMUNITY LIVING PROGRAMMES

Concepts such as normalization, independent
living, deinstitutionalization and least restrictive environment have had a dramatic effect in
recent years upon the delivery of services to
people with a disability. What is not so clear is
the secondary impact these concepts have had upon
the people themselves. Evaluations of programmes

for people with disabilities have produced equiv-
ocal results, because of a lack of attention to
the essential elements of what is being evaluated,
or a failure to recognize the social nature of
evaluation research, or conceptual and method-
ological difficulties (Emerson, 1985).

Evaluators have often failed to recognize the
origins of the two major service delivery developments: namely the emergence of the independent
living movement, largely in the context of
physical disabilities, and the deinstitutionalization process, principally in the context of
mental retardation. Both social movements have
been brought about by a variety of pressures
including the civil rights movement of the 1960s
in the United States; the development of an
articulate consumer movement; the growing public
awareness of the negative aspects of institutional
care; the growth of litigation, particularly in
the United States in the 1970s and 80s; and the
implicit assumption of policy planners that
community-based care is cheaper than institutional
services.

Too often it has been the superficial
elements of community living that have been the
focus of attention. Important as changes in the
physical environment, residents' adaptive behaviour, or provision of activities for daily living
might be, there are more critical aspects which
relate to outcomes such as client satisfaction,
social and interpersonal relationships, activity
patterns, degree of self-determination, socio-
economic factors and access to community services.
Complex as they might be to identify and measure,
outcomes which reflect a person's interaction with
his/her environment are a more valid index of the
success or otherwise of community living programmes (Bronfenbrenner, 1977; Landesman-Dwyer,
1981, 1985). Researchers, therefore, must be
guided by the fundamentally multidimensional and
co-determined nature of environments in their
design of studies to seek a genuine picture of the
degree of community integration of people with
disabilities.

If one adopts the scheme suggested by the
World Health Organization, the state of being
handicapped is relative to other people (WHO,
1980). Thus existing societal values which are
influenced by the institutional arrangements of
society are of particular importance. Understanding what constitutes a handicap depends largely

upon the setting in which the person with a disability behaves, the sociocultural system that informs those settings, and the developmental stage and age of the person. As Edgerton (1975) has suggested, we have tended to emphasize regular features or structures to the neglect of processes in our study of disability, possibly because it is easier to measure static structures more reliably or, more likely, we have tried to oversimplify the complexities of human reality.

The essentially clinical approach of medicine and psychology, the major disciplines involved in the study of the rehabilitation of people with disabilities, has resulted in a paucity of theoretical models upon which services and research have been based. Too often disability has been seen as an entity residing within an individual and rehabilitation has been seen as a process whereby the disabled person is required to adapt to his/her changed circumstances. The largely positivist nature of much of rehabilitation research has been driven by the pragmatism of the clinical approaches that have been fostered by the professionals who have dominated the field.

WHAT IS A DISABILITY?

Increasingly, disability is being studied from sociological perspectives including structural-functional, conflict, phenomenological, inter-actional and ecological. In the light of the almost total absence of sound theoretical bases for much of the research in the disability field, it is proposed to examine the concept of disability from a symbolic interactionist viewpoint. Fundamental to this approach is the principle that human experiences are mediated by interpretation (Bogdan & Kugelmass, 1984). Another basic tenet is that the 'self' arises and is maintained in a symbolic and interactive context. For instance, in addressing the question of exactly how a self comes into being, Stryker (1959) has suggested that we come to know what we are through others' response to us. In the context of the present discussion Bogdan and Kugelmass (1984) have pointed out that the word 'disability' is not a symbol for a condition that is already there in advance. Paradoxically, disability is part of the mechanism whereby the condition is created.

Physical and/or psychological impairments set the parameters in which the definitions develop, but the way in which people determine their definitions depends upon a variety of factors including personal and community attitudes toward people who appear different. Definitions and labels are influenced strongly by the degree to which people have had the opportunity to interact at a personal level with people with disabling conditions.

DISABILITY AS DEVIANCE AND THE LABELLING PERSPECTIVE

Goffman (1963) identified blindness, deafness, epilepsy and physical disfigurement as examples of stigma. This list was expanded by Clinard (1974) to include mental retardation, cerebral palsy and stuttering. Some may view the stigmatizing condition as being inherent in the individual, but Clinard (1974) maintained that the emphasis should be upon the effects of the imputed impairment, through a process of labelling, of disability onto the individual. Schur (1971), for instance, pointed out that in examining deviant human behaviour we are seeing the results of a *combination* of a personally discreditable departure from expectations and the development of certain stigmatizing reactions towards the individual. These reactions may serve to *isolate, treat, correct* or *punish* individuals who are engaged in such behaviours. Central to Schur's position is the notion that deviance is not a static entity; it is rather the dynamic outcome of the complex interactive processes ongoing in society. The process of social definition or labelling, suggested Schur (1971), includes collective rule making, interpersonal reactions, and organizational processing.

a) Collective Rule Making

Scott (1972), in his analysis of the symbolic nature of rule making, has argued that it is this dimension of the social order that is the most important one for understanding deviance. Society develops a view of reality which attempts to bring order and meaning to an otherwise random universe through the construction of a system for classifying human existence. In operational terms this results in objects, events and people having to conform to the class or category to which they have been assigned. It also requires that there are simple means available for discriminating among the classes of things. However, people with disabilities are seen as anomalous in this well-ordered view of the social order. Consequently, viewed from the perspective of a symbolic universe, the property of deviance is assigned to these anomalous individuals.

b)   The Area of Interpersonal Relations

The development of social identity or stereotyping has particular relevance for the study of deviance. McCall and Simmons (1978) have suggested that identification of persons and of other 'things' is the key to symbolic interaction; for once things are identified and their meanings for us established, we can get on with our individual pursuits. Once we categorize or place a person in a particular 'box', we know how to behave towards that person. But Schur (1971) has noted that this is a two-way process, *'Just as the individual constantly "types" other people, so he is constantly typed by others and indeed also by himself'*. For non-handicapped people, stereo-typing obviously simplifies their interaction with people who are handicapped, but this tends to limit their perception of the individual so that relationships seldom develop beyond a superficial level.

For the person with a disability there is often a lack of congruence between their desired personal identity and their assigned social identity. Hurst (1984) has commented that stereo-types focus upon generalities. This is supported by Scott's (1972) observation that society has ascribed to people with visual disabilities the attributes of *'helplessness, dependency, melancholy, docility, gravity of inner thought, (and) aestheticism'*, all traits he has suggested, *'that common sense views tell us to expect of the blind'*. The effect of this role-making process is such that the person with a disability will often not develop as an authentic person. Unfortunately people who have been assigned an identity or role in society may ultimately fulfil the expectations others have of them, thus reinforcing in the eyes of others the validity of their assessments.

11

The closer the perceptions of self by the person with a disability come to those ascribed by society, the greater is the chance that secondary deviance or career disability will emerge as the major form of role adaptation. Burbach (1981), in distinguishing between primary and secondary deviance, has suggested that the primary 'deviant' does not see his 'differentness' as defining him as a person whereas the secondary 'deviant' sees his 'differentness' as the crucial defining element in his concept of self. Career disability has been a major focus of attention of a number of writers in the field of rehabilitation (Stoddard, 1978; De Jong, 1979, 1981; Finkelstein, 1980). For instance, in his analysis of attitudes and disabled people Finkelstein (1980) has indicted professional groups as having contributed significantly to the social oppression of people with disabilities.

c) Labelling in the Organizational Context

At the public level, deviance may be regulated by bureaucracies such as education, health and community welfare departments or by large private institutions. In order to receive a 'service' it is usually necessary for deviance to be identified and assessed. In examining the role bureaucracies play in deviance creation one comes to appreciate that societies have set up political and legal structures which help them deal with the anomalous circumstances which disability produces. For instance, in the school setting children perceived as being 'difficult' or 'a problem' are almost invariably referred for assessment and diagnosis - not so much for programmatic advice, but in the expectation that they will be removed to a more 'appropriate' setting. In order to effect this transfer of responsibility, labels are attached to the child legitimizing his/her removal. Supporting this view is the work of Mercer (1973) who, in her study of mental retardation in the community setting, concluded that *'the public schools were the most significant formal organization in the social system epidemiology of mental retardation in the community'*. This view was echoed by Sarason and Doris (1979) who have strongly attacked the diagnostic and assessment procedures used in schools to define and label children. They have noted that measurement systems reflect value-laden social concepts of deviance. Categories

such as behaviour disturbance or mental retardation are whatever we choose to make them - they
are not definable as objective 'things', but are
inextricably bound to our cultural notions about
how people ought to behave.

Burton Blatt has echoed similar concerns in
his eloquent essay *Bureaucratizing Values* in which
he addressed the definition of the latest catch-
phrase *least restrictive alternative*. His
analysis is one of pessimism - pessimism that,
despite the emergence of new terms such as
individual programme plans, mainstreaming, zero
reject and least restrictive alternative,
professionals in particular will not go beyond
these terms and look at the human essence of the
problem. *'The problem with these terms and others
like them'*, he suggested, *'is that at present they
are little more than shibboleths and slogans. We
simply do not have adequate understanding of what
they mean'* (Blatt, 1981).

Legislators may act as an external force upon
service delivery agencies by mandating policies
that must be complied with. In the United States
scene an example is Public Law 94-142, the
Education for All Handicapped Children Act, which
mandated that all handicapped children receive a
free, appropriate public education in the least
restrictive environment. Paradoxically, while the
spirit of the Act attempted to encourage more
functional diagnoses of disability, the traditional categories were retained for funding purposes,
highlighting the power of the disability lobby
groups in American context. The 1981 Special
Education Act in the United Kingdom officially
abolished statutory categories of disability,
replacing them with special education needs.
However, Barton and Tomlinson (1984) have commented that *'the old labels appear to be remaining as
descriptive categories'*.

These, and similar attempts in other
countries to integrate children with disabilities
into regular schools and classes, are possibly
doomed to fail, not because of the philosophies
upon which the attempts are being based, but
because of the failure of policy planners to
address the value systems and structures which
permeate the school systems. Attempts to retain
children who are perceived as deviant within
regular classrooms will require a massive value
system reorientation by educators, their trainers
and society generally.

In summary, an examination of the processes of social definition or labelling, posited by Schur (1971), has revealed that the deviance attribute of disability is imposed by the social audience or, in the words of Becker (1983), *'Social groups create deviance by making the rules whose infraction constitutes deviance...'*. From a symbolic universe perspective rules arise in society as a result of its need to maintain an orderly view of the world. The anomalous position of people with disabilities in this universe has led to the property of deviance being assigned to these individuals. There often follows a power struggle to determine whose rules should apply. As fragmented and uncoordinated groups of individuals, people with disabilities are relatively powerless in this conflict. In the area of interpersonal relations, the lack of congruence between a personal and a socially assigned identity often prevents the person with a disability developing as a well-adjusted human being. This in turn has deleterious effects upon the quality of interpersonal relations. A brief examination of organizational structures has demonstrated how, in Schur's (1971) terms, organizations produce deviance through their attempts to regulate and control those groups that are perceived as a threat to the natural order of things.

THE IMPLICATIONS OF LABELLING FOR THE QUALITY OF LIFE QUESTION

In his illuminating analysis of the labelling issue, Burbach (1981) has suggested that it is a superficial question to ask whether we should or should not label anomalous individuals. He pointed out that labelling and categorizing people is a normal process of apprehending and organizing our world. Of more importance is *'how we label [people] and with what consequences'* (Burbach, 1981). Burbach's contention is that people with a disability are in a double bind situation. In addressing the issue of what it means to be disabled they are confronted by two messages. One comes from outside and proceeds from the social order. The other, however, comes from within and relates to what they know they can or cannot do. Thus they have to deal with the negative aspects of their personal condition and at the same time cope with the negative effects of stigmatization and stereotyping. From a philosophical point of view there is a conflict between the existential nature of the person and the social nature of human experience.

In trying to establish a coherent meaning for life as well as creating and maintaining self-esteem, the conflict between the messages the person with a disability receives often presents insuperable problems. On the one hand the person can live in a cocoon-like existence built on socially unvalidated meanings or, on the other, they can conform to the patterns of behaviour that are expected of them by society generally. Neither of these approaches leads to a satisfactory resolution to the issue of how they define their own meanings. Here, it is proposed, lies the nub of the quality of life issue. Quality of life represents the degree to which an individual has met his/her needs to create their own meanings so they can establish and sustain a viable self in the social world. The resolution proffered by Burbach draws upon the basic principles of symbolic interactionism. That is, there is a need for 'consensuality' whereby humans help each other unfold and establish contact and unity in their social existence.

In examining the outcomes of community or independent living programmes for people with disabilities, a crucial element to be examined is the degree to which these people are 'of' rather than simply 'in' a community. A measure of this will undoubtedly be the quality of their inter-personal relationships with others within their community. Here the sociological concepts of *Gemeinschaft* and *Gesellschaft* are useful analyt-ical tools. Gemeinschaft refers to a community of spirit whereas Gesellschaft describes a community organized on a formal or contractual basis where relationships are impersonal. Neither necessarily specifies a geographical or physical entity, but, from the above discussion of the development of self, it is appreciated that simply observing the superficial and outward characteristics of a community-based facility does not indicate whether it has Gemeinschaft. This reinforces the earlier discussion on the inadequacies of many outcome studies which, it is suggested, have ignored the quality of life dimension.

While there have been some attempts to rectify this, such as studies of resident satis-faction (e.g. Scheerenberger & Felsenthal, 1977;

Gollay, Freedman, Wyngaarden & Kuntz, 1978; McDevitt, Smith, Schmidt & Rosen, 1978; Birenbaum & Re, 1979; Seltzer, 1981; Bradley & Conroy, 1983; Halpern, Close & Nelson, 1986) and social and interpersonal relationships (e.g. Scheerenberger & Felsenthol, 1977; Gollay et al., 1978; Conroy, Efthemiou & Lemanowicz, 1982), much of the research suffers from being conducted in what Emerson (1985) has referred to as an *'atheoretical vacuum'*.

While not without its critics (e.g. Sharp & Green, 1975), the symbolic interaction theory has usefully contributed to our understanding of aspects of the social situation of people with disabilities. Barton and Tomlinson (1984) have suggested that this approach has at least two strengths. First, it emphasizes the viewpoint of the participants in social interaction and second, the perspective explores aspects of social life which have historically either been taken for granted or been ignored. Other sociological approaches might emphasize economic considerations and the distribution of resources in the society (e.g. structuralist neo-Marxism) or use the traditional Marxist class conflict model to explore the imbalance of power between disabled and nondisabled groups in society. These theories may not be mutually exclusive, for in the context of quality of life it is suggested that the consciousness of self and social identity, status and social role are obviously preconditions for political activism and social change.

INDEPENDENT LIVING

Viewing disability from the interactionist per-spective may also help us to provide a sounder theoretical base for the concept of independent living which has been seen as a popular outcome for rehabilitation programmes, particularly for people with physical disabilities. As well as being viewed as a dependent variable, the indepen-dent living or consumer movement can be conceptu-alized as an independent variable through its active assertion of the rights of people with disabilities. As with many concepts and terms within the disability scene, independent living suffers from semantic confusions. Conceptualiza-tions of independent living range from purely physical provisions such as attendants, personal mobility aids and adaptations to housing, as discussed by Simkins (1979) in her monograph, *The Value of Independent Living: Looking at Cost-effectiveness in the U.K.*, to more qualitative dimensions such as self-actualization, and making choices and decisions about one's life (Frieden, 1983; Zola, 1983). For instance, Zola has suggested that *'it is not the quantity of tasks we can perform without assistance but the quality of life we can live with help'*. Noble (1983) has gone further by his proposition that independent living means freedom from handicap in the sense of the World Health Organization's definition (WHO, 1980). That is, independence is seen as freedom from the disadvantages associated with impairment or disability, particularly those that are imposed by community stereotypes of what constitutes the normal range of role functioning for individuals. Noble has drawn upon the work of Rappaport in suggesting that independent living encapsulates the concept of 'empowerment' whereby people *'...gain control, find meaning, and empower their own lives'* (Rappaport, 1981).

In North America independent living as a concept has been developed from a mixture of antecedent ideologies and social movements such as normalization, social integration, demedicalization, consumerism, self-help and civil rights (De Jong, 1979). Both De Jong and Rappaport have explored the negative effects professional groups have had upon the various disabled and socially deprived people for whom they 'care'. Rappaport cited Illich (1976) who pointed out that in the domain of physical health *'the pervasive belief that experts should solve all of our problems in living has created a social and cultural iatrogenesis which extends the sense of alienation and loss of ability to control life even to one's own body'* (Rappaport, 1981).

De Jong (1981), in his development of independent living as an analytic paradigm, has argued that the independent living movement is the result of a convergence of several contemporary social movements including those referred to above. In adopting Kuhn's (1970) concept of a paradigm with its in-built notions of anomaly and paradigm shift, De Jong posited that the anomalous situation of people with severe disabilities achieving independence without the benefit of professional rehabilitation services served as the impetus for

17

the shift from a rehabilitation paradigm, characterized by professional control to the independent living paradigm, characterized by consumer control. The rehabilitation paradigm, he asserted, saw the problems residing in the individual, whereas for the emerging independent living paradigm *'the locus of the problem is not the individual but the environment that includes not only the rehabilitation process, but also the physical environment and social control mechanisms in society-at-large'* (De Jong, 1981).

Having established the independent living paradigm, De Jong proceeded to construct a research model which could be used to account for disability outcomes. To do this he reviewed the research literature on spinal cord injury outcomes in order to establish independent and dependent variables. From this analysis he hypothesized that independent living outcomes are a function of four sets of variables:

1) socio-demographic variables such as age, sex and education,
2) disability related variables such as severity and duration of disability,
3) environmental variables such as attendant care needs, transportation barriers and economic disincentives, and
4) 'interface' variables such as special equipment needs.

De Jong's choice of living arrangement and productivity as dependent variables was guided by what he described as being *'the two most relevant outcome criteria from a policy perspective'*. Whilst these variables appear on the surface overly narrow, De Jong justified their selection on the grounds that they represented historically and philosophically the major foci of the independent living paradigm. In justice to De Jong, the criteria used are broader than they appear on the surface. For instance, productivity encompassed not only gainful employment but also a wide range of contributions to family and community life. There is a strong case, however, for a much wider range of outcome variables to be considered, especially those relating to leisure time activities.

Rating scales were developed for the two outcome variables in cooperation with the Massachusetts Interagency Council on Independent Living

(ICIL). Altogether 7 living arrangement outcomes and 12 productivity outcomes were ranked by the ICIL on a scale of 0 to 10. To test the research model De Jong used as a data base the records of 111 spinal cord injured persons from ten comprehensive medical rehabilitation centres around the United States. In all, six instruments were used to collect data on the study population, including a mailed and an interview questionnaire.

Multiple regression analyses revealed that with respect to living arrangement outcomes a person's marital status, age, sex and overall station in life determined a person's residential status more than factors such as the severity of a person's disability. The most important prediction of productivity outcomes revealed a low correlation between living arrangements and productivity outcomes (r = 0.298). One of the most important findings to emerge from the regression analyses was the strong interaction between the severity of a person's disability and environmental limitations such as transportation barriers and economic disincentives. Subsequent attempts to separate out the relative effects of the variables proved abortive.

De Jong concluded that the results of the study represented only a beginning for future research on independent living issues. He maintained, however, that the results were generalizable to other spinal cord injured people, particularly for persons who did not have other unrelated medical problems. It was also claimed that the study demonstrated how theoretical rigour, based it is assumed, on the development of the independent living paradigm, provided a sound base for the empirical analyses (De Jong, 1981). However, before one can accept many of De Jong's assertions, it is necessary to examine critically his ideological and theoretical assumptions in addition to aspects of the empirical study.

While De Jong (1979) has emphasized the attributes of personal autonomy and self-direction and the need to see disability more in terms of environmental limitations than in terms of limitations within the individual, his philosophical base is somewhat narrower than the symbolic interactionist approach proposed above.

For instance, Williams (1983) has pointed out that De Jong's analysis *'assumes a one-way causal relationship between environmental contingencies and individual states, and ignores the mediating*

19

effects of symbols and contexts of social life'.
Similarly his model severely limits the influence
individual personality characteristics may have
upon defining outcomes. For instance, the question of whether 'living alone' should be seen as a
desirable outcome or not depends, in part, upon
the personality and value system of the individual
and the value he or she places upon social relationships.

The weaknesses of De Jong's theoretical and
conceptual bases are highlighted by the difficulties he had with establishing coherent independent
and dependent variables. As indicated above, the
selection of living arrangements and productivity
as outcome variables on the basis that they are
the major focus of policy planners is a somewhat
tenuous rationale, considering the intricate
social dynamics of the concept of independent
living. In respect to independent variables, De
Jong specified in his research model that four
distinct variables would predict overall independent living outcomes. This is on the face of it a
fairly arbitrary distinction, for there are likely
to be some fairly direct relationships between
these variables. For instance, marital status is
found under socio-demographic variables, but it is
possibly related to factors such as attendant
care, housing and patient role which come under
environmental variables. Of more serious concern
is that 'living with a spouse' was seen as one of
the criteria for a desirable 'living arrangement',
a dependent variable, yet marital status was
included as an independent variable under socio-
demographic details. It is also difficult to
justify interface variables which include 'unmet
equipment needs' as being independent of environmental variables such as attendant care needs.

The results of De Jong's multivariate
analyses further highlighted the conceptual
weaknesses of his model in that he found a strong
interaction between disability related and environmental factors such as transportation barriers
and economic disincentives. His attempt to use
the interaction terms (the cross product of the
two independent variables) failed because the high
degree of multicolinearity that resulted produced
highly unstable regression coefficients. As the
difficulties surrounding the multicolinearity
problem in the use of interaction terms usually
occur when inadequate data reduction procedures
have been used, Williams (1983) has questioned

whether De Jong failed to do a proper analysis of principal components, or whether his summing and separating of different independent variables were misguided.

In summary, De Jong's analyses do not offer strong justification for the validity of his research model. While he has claimed that *'independent living theory has been instrumental in focussing attention on environmental barriers as an important determinant of disability outcomes'*, a close examination of his results reveals that the picture is far less clear than this assertion implies. Nor has he presented a convincing case that he has developed an 'independent living theory', particularly as he seems to have failed to be more explicit about a number of quality of life indices such as control over one's life, meaningful participation in decision making processes, the development of an adequate self-image and satisfaction with one's life style. Before looking to other diagnostic groups to test the generalizability of his results, greater attention needs to be paid to the basic underlying ideological and theoretical assumptions concerning what independent living means. In this respect concepts such as community adjustment and quality of life may be useful avenues to follow.

COMMUNITY ADJUSTMENT

Community adjustment is a construct which has been developed to encapsulate the outcomes of pro-grammes designed to enhance the participation of people with disabilities in the milieu of the general community. Halpern (1985) suggested the concept of community adjustment as being a pre-ferred way of looking at the outcomes of transition education programmes for young people with disabilities in reaction to the 'bridges' model of transition proposed by Will (1984). Will proposed that transition be defined as *'an outcome-oriented process encompassing a broad array of services and experiences that lead to employment'*. An alterna-tive approach suggested by Halpern (1985) focused attention upon broader dimensions of community adjustment. Support for a multi-dimensional approach to outcomes in order to capture the richness and full understanding of community adjustment is found in the work of a number of authors (Heal, Sigelman & Switzky, 1978; Ward,

Parmenter, Riches & Hauritz, 1978, 1986; Irwin, Crowell & Bellamy, 1979; Brown & Hughson, 1980; Parmenter, 1980, 1987; Lakin, Bruininks & Sigford, 1981; Whelan & Speake, 1981; Emerson, 1985; Mitchell, 1986).

Working from essentially an empirical rather than a theoretical base, Halpern, Close and Nelson (1986) developed an integrated model of community adjustment which includes occupation, residential environment, social support and personal satisfaction as four key dimensions of transition from school to adult life. To test the model Halpern, Nave, Close and Nelson (1986) developed a battery of tests which tapped three variables in each of the four dimensions. Under employment were included employment status, degree of community integration and financial status; under residential were residential comfort, neighbourhood quality and access to resources; under social support were safety from minor abuse, safety from major abuse, and social support; and under satisfaction were general satisfaction, self-satisfaction and programme satisfaction. For a full description of these variables and justification for their inclusion the reader is referred to Halpern, Close and Nelson (1986) and Halpern, Nave, Close and Nelson (1986).

Measures for each of the 12 variables were given a field trial to test for internal consistency and reliability, as a part of a larger study which studied the community adjustment of adults with mental retardation who were residents of semi-independent living programmes (SILPS) in California, Oregon, Washington and Colorado. To test the model, data were gathered on the 12 variables from 257 residents (141 females, 116 males; age range 18-59, X age = 28 years), the majority of whom were classified as mildly retarded. Using both exploratory and confirmatory factor analysis techniques Halpern et al., found strong support for the proposed four-dimensional model. Inspection of Figure 1 shows that the level of association between the four factors derived from the LISREL confirmatory factor analysis was, as predicted, quite low. There were, however, significant intercorrelations with the satisfaction factor which correlated 0.41 with environment and 0.61 with social support/safety. Interestingly, occupation was quite independent of the other three factors. Of some significance was the fact that the proposed model was able to reproduce the original correlation matrix, with the average difference between the true correlations and the reproduced values at the low value of 0.04. The goodness of fit index derived from the maximum likelihood technique was 0.97, providing additional support for the robustness of the model.

FIGURE 1:   Relationships Among Factors and
Variables

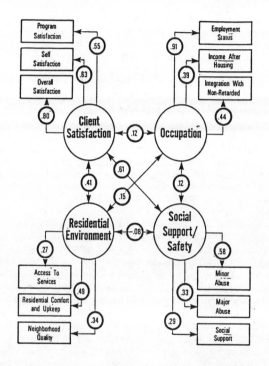

(Figure 1 reprinted with permission from Halpern, A. S., Nave, G., Close, D. W., & Nelson, D., 1986, 'An Empirical Analysis of the Dimensions of Community Adjustment for Adults with Mental Retardation,' *Australia and New Zealand Journal of Developmental Disabilities, 12*, p. 154)

The Halpern et al.[1] (1986) model of community adjustment makes a useful contribution to the analysis of quality of life for people with disabilities. While these results cannot necessarily be generalized to other populations, it is suspected that there may be a degree of concordance with populations with physical disabilities. A limitation of the study, recognized by the authors, is that the number of variables within each dimension of the model was relatively small. Also, the location of community integration within the occupation dimension may not be appropriate across other disability areas. However, their premise that opportunities for community integration for people with intellectual disabilities are generally found in the vocational setting was supported by their data for this group. This is not altogether surprising considering that work often provides the context for other, more social activities for the population in general. It may be useful to explore quality of life issues in the wider community context in order to determine if other variables may be usefully incorporated into a model of community integration.

QUALITY OF LIFE

Comparative studies to measure the quality of life (QOL) have followed three major orientations: social indicators, measures of life satisfaction, and more direct approaches. While social indicators can be measured objectively, they present a rather narrow picture even of a community's quality of life. More recently attention has shifted to the assessment of subjective or perceived quality of life in order to provide information on both individuals and community units (Andrews & Withey, 1976; Campbell, Converse & Rodgers, 1976; Hall, 1976; Atkinson, 1977, 1978a, 1978b; Marans & Wellman, 1977; Milbrath, 1977; Hawkins, 1978; Atkinson & Murray, 1979; Andrews & McKennell, 1980; Campbell, 1981; Zautra & Reich, 1983). These measures are influenced by cognitive and affective factors such as an individual's aspirations, values and immediate feeling states (McKennell & Andrews, 1983).

The third approach which appears compatible with the symbolic interactionist theoretical position assesses quality of life on the basis of a person's behaviour in response to the environment or environments in which the behaviour occurs (Evans, Burns, Robinson & Garrett, 1985). This approach also fits well into ecological theory as it focuses on the interactions which occur between individuals in the same settings in which they operate. Bogdan and Kugelmass (1984) have pointed out that, *'ecological theory further clarifies the defining process discussed extensively by symbolic interactionists in its focus upon the interaction between individuals within the context of their environment'.*

There is obviously an interaction between the affective, cognitive and behavioural components of quality of life. For instance, Andrews and McKennell argued that actions (behaviours), feelings (affect) and values (cognitions) all interact to determine a person's level of perceived wellbeing or quality of life. In order to remedy what they perceived as a dearth of studies directed towards the behaviours dimension, Evans et al. (1985) developed a Quality of Life Questionnaire which was designed to measure a person's behaviour in response to a number of ecological domains that affected him/her.

The domains selected were general wellbeing, interpersonal relations, organizational activity, occupational activity and leisure and recreational activity. Fifteen sub-domains were identified and 12 items were developed for each to constitute the Quality of Life Questionnaire. Participants in the study were 298 residents of London, Ontario. The correlation matrix of the intercorrelations among scales and the correlation between each scale and the QOL score were submitted to principal component factor analysis with varimax rotation. Five factors were described as:

1) occupational/material wellbeing,
2) social wellbeing,
3) family wellbeing,
4) personal wellbeing,
5) physical wellbeing.

With the exception of physical wellbeing, all factors had moderate loadings with the overall QOL score. A concurrent validation study indicated that there was a moderate correlation between Life Satisfaction Ratings and QOL scale scores. Particular life satisfaction measures also had moderate correlations with the overall QOL score. On this evidence, Evans et al. (1985) argued that there was support for the view expressed by several authors (Gutek, Allen, Taylor, Lou, & Majchrzak, 1983; Zautra & Reich, 1983) that functional or rewarding and enriching life experiences are necessary in order for an individual to report a high level of perceived life satisfaction or subjective wellbeing.

Milbrath (1982) proposed a research strategy for the study of ecological aspects of quality of life. He argued that studies of social ecology and studies of quality of life constitute a 'national marriage' between objective and subjective indicators. His research model allows quality of life to be analyzed either for an individual person or for a community. A basic premise is that there are interactive effects between individual and community experiences of quality of life. He has conceptualized quality of life as a result of two major classes of variables: (a) values, goals and aspirations, and (b) lifestyles. These may be viewed from either an individual or community level. Milbrath defined quality of life as the '... *fulfillment of one's values, goals, aspirations and needs*'.

In Milbrath's model, factors at the personal level affect and are in turn affected by the factors at the community level. He suggested that personal and societal learning is the main dynamic in this interaction process. For example, learning at the individual level is influenced by society's beliefs and values, but these are in turn changed by the learning of the individuals who are a part of society. New beliefs and values affect in turn the physical and economic aspects of the environment in which we live so that there is a continual process of redefinition and re-learning.

In the context of the quality of life of people with physical disabilities, the work of both Evans et al. (1985) and Milbrath (1982) has much to offer, particularly if we approach disability from a combination of the symbolic interactionist and ecological theoretical perspectives. A model of quality of life should reflect the values, beliefs, aspirations, self-perceptions, etc., of the individual, but it should also accommodate functional behaviours in a range of life domains. There should also be opportunity for societal variables to be incorporated.

A QUALITY OF LIFE MODEL

Within a symbolic interactionist/ecological theoretical framework it would seem essential to include at least three components within a quality

of life model for people with disabilities. The
first would pertain to an individual's perception
of self; the second to the individual's behaviour
in response to ecological domains that might
affect him/her; and the third to responses the
settings might make to the individual. Obviously
the model would need to be able to accommodate the
interactions which would occur among each of these
components. However, in this concluding section
it is proposed to describe briefly the subcomponents which might constitute the basis for instrument development for subsequent testing of the
model. Figure 2 illustrates the components of the
model.

FIGURE 2:   A Model for Quality of Life of People
            with Disabilities

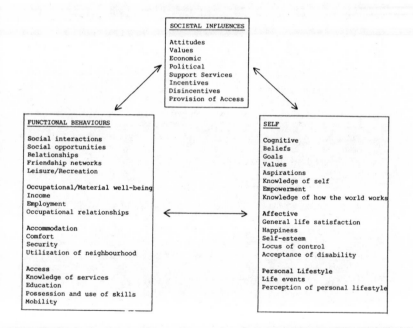

a)   Self

The subcomponents of self have been arbitrarily
classified under cognitive and affective, given
that they are highly interactive. A further
moderating dimension, personal lifestyle, has also

27

been included under self. Under the cognitive
dimension are included beliefs, goals, values,
aspirations, knowledge of self, knowledge of how
the world works, and empowerment. The latter
refers to strategies such as risk-taking and
decision-making which may lead to greater levels
of autonomy and self-determination. The facets of
the affective dimension include general life
satisfaction, happiness, self-esteem, locus of
control and acceptance of disability. It is
anticipated that life events and perception of
one's personal lifestyle would affect both the
cognitive and affective dimensions.

b)   Functional Behaviours

These elements, which may be directly observed,
have been grouped into four categories. The first
has been termed social interaction, which includes
social opportunities, relationships and friendship
networks, leisure/recreational activities and
communications. The second has been described as
occupational/material well-being and incorporates
income, employment and occupational relationships.
Under accommodation, the third subcomponent, are
included comfort, security and utilization of
neighbourhood resources. The fourth subcomponent,
access, includes knowledge of and use of services,
education, possession and use of skills, and
mobility.

c)   Societal Factors

As the individual with a disability comes to a
view of his/her quality of life in the context of
the environment in which he/she lives, it is
essential that a model incorporate those societal
factors which may influence the person's subjective wellbeing. Hence the following elements are
suggested: community attitudes towards disability, community values, state of the economy,
political values, support provisions, incentives,
disincentives and provision of access.

Within these three components the list of
subcomponents is presently tentative but, from an
examination of the research literature, together
with the issues explored under the symbolic
interactionist rubric, and from the results of the
pilot study, it would appear they represent
important elements of a model.

In terms of interactions, it is proposed that each component interacts with the other. The development of self is largely influenced by both functional and societal factors. Functional behaviours are in turn affected by societal influences and the level of self development. Societal influences possibly exert a strong moderating force upon both of the other components. However, societal influences are also amenable to change, particularly if people with disabilities are assertive and demonstrate skilful control over their lives.

CONCLUSIONS

It is imperative that in the current social, economic and political climate in which the efficacy of community living programmes is being scrutinized, partly as a result of shrinking economies in industrialized countries, that more effective evaluative tools be developed. A number of problems which this chapter has addressed have existed in previous work. Insufficient attention has been paid to the major aims, values and goals which underpin the movement towards community living for people with disabilities. In this respect it has been argued that the basic meaning of disability should be examined in its social context. If this is done, the focus of evaluation studies will include not only an examination of the individual's functional skills and his/her adjustment to the environment, but also the important issue of how well the person with a disability perceives him/herself within the community setting. What becomes paramount is how that person grows and develops as an autonomous individual, with an opportunity to achieve his/her hopes and aspirations.

Obviously there is also a need to explore how the environment reacts to people with disabilities, particularly the extent to which it encourages their personal and social integration into the community. It is hoped that the suggested quality of life model may go some way in meeting our needs for a more sensitive approach to evaluation. What remains are its validation and the use of adequate evaluation designs which will give answers to the real issues underlying the level of participation and equity of people with disabilities in their communities.

SUMMARY

This chapter has explored the need for a more comprehensive set of outcome criteria for community living programmes for people with disabilities. It has proposed that a quality of life model, derived from a symbolic interactionist perspective has the potential to provide a set of measures which can capture the richness of community integration.

De Jong's (1981) independent living paradigm was critically analyzed and was found to be inadequate on a number of counts. The community adjustment model proposed by Halpern et al. (1986) provided a more useful approach, but it, too, was found to be somewhat limited in the range of variables it included.

A pilot study, designed to investigate aspects of the quality of life of a sample of people with physical disabilities who had been in a community living programme, was described. This study emphasized the subjective dimensions of quality of life such as general life satisfaction.

Finally a model of quality of life was proposed.

REFERENCES

Andrews, F. M. & McKennell, A. C. (1980) 'Measure of Self-reported Well-being: Their Affective, Cognitive and Other Components,' *Social Indicators Research, 8,* 127-155.

Andrews, F. & Withey, S. B. (1976) *Social Indicators of Well-being: America's Perceptions of Life Quality,* Plenum Press, New York.

Atkinson, T. (1977) 'Is Satisfaction a Good Measure of the Perceived Quality of Life?', Institute of Behavioral Research, York University, Toronto. Mimeo.

Atkinson, T. (1978a) 'Trends in Life Satisfaction Among Canadians, 1968-1977,' Paper Delivered at the IX World Congress of Sociology, Uppsala, Sweden.

Atkinson, T. (1978b) 'Public Perceptions on the Quality of Life,' Institute of Behavioral Research, York University, Toronto. Mimeo. Also published in *Statistics Canada: Perspectives Canada III,* Minister of Supply and Services, Ottawa, Canada, 1980.

Atkinson, T. & Murray, M. (1979) 'Values, Domains and the Perceived Quality of Life,' Paper presented at the American Psychological Association Annual Meeting, New York.

Barton, L. & Tomlinson, S. (1984) 'The Politics of Integration in England,' in L. Barton & S. Tomlinson (eds.), *Special Education and Social Interests,* Croom Helm, London/Nichols, New York.

Becker, H. S. (1983) *Outsiders: Studies in the Sociology of Deviance,* The Free Press, New York.

Birenbaum, A. & Re, M. (1979) 'Resettling Mentally Retarded Adults in the Community - Almost Four Years Later,' *American Journal of Mental Deficiency, 83,* 323-329.

Blatt, B. (1981) *In and Out of Mental Retardation. Essays on Educability, Disability, and Human Policy,* University Park Press, Baltimore.

Bogdan, R. & Kugelmass, J. (1984) 'Case Studies of Mainstreaming. A Symbolic Interactionist Approach to Special Schooling,' in L. Barton & S. Tomlinson (eds.), *Special Education and Social Interests,* Croom Helm, London/Nichols, New York.

Bradley, V. J. & Conroy, J. W. (1983) 'Third Year Comprehensive Report of the Penshurst Longitudinal Study,' Temple University Developmental Disabilities Center, Philadelphia.

Bronfenbrenner, U. (1977) 'Toward an Experimental Ecology of Human Development,' *American Psychologist, 32,* 513-531.

Brown, R. I. & Hughson, E. A. (1980) *Training of the Developmentally Handicapped Adult,* Charles C. Thomas, Springfield, IL.

Burbach, H. J. (1981) 'The Labeling Process. A Sociological Analysis,' in J. M. Kauffman & D. P. Hallahan (eds.), *Handbook of Special Education,* Prentice Hall, Englewood Cliffs, N.J.

Campbell, A. (1981) *The Sense of Well-being in America,* McGraw Hill, New York.

Campbell, A., Converse, P. E., & Rodgers, W. L. (1976) *The Quality of American Life: Perceptions, Evaluations, and Satisfactions,* Russell Sage, New York.

Clinard, M. B. (1974) *Sociology of Deviant Behavior,* Holt, Rinehart & Winston, New York.

Conroy, J., Efthemiou, J., & Lemanowicz, J. (1982)
    'A Matched Comparison of the Developmental
    Growth of Institutionalized and Deinstitu-
    tionalized Mentally Retarded Citizens,'
    American Journal of Mental Deficiency, 86,
    581-587.
De Jong, G. (1979) *The Movement for Independent
    Living. Origins, Ideology and Implications
    for Disability Research*, University Center
    for International Rehabilitation, Michigan
    State University.
De Jong, G. (1981) *Environmental Accessibility
    and Independent Living Outcomes. Directions
    for Disability Policy and Research*, Univer-
    sity Center for International Rehabilitation,
    Michigan State University.
Edgerton, R. B. (1975) 'Issues Relating to the
    Quality of Life Among Mentally Retarded
    Persons,' in M. J. Begab & S. A. Richardson
    (eds.), *The Mentally Retarded and Society*,
    University Park Press, Baltimore.
Emerson, E. B. (1985) 'Evaluating the Impact of
    Deinstitutionalization on the Lives of
    Mentally Retarded People,' *American Journal
    of Mental Deficiency, 90*, 277-288.
Evans, D. R., Burns, J. E., Robinson, W. E., &
    Garrett, O. J. (1985) 'The Quality of Life
    Questionnaire: A Multidimensional Measure,'
    American Journal of Community Psychology, 13,
    305-322.
Finkelstein, V. (1980) *Attitudes and Disabled
    People: Issues for Discussion*, World Rehab-
    ilitation Fund, Inc., New York.
Frieden, L. (1983) 'Defining Independence,' in D.
    G. Tate & L. M. Chadderdon (eds.), *Inter-
    national Perspectives about Independent
    Living*, University Center for International
    Rehabilitation, Michigan State University.
Goffman, E. (1963) *Stigma: Notes on the Manage-
    ment of Spoiled Identity*, Prentice Hall,
    Englewood Cliffs, N.J.
Gollay, E., Freedman, R., Wyngaarden, M., & Kuntz,
    N. R. (1978) *Coming Back: The Community
    Experiences of Institutionalized Mentally
    Retarded People*, Abt Books, Cambridge, MA.
Gutek, B. A., Allen, H., Taylor, T. R., Lou, R.
    R., & Majchrzak, A. (1983) 'The Importance
    of Internal Referents as Determinants of
    Satisfaction,' *Journal of Community Psych-
    ology, 11*, 111-120.

Hall, J. (1976) 'Subjective Memories of Quality of Life in Britain: 1971 to 1975, Some Developments and Trends,' *Social Trends, No. 7,* Her Majesty's Stationery Office, London.

Halpern, A. S. (1985) 'Transition: A Look at the Foundations,' *Exceptional Children, 51,* 479-486.

Halpern, A. S., Close, D. W., & Nelson, D. J. (1986) *On My Own. The Impact of Semi-independent Living Programs for Adults with Mental Retardation,* Paul H. Brookes, Baltimore.

Halpern, A. S., Nave, G., Close, D. W., & Nelson, D. (1986) 'An Empirical Analysis of the Dimensions of Community Adjustment for Adults with Mental Retardation,' *Australia and New Zealand Journal of Developmental Disabilities, 12,* 147-157.

Hawkins, E. (1978) 'Quality of Life Models,' in *Indicators of Environmental Quality and Quality of Life,* UNESCO Reports and Papers in the Social Sciences, Paris.

Heal, L. W., Sigelman, C. K., & Switzky, H. N. (1978) 'Research on Community Residential Alternatives for the Mentally Retarded,' in N. R. Ellis (ed.), *International Review of Research on Mental Retardation,* (Vol. 9), Academic Press, New York.

Hurst, A. (1984) 'Adolescence and Physical Impairment: An Interactionist View,' in L. Barton & S. Tomlinson (eds.), *Special Education and Social Interest,* Croom Helm, London/Nichols, New York.

Illich, I. (1976) *Medical Nemesis: The Exploration of Health,* Pantheon, New York.

Irwin, L. K., Crowell, F., & Bellamy, G. T. (1979) 'Multiple Assessment Evaluation of Programs for Severely Retarded Adults,' *Mental Retardation, 17,* 123-128.

Kuhn, T. (1970) *The Structure of Scientific Revolutions,* University of Chicago, Chicago.

Lakin, K. C., Bruininks, R. H., & Sigford, B. B. (1981) 'Deinstitutionalization and Community-based Residential Adjustment: A Summary of Research and Issues,' in R. H. Bruininks, C. E. Meyers, B. B. Sigford & K. C. Lakin (eds.), *Deinstitutionalization and Community Adjustment of Mentally Retarded People,* American Association on Mental Deficiency, Washington, D.C.

Landesman-Dwyer, S. (1981) 'Living in the
    Community,' *American Journal of Mental
    Deficiency, 86,* 223-234.
Landesman-Dwyer, S. (1985) 'Describing and
    Evaluating Residential Environments,' in R.
    H. Bruininks & K. C. Lakin (eds.), *Living and
    Learning in the Least Restrictive Environ-
    ment,* Paul H. Brookes, Baltimore.
McCall, G. J. & Simmons, J. L. (1978) *Identities
    and Interactions: An Examination of Human
    Association in Everyday Life,* The Free Press,
    New York.
McDevitt, S. C., Smith, P. M., Schmidt, D. W., &
    Rosen, M. (1978) 'The Deinstitutionalized
    Citizen: Adjustment and Quality of Life,'
    Mental Retardation, 16, 23-24.
McKennell, A. C. & Andrews, F. M. (1983) 'Compon-
    ents of Perceived Life Quality,' *Journal of
    Community Psychology, 11,* 98-110.
Marans, R. W. & Wellman, J. D. (1977) 'The
    Quality of Non-metropolitan Living: Evalua-
    tion, Behaviors, and Expectations of Northern
    Michigan Residents,' University of Michigan
    Institute for Social Research, Ann Arbor.
Mercer, J. R. (1973) *Labeling the Mentally
    Retarded,* University of California Press,
    Berkeley.
Milbrath, L. W. (1977) 'Quality of Life on the
    Niagara Frontier Region of New York State,'
    Environmental Studies Center, State Univer-
    sity of New York at Buffalo. Mimeo.
Milbrath, L. W. (1982) 'A Conceptualization and
    Research Strategy for the Study of Ecological
    Aspects of the Quality of Life,' *Social
    Indicators Research, 10,* 133-157.
Mitchell, D. R. (1986) 'A Developmental Systems
    Approach to Planning and Evaluating Services
    for Persons with Handicaps,' in R. I. Brown
    (ed.), *Management and Administration of
    Rehabilitation Programmes,* Croom Helm,
    London/College-Hill Press, San Diego.
Noble, I. H. (1983) 'Defining Independence,' in
    D. G. Tate & L. M. Chadderdon (eds.), *Inter-
    national Perspectives about Independent
    Living,* University Center for International
    Rehabilitation, Michigan State University.
Parmenter, T. R. (1980) *Vocational Training for
    Independent Living,* World Rehabilitation
    Fund, Inc., New York.

Parmenter, T. R. (1986) *Bridges from School to Working Life for Handicapped Youth: The View from Australia,* World Rehabilitation Fund, Inc., New York.

Parmenter, T. R. (1987) 'Quality of Life of People with Physical Disabilities,' Macquarie University. Mimeo.

Rappaport, J. (1981) 'In Praise of Paradox: A Social Policy of Empowerment over Prevention,' *American Journal of Community Psychology, 9,* 1-25.

Sarason, S. B. & Doris, J. (1979) *Educational Handicap, Public Policy, and Social History,* Macmillan, New York.

Scheerenberger, R. C. & Felsenthol, D. (1977) 'Community Settings for Mentally Retarded Persons: Satisfaction and Activities,' *Mental Retardation, 15,* 3-7.

Schur, E. M. (1971) *Labeling Deviant Behavior: Its Sociological Implications,* Harper & Row, New York.

Scott, R. A. (1972) 'A Proposed Framework for Analyzing Deviance as a Property of Social Order,' in R. A. Scott & J. D. Douglass (eds.), *Theoretical Perspectives on Deviance,* Basic Books, New York.

Seltzer, G. B. (1981) 'Community Residential Adjustment: The Relationship Among Environment, Performance, and Satisfaction,' *American Journal of Mental Deficiency, 85,* 624-630.

Sharp, R. & Green, A. (1975) *Education and Social Control,* Routledge and Kegan Paul, London.

Simkins, J. (1979) *The Value of Independent Living: Looking at Cost-effectiveness in the United Kingdom,* World Rehabilitation Fund Inc., New York.

Stoddard, S. (1978) 'Independent Living: Concepts and Programs,' *American Rehabilitation, 3,* 2-5.

Stryker, S. (1959) 'Symbolic Interaction as an Approach to Family Research,' *Marriage and Family Living, 21,* 111-119.

Ward, J., Parmenter, T. R., Riches, V., & Hauritz, M. (1978) 'Adjustment to Work: A Follow-up of Mildly Handicapped Adolescents Who Have Undergone Training in a Work Preparation Centre.' *National Rehabilitation Digest, 2,* 34-38.

Ward, J., Parmenter, T. R., Riches, V., & Hauritz, M. (1986) 'A Summative Report of a Work Preparation Program for Mildly Intellectually Disabled Schoolleavers,' *Australian Disability Review*, *3*, 7-15.

Whelan, E. & Speake, B. (1981) *Getting to Work*, Souvenir Press, London.

Will, M. (1984) *OSERS Programming for the Transition of Youth with Disabilities: Bridges from School to Working Life*, Office of Special Education and Rehabilitation Services, Washington, D.C.

Williams, G. H. (1983) 'The Movement for Independent Living: An Evaluation and Critique,' *Social Science and Medicine*, *17*, 1003-1010.

World Health Organization (1980) *International Classification of Impairments, Disabilities, and Handicaps*, WHO, Geneva.

Zautra, A. J. & Reich, J. W. (1983) 'Life Events and Perceptions of Life Quality: Developments in a Two-factor Approach,' *Journal of Community Psychology*, *11*, 121-132.

Zola, I. K. (1983) 'Defining Independence,' in D. G. Tate & L. M. Chadderdon (eds.), *International Perspectives About Independent Living*, University Center for International Rehabilitation, Michigan State University.

Chapter Three

QUALITY OF LIFE IN PERSONS WITH DISABILITIES:
ISSUES IN THE DEVELOPMENT OF SERVICES[1]

Roger Blunden

SERVICES AND QUALITY OF LIFE

In researching and developing services for people
with disabilities, we often make tacit assumptions
about the quality of life of service users. For
example, we assume that a person's quality of life
is adversely affected in some way by his or her
disability and that the provision of services
will, to some extent, contribute towards an
improvement in this quality of life. However, the
term *quality of life* is usually left undefined and
means different things to different people under
different circumstances. In this chapter we first
examine the concept of quality of life, and then
explore some dimensions along which quality might
be judged, and examine how services influence the
quality of their users' lives, in both positive
and negative ways. The aim of the chapter is to
raise ideas and issues for discussion and to
suggest some ways in which service personnel and
researchers might help promote the quality of life
of service users.
      The importance of quality of life issues in
the context of service design and evaluation is
now being recognized. For example, Landesman
(1986) suggested that the American Association on
Mental Deficiency should take a leading role in
defining the terms quality of life and personal
life satisfaction and developing guidelines for
the measurement of programme effectiveness in
terms of the lifestyles of their users. In Wales,
an important aspect of the evaluation of the
All-Wales Strategy for the Development of Services
for People with Mental Handicap (Welsh Office,

37

1983) is an assessment of user lifestyles (Evans, Beyer & Todd; in preparation).

Some Dimensions of Quality of Life

Figure 1 shows four major dimensions along which quality of life is often judged. It should be emphasized that these are not mutually exclusive or independent: changes along one dimension may well influence another. However they do relate to the major ways in which quality of life is intuitively discussed.

FIGURE 1: Some Dimensions of Quality of Life

1. PHYSICAL WELLBEING
       Health
       Fitness
       Absence of disability

2. COGNITIVE WELLBEING
       Satisfaction with life
       Positive 'story'

3. MATERIAL WELLBEING
       Adequate income
       A home
       Means of transport

4. SOCIAL WELLBEING
       Community presence
       Choice
       Competence
       Respect
       Valued relationships

Physical Wellbeing

Physical wellbeing can be defined as the ability to use one's body in as effective a way as possible. This encompasses good health and fitness and the absence of disability. Many people place physical wellbeing high on their list of priorities when asked about quality of life.

Material Wellbeing

Quality of life within our own Western culture is often judged in terms of material wellbeing. We place great emphasis on the material aspects of life - income, housing, means of transport and other possessions. Whilst we sometimes acknowledge that such material aspects are not 'really' important, nevertheless we are encouraged through our education system and the advertising media to place the improvement of our material wellbeing high on our list of priorities.

Social Wellbeing

This fourth dimension of quality of life is often neglected, particularly in the context of services for people with disabilities. The term is used to refer to the extent to which an individual is able to enter into rewarding social relationships with others. O'Brien (1987) has usefully identified some important aspects of social wellbeing which have particular relevance in the context of services for people with disabilities.

Community presence refers to the basic ability of a person to live their lives in the company of other valued human beings. Regimes which deny this ability (such as the apartheid system, prisons and institutions for people with disabilities) prevent people from establishing rewarding social relationships.

Choice is another aspect of social wellbeing. It includes the ability to make small, everyday decisions like what to wear or what to eat, as well as major decisions such as where to live or work or with whom to live. Another important choice is the right to refuse to do something.

Competence is a facet of social wellbeing which is often taken for granted. The ability and opportunity to perform basic skills in such areas as mobility and communication play a vitally important part in our social wellbeing.

Respect is a further important component. The literature on devaluation (for example Wolfensberger, 1972) demonstrates how groups of people who are perceived as 'different' from the rest of society often acquire an undeserved bad reputation and become treated as second-class citizens.

The net result of a high level of social wellbeing is that a person enters into a series of valued relationships with others. They have a network of friends, relatives, colleagues and acquaintances and enjoy a mutually rewarding set of interactions with these people.

Cognitive Wellbeing

Much of the literature on quality of life concentrates on the area of life satisfaction. It is assumed that the 'real' test of quality is whether or not the individual expresses satisfaction and happiness with his/her life. One way of looking at this is that the person has a positive interpretation or 'story' about their life, which they tell both to themselves and to others. The assumption is often made that the cognitive aspects of wellbeing are the real dependent variables; if the other dimensions are satisfactory, then the person has a high degree of life satisfaction. This is not necessarily the case. There are examples of people who are physically fit and healthy and who are materially well off, but who are grossly dissatisfied with their lives, perhaps to the extent of being suicidal. On the other hand, it is possible to find people who are disabled or sick and who live materially and socially deprived lives, but who express a high level of satisfaction with their lives. Thus, whilst there clearly is a level of correlation between cognitive wellbeing and the other aspects of quality of life examined here, it is by no means clear that a simple relationship exists.

SOME TYPES OF SERVICE PROVISION AND THEIR IMPACT ON QUALITY OF LIFE

The above discussion has outlined some ways of considering the quality of life of an individual. In order to examine the impact of service provision on quality of life, it is worth considering the types of service which are available to people with disabilities. Figure 2 shows some common categories of service provision. It is perhaps important to emphasize that particular professions

may well work within more than one of the modes of
service provision identified in Figure 2. Having
identified some broad service types, it is also
possible to describe their intended impact on the
quality of life of their users.

FIGURE 2: Some Types of Service Provision

Health care
    Medical
    Surgical
    Audiological,
    Ophthalmological
    Dental

Resource access
    Housing services
    Job-finding & support
    Benefits

Rehabilitative
    Therapies (physio,
    etc.)
    Psychology
    Teaching/education
    Training
    Aids & adaptations

Support
    Domiciliary support
    Family relief
    Volunteer services

Counselling
    Social work
    Counselling therapies

Prosthetic
environments
    Social clubs
    Day care
    Residential care

Health Care

Health care services are directed towards the
prevention and cure of disease. They include a
range of both general and specialist services,
including, for example, general practitioner,
surgical, medical, dental, ophthalmological. In
general, people with disabilities will have the
same need for health care services as others,
although certain forms of disability may be
associated with particular clinical conditions
which will require specialist treatment.
    Health care services are mainly directed
towards aspects of people's physical wellbeing,
ensuring that the body operates in as effective a
way as possible. A good health care service will
also be concerned with the other aspects of
wellbeing, encouraging a positive attitude and
ensuring that the material and social aspects of
people's lives are supporting a healthy life.

Rehabilitative

Some forms of service provision are specifically habilitative, in that they are directed towards increasing or maintaining a person's competence in particular areas of functioning. Habilitative services include those offered by psychologists, teachers, therapists (physio, speech, occupational, etc.) and would include skills training and the provision of aids and adaptations.

Rehabilitative services are primarily directed towards aspects of physical and social wellbeing, helping people to overcome physical disabilities and being concerned with social aspects of competence.

For some forms of disability, prosthetic devices have an important part to play in the rehabilitation process. For example, walking aids, hearing aids and spectacles feature prominently in everyday life and assist their users to participate more fully in a wide range of activities. Other prosthetic devices (for example, wheelchairs or goecial computer communication systems) may help their users in some situations but not in others. In these instances, a careful judgment has to be made between possible alternative approaches, their feasibility and their effect on the user's life. For example, if it is possible to teach someone to walk without a wheelchair or to communicate without a computer, this may be preferable to the limitations imposed by these devices.

Counselling

Other forms of service provision are oriented more generally towards the provision of advice or helping people to resolve their problems. Social work is often concerned with counselling, as are various therapies such as psychoanalysis and marriage guidance.

Counselling services are aimed primarily at the cognitive aspects of wellbeing. Essentially the services work on the 'story' that people have about their lives. The counsellor may help the client to 'come to terms with' a particular situation or disability (in other words accept that things are as they are) or she may help the client to work out an alternative, more functional approach to his life.

Resource Access

Other services are specifically directed towards obtaining resources for people. Examples here would include housing services, job finding and support and services which allocate financial benefits to people.
Resource access services are directed towards material aspects of wellbeing, assisting the client to obtain financial or other resources which will help overcome the problems caused by the disability.

Support Services

Support services exist to enable people to continue living or working within a given environment. For example a range of domiciliary support services exist to help individuals to remain in their own homes. These may include home helps, meals on wheels and domiciliary nursing. Other forms of support may be more directed towards supporting other members of the family, such as sitting in or short term care. Volunteer services may be directed towards supporting the disabled person within a wider social or community network.
Support services are usually aimed at aspects of social wellbeing, assisting the disabled person or carers to enjoy a more varied or rewarding social life.

Prosthetic Environments

A further set of services have been labelled prosthetic environments. In this case the service system establishes an 'artificial' environment for some or all aspects of people's lives. Examples include social clubs for disabled people, day care and residential care. In all of these examples it is usual to find groups of disabled people congregated within one environment.
Prosthetic environments differ from the other types of service in that they have a much more general impact, usually on most aspects of wellbeing. Most day and residential services take over responsibility for the physical wellbeing of their clients, by providing separate health care services, or at least by channelling access to such services. Prosthetic environments may or may

not take responsibility for their clients' cognitive wellbeing, but they are likely to be a major influence on the interpretation people have of their own lives. Material aspects of wellbeing, such as income and means of transport are likely to be controlled by the service environment, and in the case of residential services, the person's home environment will also be in the control of the service system.

Some Unintended Negative Consequences of a Service's Approach

As well as the benefits of various types of service on their users' lifestyle, it is clear that many forms of service provision can cause harm to their users. This harm is usually unintentional and is often brought about by the organizational constraints within which the service operates.

In the area of physical wellbeing, services can be responsible for neglect or damage to their users' health. It is not uncommon to find people in institutional provision, often provided by a health authority, who have suffered considerably from disease (for example, hepatitis), poor nutrition, or lack of attention to dental, sight or hearing problems. It may be more difficult for aging or handicapped persons to gain access to health services than for other members of society. 'Special' services may be provided, which in effect provide a lower level of access than for the general population. For example, in many areas a separate physiotherapy service is provided for people with mental handicap, but this is often understaffed and much less accessible than the generic service.

Services may also have a negative effect on their users' cognitive wellbeing. People may be treated as problems ('Here's an interesting behaviour problem... senile dementia... xyz syndrome... partial paralysis...'). The service may encourage the user to feel devalued. Placing people in shabby surroundings, treating them as less than human, violating their privacy can all have a major detrimental effect on people's 'story' about themselves.

People who are dependent on organized service provision often suffer materially. Their disposable income is usually negligible, they may be deprived of personal possessions, and the physical environment in which they live or spend large portions of their life may be extremely impoverished.

Services can also damage their users' social wellbeing. It is still common to segregate people who are aging or disabled into isolated large group living or day environments. This sets them apart from other members of society and virtually eliminates the possibility of forming valued social relationships with non-disabled people. Lack of choice, decreasing competence, and lack of status and respect can all be negative consequences on social wellbeing as a result of the way that services are organized for people who are aging or disabled.

We have seen then in this part of the discussion that quality of life is a complex, multidimensional phenomenon which involves physical, cognitive, material and social aspects of wellbeing. Services are clearly aimed at improving some of these aspects of the lives of their users. However it is also apparent that the design and organization of services can have a major detrimental effect on some aspects of their users' lives. This problem may be particularly acute in prosthetic environments, which take over responsibility for many major aspects of their clients' lives. The aim for services must be the maximize their positive impact on the lifestyle of their users and to minimize the damage caused. In the remainder of this chapter, we look briefly at ways in which both service providers and researchers can contribute to this endeavour.

PURSUING QUALITY IN SERVICES

Given the influence which services can have on people's lives and the dangers which have just been discussed, what can be done in the design and organization of services to maximize the benefits and minimize the damage? When considering quality in services, two aspects become apparent. The first of these, borrowing from computer jargon, may be called 'user-friendliness'. This has to do with the service process. How accessible is the service to its users? Is it readily available? Can potential users afford it? Is it jargon free? Are services 'customized' to meet the needs of individual users? These are all important issues if it can be assumed that the service is of basic benefit to its users. (If the service does not effectively help its users, then user-friendliness becomes rather an irrelevance).

The second aspect of service quality is then effectiveness. Following the earlier discussion in this chapter, we might consider effectiveness in the light of the dimensions of quality of life discussed above. An effective service is one which has a positive impact on the physical, cognitive, material and social aspects of its users' wellbeing and much minimizes the damage to these. What can be done to promote the effectiveness of a service?

Traditionally this has been the task of monitoring. However, in the United Kingdom at least, there have been major problems in attempting to implement effective monitoring of services for people with disabilities. One reason for this is lack of clarity about the values, objectives or criteria on which a quality service is based. It is difficult to monitor the quality of a service in the absence of a clearly defined notion of what quality is.

Another problem in the context of services for people who are aging or with disabilities in the United Kingdom has been a concern with minimum standards. Monitoring has sometimes been introduced as a response to scandals and the primary concern is to avoid a repetition of situations which hit newspaper headlines. Monitoring is also often seen as predominantly an information gathering exercise, divorced from action. Information is often channelled up the service delivery system with little expectation that any changes will result.

Where monitoring does take place, it is often concerned with the service process, rather than client outcomes. Thus the activities of professionals are monitored, for example, in terms of the way they complete records or identify clients or make assessments or obtain funding, rather than in terms of the effect that all of these activities have on service users.

In Britain in particular, monitoring has a bad reputation for being negative and bureaucratic. As a race we often find it difficult to celebrate positive achievements and find it much easier to criticize and complain about deficiencies. The notion of monitoring being a positive process is seldom encountered this side of the Atlantic.

One recent British attempt to engage in a more effective form of monitoring has been set out by the Independent Council (1986). They suggest that 'stakeholders', those with an interest in the service either as consumers or providers, should form Quality Action groups, committed to reviewing the service's quality and taking action to improve it. The group should first clarify the values underpinning the service. What are the major assumptions about the value of the service's clients as individuals and what, in general terms, is the service setting out to achieve for its clients?

The group then focuses more specifically on the ways in which the service aims to influence the lives of its users. These 'accomplishments' concentrate on client outcomes rather than service processes, for example:

> *'people make use of facilities in the community',*

> *'people participate in a wider range of community activities',*

> *'people have friends',*

> *'people are more independent in their domestic and personal lives',*

> *'people live in accommodation of their choice, with other people of their choice'.*

Having defined the general accomplishments of the service, the group then focuses on one or more of these for further investigation. They collect and review evidence on the extent to which the service attains its client outcomes in this area, agree on goals for the improvement of the service's performance, and implement these goals. At this stage a further accomplishment is selected and the cycle of review and action is repeated.

Although this process is in its infancy, early experience (Beyer, 1987) suggests that it may be a useful means of ensuring that services become more responsive to the quality of life of their users than has often been the case in the past.

Implications for Research

This chapter ends with a brief account of how the notion of quality of life has influenced work carried out in recent years by researchers in the Mental Handicap in Wales Applied Research Unit, Cardiff. It also looks to the future and discusses some developments in research methodology which may contribute towards the development and evaluation of quality-oriented service systems.

Measurement of client outcomes has always been a major feature of the Unit's work. Early studies involved the use of 'engagement' as a key dependent variable (Porterfield, Blunden & Blewitt, 1980). Engagement is a measure of the extent to which service users interact in a constructive manner with their environment (for example, by manipulating objects or by interacting with other people). This can be thought of as one indication of social wellbeing. These early studies were particularly concerned with evaluating changes in the organizational aspects of day and residential services. Briefly, it proved possible to improve the quality of lives of profoundly handicapped people, as reflected in levels of engagement, by a change in the way in which staff were organized and interacted with their clients.

More recently there has been an increasing emphasis on the development and evaluation of community based services for people with mental handicap. In 1980 a major evaluation was started by NIMROD, a pilot comprehensive, community based service in the city of Cardiff. At the time the evaluation was started, client competence, as reflected in increases in skill levels, was considered to be the major client outcome to be measured. Clients' use of community facilities and contact with friends and relatives were also examined (Humphreys, 1986). These reflect further aspects of social wellbeing. Data were also collected on accidents and illnesses, important aspects of physical wellbeing. The long term evaluation strategy adopted for the NIMROD research, included repeated assessments of these variables. More recently data have been collected on the views of some of the handicapped users of the service and this will partly reflect some aspects of people's cognitive wellbeing. This five-year evaluation period is now drawing to an end and data are now being analyzed.

In order to explore further one aspect of the impact of NIMROD on the quality of life of its users, a short term study was undertaken (Evans, Todd, Blunden, Porterfield & Ager, 1987) to measure the impact on clients' lifestyle of moving into an ordinary house. This study involved the use of diaries, interview and observational data to chart changes in people's location, activity and contact before and after the move. Again this study concentrated primarily on aspects of social wellbeing.

At the present time the Unit has embarked upon an evaluation of the All Wales Mental Handicap Strategy, a national initiative to promote the development of community based services throughout Wales. A long term evaluation of this strategy is again concentrating on service users' lifestyle as the major dependent variable (Evans, Beyer & Todd, in preparation). This examines in some detail, aspects of physical, material and social wellbeing and will be used both as a guide to local planning and as a means of evaluating the effectiveness of the strategy over time.

The above suggests some ways in which evaluative research can contribute to the promotion of quality of life in services for disabled people. By measuring and providing feedback on aspects of people's wellbeing, research can influence both the design of new services and the way in which they develop over time, hopefully making them more responsive to the quality of life of their users.

Other styles of research make a more direct contribution to the development of quality-oriented services. Many of the issues concerning this direct relationship between research and practice were discussed by Westwood (1986). We briefly consider below three action research strategies which are also being developed in the context of Welsh research in the field of mental handicap.

Evaluability assessment (Wholey, 1977) requires service personnel and researchers to consider jointly aspects of an evaluation before embarking upon any such research. Several key questions are in order to judge the extent to which it makes sense to evaluate a programme. These include:

What is being evaluated? - Is it possible to define the service or services which are the subject of the evaluation sufficiently precisely?

What are the programme's objectives for its clients? - Is it possible to identify precisely those aspects of clients' quality of life which will determine the success or otherwise of the programme?

Are these objectives measurable?

Does the programme design logically lead to the achievement of these outcomes?

What decisions are to be made on the basis of the evaluation, and will the exercise provide relevant information to enable these decisions to be taken?

These are crucial questions which are often left unstated at the outset of an evaluative research exercise. The point is made by Wholey that, unless these issues are clarified, there is little point in embarking on an evaluation. The methodology of evaluability assessment provides a systematic way of investigating these questions. Early experience in this Research Unit (Beyer, Evans & Todd, 1987) suggests that this is a fruitful way of ensuring that evaluative research will be relevant to the development of services which promote quality of life amongst their users.

Another way of ensuring that research is relevant to professionals and service users is for them to be explicitly involved in the research process. The method of collaborative evaluation (Patton, 1982) offers one way of achieving this. A 'task force' is formed consisting of all those with an interest in the evaluation. This can include staff, family members and service users, as well as researchers. The group first focuses the evaluation by deciding what questions need to be asked and how the answers to these are to be used. This is a crucial and often difficult part of the evaluation process. It is often much easier to decide what information to collect than to decide how it is to be used. The evaluation can then be designed with these specific uses in mind. The collection, analysis and interpretation of data are also conducted jointly by the task force, who then apply and disseminate the findings. It is at this stage that the early emphasis on the use of the evaluation pays off.

The Mental Handicap in Wales Applied Research Unit has successfully adopted this approach in two recent research projects. Evans and Blunden (1984) described an evaluation of a short term care service, conducted collaboratively with service personnel and consumers. Humphreys and Blunden (1987) reported a collaborative evaluation of the individual planning system within the NIMROD service in Cardiff. Both evaluations demonstrated the feasibility and beneficial results of including consumers and service users in the evaluation process, ensuring that the research was of direct relevance to service consumers and staff.

A third research methodology which can potentially make a direct contribution to the development of quality-oriented services is soft systems analysis (Checkland, 1981). This is a form of systems analysis which recognizes that human systems cannot be treated in the same rigorously mathematical way as can other more mechanical systems. It is often more difficult to define clear goals and to obtain agreement on these. Different actors in the situation will have different perceptions and priorities.

In a very readable introduction to soft systems analysis, Naughton (1984) describes seven practical stages.

Stage 1: The problem situation unstructured. The analysis usually begins with a 'mess', rather than a clearly identified problem. Different actors in the situation have different perspectives.

Stage 2: Rich picture. The situation, in all its complexity, is summarized in pictorial form.

Stage 3: Relevant systems and root definitions. From the rich picture a number of specific systems are defined in terms of inputs, outputs and trans-formational processes.

Stage 4: Conceptual model. An abstract model of the system is built, showing the logical stages necessary to move from inputs to outputs.

Stage 5: Comparison of conceptual model with rich picture. At this stage the abstract conceptual model is brought back into the real world and compared with the real situation contained in the rich picture.

Stage 6: Debate with the people involved in the situation. The ideas developed are discussed with a view to determining their desirability and feasibility. It is recognized that new ideas, however worthy, are unlikely to be accepted without the support of the people in the situation.

Stage 7: Implementation of agreed changes. Only when the above stages have been completed is there an attempt to implement changes to the situation.

Soft systems analysis provides a systematic basis for clarifying a problem situation involving human actors, and working out negotiated solutions based on a logical analysis. As such it has great potential in the field of services for disabled people as a research and development tool which will directly address issues of service quality.

CONCLUSIONS

This chapter has reviewed the issue of quality of life in the context of services for people with disabilities. It has been suggested that quality of life is multi-dimensional, and a framework for examining quality in terms of four key areas of wellbeing has been set out.
In summary, this chapter suggests:

1.   that it might be useful to examine quality of life in terms of:
       - physical wellbeing,
       - material wellbeing,
       - social wellbeing,
       - cognitive wellbeing;
2.   that various forms of service provision:
       - health care,
       - habilitative,
       - counselling,
       - resource access,
       - support,
       - prosthetic environments,
       are agreed towards different aspects of quality of life;

3. that services can also have unintended
    negative effects on the various aspects of
    wellbeing identified above;
4. that there is a major service task in
    pursuing quality in terms of the impact of
    services on people's lives. Some early
    British experience in this area was outlined;
5. that the notion of quality of life has
    important implications for resarchers, in
    terms of:
    - measurement of client outcomes,
    - action research strategies;
6. that the following action research strategies
    are worthy of further attention:
    - evaluability assessment,
    - collaborative evaluation,
    - soft systems analysis.

REFERENCES

Beyer, S. (1987) 'Pursuing Quality through a
    Quality Action Group: Experiences in the
    CUSS Home Support Service,' in L. Ward (ed.),
    *Getting Better All the Time: Issues and
    Strategies for Ensuring Quality in Community
    Services for People with Mental Handicap*,
    King's Fund Centre, London.

Beyer, S., Evans, G., & Todd, S. (1987) *The West
    Glamorgan Staff Development Initiative: An
    Example of Evaluability Assessment*, Mental
    Handicap in Wales - Applied Research Unit,
    Cardiff, U.K.

Checkland, P. (1981) *Systems Thinking, Systems
    Practice*, John Wiley & Sons, Chichester & New
    York.

Evans, G., Beyer, S., & Todd, S. (in preparation)
    *Evaluating the Impact of the All-Wales
    Strategy on the Lifestyles of People with
    Mental Handicap: A Research Methodology*,
    Mental Handicap in Wales - Applied Research
    Unit, Cardiff, U.K.

Evans, G. & Blunden, R. (1984) 'A Collaborative
    Approach to Evaluation,' *Journal of Practical
    Approaches to Developmental Handicap, 8*,
    14-18.

Evans, G., Todd, S., Blunden, R., Porterfield, J.,
    & Ager, A. (1987) 'Evaluating the Impact of
    a Move to Ordinary Housing,' *British Journal
    of Mental Subnormality* (in press).

Humphreys, S. (1986) 'Evaluation of the NIMROD Project,' in N. Eisenberg & D. Glasgow (eds.), *Current Issues in Clinical Psychology: 1985 Annual Merseyside Course in Clinical Psychology*, Gower, Aldershot.

Humphreys, S. & Blunden, R. (1987) 'A Collaborative Evaluation of an Individual Plan System,' *British Journal of Mental Subnormality, xxxiii*, 19-30.

Independent Development Council for People with Mental Handicap (1986) *Pursuing Quality: How Good Are Your Local Services for People with Mental Handicap?* Available from IDC, 126 Albert Street, London NW1 7NF.

Landesman, S. (1986) 'Quality of Life and Personal Life Satisfaction: Definition and Measurement Issues,' *Mental Retardation, 24*, 141-143.

Naughton, J. (1984) *Soft Systems Analysis: An Introductory Guide* (T301 Block IV SSA: Guide). The Open University Press, Milton Keynes.

O'Brien, J. (1987) 'A Guide to Personal Futures Planning,' in G. T. Bellamy and B. Wilcox (eds.), *A Comprehensive Guide to the Activities Catalog: An Alternative Curriculum for Youth and Adults with Severe Disabilities*, Paul H. Brookes, Baltimore, Maryland.

Patton, M. Q. (1982) *Practical Evaluation*, Sage Publications, London and Beverly Hills.

Porterfield, J., Blunden, R., & Blewitt, E. (1980) 'Improving Environments for Profoundly Handicapped Adults: Establishing Staff Routines for High Client Engagement,' *Behavior Modification, 4*, 225-241.

Welsh Office (1983) *All-Wales Strategy for the Development of Services for Mentally Handicapped People*, Welsh Office, Cardiff.

Westwood, R. (1986) 'Conjoint Evaluation as a Programme Development Strategy,' in R. Brown (ed.), *Management and Administration of Rehabilitation Programmes*, Croom Helm, London/College-Hill Press, San Diego.

Wholey, J. S. (1977) 'Evaluability Assessment,' in L. Rutman (ed.), *Evaluation Research Methods: A Basic Guide*, Sage Publications, Beverly Hills.

Wolfensberger, W. (1972) *The Principle of Normalization in Human Services*, National Institute on Mental Retardation, Toronto, Canada.

NOTE

1. This chapter was based on a paper presented to the International Conference on Aging and Disabilities, University of Calgary, July 1986. The Mental Handicap in Wales Applied Research Unit is funded by the Department of Health and Social Security and the Welsh Office.

Chapter Four

INTEGRATED CHILD DEVELOPMENT SERVICES (ICDS)
PROGRAMMES AND QUALITY OF LIFE OF CHILDREN

Tehal Kohli

ICDS IN INDIA

Growth of a country depends to a large degree on
integrated development of the children of that
country, who are its most valuable resource.
Hence all relevant agencies and procedures
contributing to or responsible for this growth
should be integrated in order to ensure all round
development of the children. India is the second
most populous and the seventh largest country in
the world, with only 2.4 per cent of the world's
land area supporting 15 per cent of the world's
total population (Census of India, 1981). A
majority of its 272 million children below 14
years and 121 million children below 6 years
(Census of India, 1981) live in impoverished
conditions which impede their physical and mental
development. As a response to the unmet needs of
this vast and vulnerable population, and in
pursuance of the National Policy for Children
(Ministry of Social Welfare, 1974), the Government
of India launched upon its most ambitious and
comprehensive plan to increase child survival rate
among the poorest and enhance the health, nutrition and learning opportunities of pre-school
children and their mothers. Drawing upon experience culled from 20 years of planned social
development, the ICDS scheme is designed both as a
preventive and as a developmental effort. It
extends beyond the existing health and education
systems to reach children and their mothers in
villages, tribal areas and urban slums and deliver
to them an integrated package of essential early
childhood services such as non-formal pre-school
education, immunization, and health check-ups, as

shown in Figure 1, where *'the convergence of inputs and services of ICDS is a clear trend which cuts across all levels of the planning and implementation process'* (Sadka, 1984).

FIGURE 1: Integrated Services

Source: Ministry of Human Resource Development, 1986.

The above pattern is based on the concept that services for children must collaborate and function in tandem if they are to have lasting value, and if their total impact is to be more than the sum of their separate efforts. Figure 2 clarifies this point further.

FIGURE 2: Services for Children and Mothers

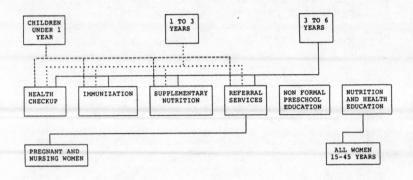

The blueprint for the ICDS scheme was drawn up by the Ministry of Social Welfare[1], Government of India, in 1975 and has called for coordinated and concerted effort by different ministries, departments and voluntary organizations (Figure 1). The ICDS scheme was launched on an experimental basis in 33 areas on October 2, 1975, i.e. on the 106th birthday of Mahatma Gandhi, the Father of the Nation. Subsequently, encouraged by the progress registered by these projects, the programme was expanded and by 1979-80 a total of 150 projects were sanctioned. During the Sixth Five Year Plan, i.e. from 1980-81 to 1984-85, 869 projects were sanctioned and, during 1985-86, 210 more projects were sanctioned, bringing the total number to 1,229 projects located in villages and urban slum communities in every state and Union Territory of India (Figure 3). Now by the end of September 1986, there are already 1,605 ICDS projects (Ministry of Human Resource Development, 1986). Ethically speaking, every child should be assured access to the fulfilment of all basic needs. Yet, facing the existing realities of outreach and utilization, it is suggested that 70 per cent of the target groups (children 0-6 years) should be covered by all services by 2000 AD, whereas health and nutrition services should be extended to all the needy groups as early as possible. By the end of the Seventh Plan, a modest network of ECCE facilities should be established in all tribal development blocks, blocks having substantial scheduled caste population and slums in large cities. A minimum of 250,000 lakh centres should be established by 1990. Though various schemes need to be improved and expanded, this coverage will be predominantly achieved by expansion of ICDS. ECCE will be expanded to a level of one million lakh centres by 1995 and two million lakh by the year 2000. Most of the coverage will be through ICDS, but diverse kinds of pre-primary education centres and day care centres will also be encouraged and supported. Besides these centrally sponsored projects, 129 additional projects are being run by the State sector. Further, central government plans to launch a total of 2,000 projects all over the country to achieve the targets set-up for the Seventh Five Year Plan of India. These services exemplify a number of major points:

1. The services are cost effective. The cost of feeding each child is Rs. 0.50 per day for 270 days a year, or Rs. 135.00 per child per year. Supplementary nutrition can be provided by each state from its own resources.
2. The services are directly linked to the existing government infrastructure.
3. Services are community based and can freely make use of the resources in non-governmental agencies and academic institutions.

Figure 3 represents the year-wise expansion and expenditure of ICDS.

Figure 4 represents the targets of various services to be reached during the Sixth Five Year Plan.

Aims and Objectives of ICDS

The major or ultimate goal of ICDS is to bring about total development of the child physically, mentally and socially. This goal can be broken up into a number of specific objectives (Figure 5).

FIGURE 3:   Integrated Child Development Services

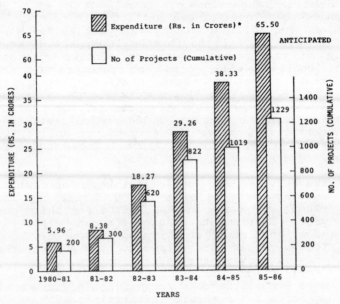

Total AWs in India: 63,267

Total 0-6 yrs. beneficiaries: 3,420,000

*1 crore = 10 million

Source: Ministry of Human Resource Development, 1986.

FIGURE 4:   Targets of the Sixth Five Year Plan, 1980-85

IMMUNIZATION & HEALTH CHECKUPS	10.4 million children
SUPPLEMENTARY NUTRITION	6.1 million children 1.2 million women
PRE-SCHOOL EDUCATION	3.0 million children
NON-FORMAL EDUCATION	2.4 million women

Source: Sadka, 1984.

Beneficiaries of ICDS

Beneficiaries of ICDS services are as follows:

Beneficiaries:	Services:
1. Expectant and lactating mothers	i) Health check-up ii) Immunization of expectant mothers against tetanus iii) Supplementary nutrition iv) Nutrition and health education
2. Other women between 15 and 45 years	Nutrition and health education
3. Children less than 1 year	i) Supplementary nutrition ii) Immunization iii) Health check-ups iv) Referral services
4. Children from 1 to 6 years	i) Supplementary nutrition ii) Immunization iii) Health check-up iv) Referral services v) Non-formal pre-school education

In the selection of ICDS projects in rural areas, priority consideration is given to:

1) areas predominantly inhabited by tribes, particularly backward tribes,
2) backward areas,
3) drought-prone areas,
4) areas inhabited by scheduled castes,
5) nutritionally deficient areas, and
6) areas poor in development of social services.

In the selection of the projects in urban areas, priority consideration is given to: (1) slum locations, and (2) areas predominantly inhabited by scheduled castes.

FIGURE 5: Aims and Objectives of the ICDS

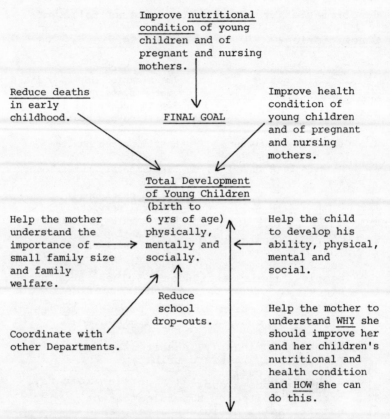

These aims and objectives can be achieved only if the community is interested in all these things happening. This is the foundation of the whole programme. We call this COMMUNITY INVOLVEMENT.

Source: National Institute of Public Cooperation and Child Development, 1984.

Functionaries of ICDS Centres (Anganwadis)

The major ICDS functionaries are:

1) Child Development Project Officer (CDPO),
2) Supervisors (Mukhayasevikas),
3) Anganwadi workers (AWWs), and
4) Helpers (AWHs).

The institution through which all services are provided is known as an anganwadi (AW). This concept was taken from the Gujarati language and it means 'courtyard's garden' (angan - courtyard, wadi - garden), and has had a deep rooted impact on the philosophy of child development. The term was first used officially in the Report of the Mina Swaminthan Committee on pre-school education in 1972. The AWWs are at the grass-root level of the programmes. Each AWW has a pivotal role to play in the structure. She is a multi-purpose agent of change and is selected from the community which she has to serve.

The AWW is a frontline field worker who performs a wide range of multi-faceted duties to direct and support the parents for the integrated development of their children. Some of the important tasks (NIPCCD, 1984) carried out by AWWs who are in charge of the AWs are as follows:

1. Getting the people/community involved in the local programme. This involves the worker familiarizing herself personally with local people, their attitudes, values and practices, in order to gain their confidence for convincing people that ICDS is their programme.

2. Identifying the most malnourished children through observation of age, growth and available food, and providing supplementary nutrition. Also selecting the most needy and malnourished pregnant and nursing mothers.

3. Coordinating with the Auxiliary Nurse Midwife (ANM) or Lady Health Visitor (LHV) in carrying out and encouraging use of an immunization programme through activities such as informing mothers about immunization.

4. Carrying out health check-ups and keeping a look-out for all illnesses in the village and referring to other services as appropriate.

5. Conducting non-formal pre-school education. The AWW is supposed to prepare an 'education kit' including charts, play material from local wastes and inexpensive materials, etc. She is to work as a catalytic agent by using local resources for meeting the basic needs of children.

6. Providing services of nutrition, health and population education by helping women understand what will keep their families strong and healthy.

63

7. Providing services of functional literacy for adult women by conducting these classes.

Coverage

While the demographic and other characteristics may differ from one project to another, a rural project (a community development block) is assumed to have a population of 100,000 of which 17 per cent, i.e. 17,000, are expected to be less than 6 years of age (3 per cent, i.e. 3,000, less than 1 year, 6 per cent, i.e. 6,000, in the age group 1-2 years and 8 per cent, i.e. 8,000, in the age group 3-5). The number of women in the age group 15-45 years is assumed to be 20,000, of which 4,000 are anticipated to be nursing and expectant mothers. The number of villages in a rural project is assumed to be 100.

A tribal project (tribes are recognized under the Indian constitution in many states) is assumed to have a population of 35,000, of which 17 per cent, i.e. 5,950, are expected to be of less than 6 years (3 per cent, i.e. 1,050, less than 1 year, 6 per cent, i.e. 2,100, in the age group 1-2 years and 8 per cent, i.e. 2,800, in the age group 3-5). The number of women in the age group 15-45 years is estimated at 7,000, of which 1,400 are expected to be expectant and nursing mothers. The number of villages in a tribal project is assumed to be 50.

An urban project (one or more wards/slums) is assumed to have the same demographic characteristics as a rural project (Manual on ICDS, NIPCCD, 1984).

The National Institute of Public Cooperation and Child Development (NIPCCD) is an institution which is actively involved in relation to training, research, evaluation and monitoring components of the scheme. The institution is often called upon to bear the responsibility of organizing a series of regional/national workshops for various levels of ICDS functionaries.

ICDS AND QUALITY OF LIFE OF CHILDREN IN GENERAL

In order to achieve its objectives, the ICDS scheme envisages the delivery of a package of six services by its functionaries, particularly AWWs. There are one AWW and one AWH attached to each of the anganwadi centres.

The training of functionaries of ICDS is an important function. Involvement and participation of the community is critical and facilitates the delivery of the services. When millions of rupees are being spent on the scheme, the objectives of the scheme have to be concrete, measured and evaluated in terms of 'output' variables which will throw light on the effectiveness and accountability for the services implemented. These will, of course, ultimately affect the quality of life of children which can be measured qualitatively or quantitatively as follows:

Inputs/Services	Quality of Life	Indicators
Immunization	Physical and/or	Infant mortality
Health checking	psychological	rate
Referral services	development of	Morbidity
Supplementary	the child	Maternal mortality
nutrition		Malnutrition
Nutrition and		Reducing drop-outs
health education		Increasing enrolment
Pre-school		Motor, cognitive,
education		emotional, social
		development
		Development of
		self-help skills
		Psychological
		wellbeing

High infant mortality rate, high levels of morbidity, high incidence of malnutrition and nutrition related diseases, temporary or irreversible diseases, low literacy rates - these are some of the prospects staring at the 110 million children under six years of age in India. (Ministry of Human Resource Development, 1985)

However, the evolution of ICDS services in terms of tangible benefits accruing to the community during its first decade (1975-85) indicates that *'it has the potential of becoming a silent revolution - a profound instrument of community and human resource development'* (Ministry of Human Resource Development, 1985). Impact of the ICDS on the quality of life of children will be reviewed within the framework of the above eight inputs.

Immunization - Immunization against tuberculosis, whooping cough, diptheria, tetanus, polio and measles for all children below one year of age and immunization against tetanus for all expectant mothers have been covered under the ICDS scheme. The Ministry of Human Resource Development in its document *A Decade of ICDS* (1985) has reported on the basis of surveys, starting from base-line surveys of 21.0, 4.9 and 9.2 per cent for BCG, DPT and polio vaccination respectively in 1976, that coverage rose in 1983 to 64.6, 61.0 and 59.6 per cent in ICDS blocks as compared to 29.4, 21.4 and 16.6 per cent in non-ICDS blocks. This led to a reduction in infant mortality. In 1981 the national infant mortality was 110 average per 1,000 births but only 88.2 in ICDS projects in 1982-83. Mortality due to severe malnutrition declined from 15.0 to 3.0 per cent (Ministry of Human Resource Development, 1985), but there was a greater reduction for females than males.

A quiet influence of family planning was evident from the decline in birth rate to 24.2 as against the national average of 33 per cent in 1983 (Ministry of Human Resource Development, 1985). Vasundhra and Srinivasan (1985) also found that the acceptance of education relating to child birth and birth spacing was higher among ICDS beneficiary couples (33.3 per cent) than among the ICDS non-beneficiary couples (26.8 per cent).

Health Check-up - This service includes antenatal care of expectant mothers, postnatal care of nursing mothers and care of newborns and children under 6 years of age. This service is carried out at three different levels, i.e. by the AWW at AW, by the ANM/LHV at the sub-centre or by the medical officer (MO) at the Primary Health Centre (PHC). In Ministry of Human Resource Development (1985) an increase in antenatal care of pregnant women is reported using the observed baselines of 6.0, 18.6 and 19.6 per cent when the family welfare programmes were started in 1976 for tetanus, toxoid, iron and folic acid and health check-ups. The comparable 1983 figures for ICDS blocks are 33.1, 47.9 and 59.3 per cent through the use of trained personnel while 28.9, 18.6 and 19.6 per cent are the respective figures in non-ICDS blocks. Thus there appears to have been general improvement over time, but that improvement is particularly marked in the ICDS blocks.

Overall there was an increase in maternity assistance through trained personnel and post-natal care which rose to about 60 per cent.

Besides, the upward trend in coverage of pre-school children through health check-ups has been reported to increase 2-4-fold (i.e. from 15 to 30 to 60 per cent) of the number in non-ICDS projects (Sahai & Mahajan, 1986). However, the qualitative and depth analysis of the projects shows that the health standards are far from satisfactory and need further intensive probing and extensive expansion. Krishna and Nadkarni (1983) also stressed similar findings. Results of their study revealed that though health coverage in general, and immunization in particular, improved and went beyond 50 per cent, there was a high drop-out rate in vaccination administered in series. They also found that important drugs were generally not available when needed, especially in rural and tribal blocks.

Referral Services - Referral services provide relevant medical care according to the seriousness of the disease as well as follow-up care of cases that have been treated or given medical attention at appropriate levels. Studies have shown that, despite a well thought out system of referral from peripheral points to apex institutions, health services were not utilized extensively, e.g. a referral study in 406 AWs where 4,292 children with severe malnutrition were followed up every week for 12 weeks, revealed that half the children could not use the facilities (Tandon & Sahai, 1984). This was due to beneficiaries not respond-ing to scheduled dates, medicine not provided in time, or the beneficiaries being too far away.

Supplementary Nutrition - This service aims to identify and replace deficiencies in calories, proteins, essential vitamins and minerals in existing diets, reduce cut-backs in the family diet, and take other measures for the nutritional rehabilitation of children below 6 years of age, as well as expectant and nursing mothers from low income families. The AWW is the key local func-tionary for the nutrition component of the ICDS scheme. Food is the most costly (more than half the ICDS budget - Krishna & Nadkarni, 1983) and an attractive component of the package of services of ICDS. The cost is Rs. 225.00 per child per year. Figures from the annual surveys of the Central Technical Cell on ICDS (1983) reveal that the prophylaxis coverage of vitamin A increased from 9.9 in non-ICDS to 59.5 per cent in ICDS blocks, and iron and folic acid increased from 8.4 to 26.3 per cent. Reports show that this led to considerable decline in the prevalence of malnutrition from an overall baseline of 19.1 per cent in 1976 to 7.8 per cent in ICDS blocks and 11.4 in non-ICDS blocks in 1983.

<u>Nutrition and Health Education</u> - *'The Nutrition and Health Education component of the ICDS scheme aims to effectively communicate certain basic health and nutrition messages with a view to enhancing the mother's awareness of the child's needs and her capacity to look after these within the family environment'* (Manual on ICDS, NIPCCD, 1984). This service is meant for all women in the age group 15-45 years and, if possible, other members of the family. Problems of ignorance, ill-health and malnutrition are interlinked. The AWW gets very little time for this service. Although there is very little published work to stress the impact of this service, unpublished studies have confirmed that it does have lasting returns in terms of improved health and nutritional status of women and children.

<u>Non-Formal Pre-School Education</u> - Non-formal pre-school education is an important component of the package of services imparted under the ICDS scheme. It aims at laying appropriate foundations for physical, psychological and social development of the child, and thus develops desirable social attitudes, values and behavioural patterns as well as providing early environmental stimulation. All this is to be done by AWWs who are supposed to prepare their own pre-school kit by utilizing local wastes, inexpensive play materials, charts, etc. Each AWW is responsible for organizing pre-school activities for about 40 children admitted in the AW in the age group 3 to 5 years. She has to play the role of a friend, an elderly playmate, and a guide, while imparting pre-school education. The modus operandi is that *'there has to be flexibility in the programme content and methods and the child is to be encouraged and stimulated to grow at his own pace'* (Manual on ICDS, NIPCCD, 1984).

Many published and unpublished studies in ICDS show the beneficial effects of pre-school education on enhanced regular school enrolment (Lal & Wati, 1986), cognitive, language and other areas of child development (Krishna & Nadkarni,

1983; Khosla, 1986; Muralidharan & Kaur, 1986). Research in this area, however, is too scanty to make firm conclusions, particularly with regard to the drop-out rate of children with ICDS experiences and the impact of pre-school education on social and emotional development and development of self-help skills.

For the above reasons, time and again it was recommended by NIPCCD (1983, 1986) that increased 'refresher training' in pre-school education should be imparted to AWWs and helpers so that this service could be made more effective.

Besides the above inputs making impact on the quality of life of slum dwellers, community involvement is a very important factor in obtaining successful impact. This would assist the ICDS functionaries in running the project and ensure better care of children under 6 years of age.

Lastly, regular training, orientation and refresher courses of ICDS functionaries would lead to better utilization of human resources, and functionaries would be more effective in delivering all aspects of the ICDS scheme.

ICDS AND THE QUALITY OF LIFE OF DEVELOPMENTALLY DELAYED CHILDREN

Developmentally delayed children are those children who have retarded or delayed development in one or more areas of child development. Such children are usually neglected in ICDS centres or by AWs because personnel, unless or until they are trained, are not able to identify mild delays. Such deficits consequently lead to mental retardation. About 80 per cent of the developmentally delayed children are due to environmental influences such as abnormal mother-child relations, deprivation in environmental stimulations in the formative years of life, birth injury, difficult labour, forced delivery, postnatal hazards such as viral infections, or inflammation of the brain.

Role of AWWs in Prevention of Developmental Deficits of Children

The high prevalence of developmental deficits in children of ICDS centres (anganwadis) is a sad fact, but the most relevant and heartwarming point is the etiology of the developmental deficits

GOVERNORS STATE UNIVERSITY
UNIVERSITY PARK
IL 60466

which discloses the fact that 80 per cent of developmental deficits in children are due to environmental influences, many of which can be prevented from occurring. ICDS's stress on integration of various services and special focus on grass-root level workers such as AWWs and AWHs (anganwadi helpers) to deliver these basic services can help in prevention of many of the developmental deficits in expectant and nursing mothers, who are one of the major beneficiaries of the scheme. AWWs can be particularly helpful in creating conditions for 'primary intervention' by making the expectant mothers aware of the importance of immunization, and helping them to minimize deleterious factors in pregnancy such as use of a wide range of drugs, the involvement of teratogenic agents which harm the developing fetus, and harmful toxic environmental factors and also by informing the mothers of the adverse effects of too much radiation exposure and the value of improved prenatal and perinatal care and conditions. They can provide family counselling where needed, and help the lady health visitors in distributing tonics and micronutrients as well as food supplements to expectant mothers.

Role of AWWs in Early Detection of Developmental Deficits of Young Children

The role of AWWs is critical yet complicated. They need ingenuity and an interest in the welfare of children under their custody. Since AWWs maintain the growth charts of all children in anganwadi centres, they can easily spot the underweight and extremely undernourished children. Malnutrition and undernourishment are the major causes of developmental delays. Special diets can be prescribed for such children by the doctors of the area. Figure 6, which represents the weight curve from 0 to 5 years, offers a guideline to the identification of such children.

AWWs can act as 'mini psychologists' and can be made aware of the milestones of child development from birth to 6 years so that they can detect those children who are grossly lagging behind the expected developmental milestones or who are 'high risk' children for developmental delay. UNESCO's (1976) guidelines *The Child and His Development from Birth to Six Years Old*, can be safely used

GOVERNORS STATE UNIVERSITY
UNIVERSITY PARK
IL. 60466

by these paraprofessionals (AWWs) to ascertain the satisfactory or delayed development of the children (Prakasha, Digest III, 1983).

If AWWs are duly informed about the obstacles to child development (Prakasha, Digest IV, 1984), such as (1) malnutrition, (2) accidents, and (3) non-fulfilment of basic physiological and psycho-social needs during their training period, they can further probe into the causes of deficit in children and help families realize the importance of removing these obstacles. Early detection, followed by timely and appropriate intervention initiated by AWWs, can help accelerate the cause of normal development of the pre-school developmentally delayed children or, at least, the impact of the deficits on the everyday life of the children can be diminished. AWWs can always approach the Mukhyasevika (supervisor) or the child development programme officer (CIPO) or the medical specialist if and when required.

FIGURE 6:   Growth Chart from Birth to 5 Years of Age

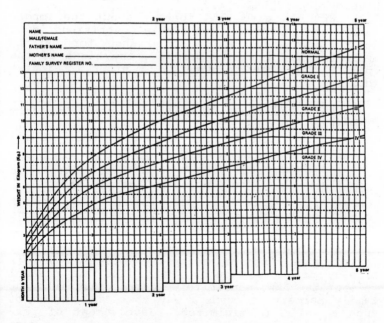

SOURCE: Sadka, 1984.

Role of AWWs in Training of Mothers to Reduce Developmental Deficits of Their Children

AWWs and the Expectant Mothers - It is the AWW who is at the grass-root level and actively involves the mothers in any prevention and intervention programme. Since the expectant mothers visit ICDS centres for antenatal check-ups, AWWs can take advantage of the opportunity and provide important information about health development. They can be of great help during mothers' pregnancy, thus reducing the chances of complications. This, too, can reduce the incidence of subnormal children.

The AWW is also responsible for preparing the mother mentally to accept the arrival of the child. If a mother does not want more children, advice about the avoidance of further pregnancies and the importance of spacing between two children is provided, but the child who is to arrive in this world must feel wanted and craved for, otherwise the negative attitude of the parents, particularly the mothers, is likely to mar the normal development of the child.

AWWs can also tell mothers about the importance of balanced, affordable nutritious diet during pregnancy, and also arrange for her to learn about child care prior to the birth of the child. This can be done in a group or individually.

AWWs and the Mothers of Children with Developmental Deficits

> *It is a platitude and also a truth that it can be one of the easiest things in the world to become and one of the hardest things in the world to be a parent.* (Loewy, 1955)

Another platitude that is beyond doubt is that it is one of the hardest things to be parents of a developmentally delayed child, but the AWW who has been able to detect a developmental deficit should not dramatize the situation that is already dramatic enough. Here lies the crucial role of the AWW, who is to weld the child into the family pattern in such a way that the burden of such a child is minimized. Involvement of parents, particularly mothers, is a must to reduce the deficits of infants and young children.

Bronfenbrenner (1974) has rightly pointed out that:

> *The involvement of the child's family as an active participant is critical to the success of an intervention programme. Without such family involvement, any effect of intervention appears to erode fairly rapidly once the programme ends. In contrast, the involvement of the parents as partners in the enterprise provides an ongoing system which can reinforce the effects of the programme while it is in operation and help to sustain that after the programme ends.*

UNESCO/UNICEF Cooperative Programme undertaken by Prakasha (Digest III, 1983) states:

> *The need for the home and the pre-school institution where one exists, to move closer to each other in the interest of the child cannot be over stressed. The influence of the home can easily undo anything that the school achieves. Hopefully, there is a growing awareness of this extremely important desideratum, whose realization deserves every encouragement from the educational administrator and policy maker.*

Obviously, AWWs as para-professionals must have parental involvement in reducing the developmental deficits of their children. They can help mothers in the following ways:

1. Help the mother in early detection of impairment and disability. If this is followed by appropriate intervention, it can significantly reduce the functional limitations that can take place and can further lead to arrest of a progression from impairment to disability and further handicap.
2. Help the mother in accepting a developmentally delayed child. Neglect or abuse is bound to have a worsening effect on deficits.
3. Reduce mothers' undue anxiety about possible deficits. For example she should not have feelings of guilt, shame, abasement or inferiority for having given birth to such a child. Excessive petting and 'mollycoddling' for such a child should also be avoided.

She should be as normal with this child as she is with others.

4. Tell the mother about the degree of deficit. Of course, the AWW is not a professional, but she can always use the assistance of expertise attached to the ICDS centres. Sometimes developmental deficits are pseudo deficits and can be easily overcome if nipped in the bud. Sometimes these deficits are mild and can be removed or reduced through early stimulation.

5. Encourage mothers of children with similar disabilities to organize community activities such as child care centres or to form 'self-help groups'. Experimental findings have confirmed the utility and therapeutic value of such groups where mothers work in coopera-tion to cope with the problems of their delayed children (Kohli, 1986).

6. Help mothers to make use of play activities and toys in reducing the deficits of their children or to enhance the development of their children. Action games and play activities can contribute a lot in reducing the deficits of children in all areas of development. Cheap toys can also be made out of 'throw-aways' and cost-effective material.

7. Lastly, much can happen at home and mothers can be wonderful non-professional therapists (Kohli, 1985a) in training their children step-by-step to reduce their deficits. Particularly, the Portage Training project, which is the focus of a later part of the present chapter, if implemented properly by AWWs with the help of the mothers, can assist such children and encourage more normal development. This technique of behaviour modification basically follows the sequence of six stages (Worell & Nelson, 1974), as follows:

1) select a target behaviour for the child;
2) measure and record baseline;
3) develop an ABC analysis, i.e. antece-dents (A) that may contribute to the occurrence of the behaviour (B) and the consequences (C);
4) initiate an intervention strategy;
5) evaluate results after intervention; and, finally,

6) communicate results and positive progress to the child as well as others
involved in the intervention programme.

It is important to be aware of the limited
comprehension and low educational level of the
AWWs and the clientele with whom they work. Yet
experience over a number of years suggests that
the capabilities of these para-professionals
(AWWs) in training the mothers with delayed
children are sufficient for the needs. This view
is supported by similar experiences with other
developing areas (e.g. the pre-school intervention
programme in Gaza; Abu Ghazaleh, 1986). In fact
illiterate parents of these children from slums
and deprived environments understand the language
of the semi-literate anganwadi workers much better
than the language of the highly sophisticated
professionals, an argument which is supported in
the discussion of models of rehabilitation by
Brown and Hughson (1987). Parents can freely talk
with them and it has been observed that professionals have to depend upon and request the
assistance of these grass-root workers to probe
into the local conditions in order to make
intervention programmes more effective. AWWs,
thus, can do much in training the parents,
particularly the mothers of developmentally
delayed children. This approach is consistent
with the widely stressed general principle of
'costs low - benefits high'. Mothers, with the
help of AWWs, can provide their delayed children
with socially rich, emotionally satisfying and
intellectually stimulating environments at
negligible additional expense to the government.

AWWs as Change Agents for Reducing the Develop-
mental Handicaps of the 'Under Sixes' - Some
Research Findings

Success of earlier research (Kohli, 1983)
encouraged the author and her team of research
workers to extend the Portage Training to ICDS
centres which needed cost effective intervention
programmes for those living in extreme slum
conditions. These studies are reviewed below.
The major objectives of the studies were:

1) to try different Portage Models, and examine
their effectiveness and practical usefulness

75

for training of pre-school MR children with various developmental delays,

2) to individualize Portage Training for the above children according to their specific needs,

3) to involve AW functionaries and parents in imparting the training. Their importance in making early detection of delayed children and in the training of mothers to reduce the deficits has been stressed by Kohli (1985b).

One of the research studies in Chandigarh entitled 'Effect of Early Stimulation on Developmental Deficits of Infants under ICDS Scheme' was conducted under the supervision of the present author and reported at the 7th International Congress of IASSMD (Kohli & Saggar, 1985). This model was centre-based and involved the Portage Project Training being given to infants below 6 months who came to ICDS centres. The project was directed to all-round development of children below 6 years of age. The results of Portage intervention showed positive gains. A similar study on the acquisition of language was conducted by Grewal (1984). Parents acted as effective therapists for their children under the direction of the AWWs.

Another study, which was conducted by Datta (1986) under the supervision of the author, is entitled 'Effect of Different Portage Training Intervention Models on Motor Development of Pre-School MR Children'. Four different models of Portage Training were utilized in reducing the motor-deficits of mentally handicapped children:

(i) Portage Training used by literate parents of high socio-economic groups,

(ii) Portage Training used by teachers of an institution with children of well-to-do families,

(iii) home-based Portage Training given by parents from slum areas to their children from 0 to 6 years and admitted to ICDS centres, and

(iv) Portage Training given by anganwadi workers (AWWs) of ICDS centres.

All four models proved effective, but the largest gains were evident in Model (ii) of the study.

The present author has also been involved in a major UNICEF sponsored project concerned with the impact of a home-centre based training programme on disadvantaged young children. This was carried out under the ICDS scheme in Chandigarh. The project, with a team of four research scholars, has been in progress since January 1985. So far, out of a sample of around 4,000 children with age range of 0-6 years, 120 mentally handicapped children have been identified using developmental quotients from three different tests of intelligence. The Portage Training has been provided over the past 16 months. A combination of the various models tried earlier has been used and the Portage Project Training is being given to them in all areas of developmental deficit as follows:

1) infant stimulation,
2) cognitive development,
3) social and emotional development,
4) motor-development,
5) self-help skills, and
6) language development.

The total Portage Project material of 580 items including the developmental procedures has been translated and adapted to Indian conditions. It is hoped that the present project of approximately three years will provide further guidelines for those working in the field and may be safely extended to AWs all over India.

Major Findings

1. If AWWs are given some basic training, they can be effective in early detection and prevention of developmental deficits.
2. AWWs, despite their low literacy level, can play the role of 'change agents' in reducing the developmental handicaps of the children coming to AWs.
3. The earlier the stimulation, the better are the chances of the children coming nearer to the average norms of development (Kohli, 1986).
4. The Portage Training programme has much potential. It should be included in the training programme of AWWs and does not add much additional cost to government or non-government agencies.

77

RECOMMENDATIONS FOR THE FUTURE

To conclude, society owes a special obligation towards children for their development into healthy and enlightened citizens. The ICDS scheme is a single strategy being implemented on a very large scale to provide basic services to children in an integrated manner compared with earlier approaches which were fragmented in their approach. An overview of ICDS and its impact on the quality of life of children during the past decade indicates it is rendering valuable service.

Estimates of pre-school education in India show about 1.2 million children are covered, which is about 1.5 per cent of the total population in the 3-6 year age group. ICDS meets this need by stressing access to children, particularly those from lower socio-economic groups in backward rural and tribal areas and in urban slums. A healthy move at present is that all children in this age group should be covered under this scheme.

ICDS has filled many gaps by reducing disparities between tribal, rural and urban people in terms of social, psychological and educational variables, and, to some extent, on the economic front by breaking down social barriers of scheduled caste population of India, who are encouraged to mix with each other. Children are oriented to pre-schooling and prepared for regular schooling. Yet, despite the present efforts, many segments of the scheme still remain relatively weak. The Central Task Force should work out plans and proposals based on priorities and programme strategies - developing new approaches, revising programme content and delineating budgetary allocations. In working out these plans and proposals some further considerations should be kept in mind.

1. Programmes/plans should fall within the existing priorities laid down by the state governments and Union Territories administration.
2. Organizational and administrative infrastructure should be activated at the various levels.
3. Plans and proposals should be capable of being replicated.
4. All other social welfare programmes should be properly integrated and suitably dovetailed with the ICDS programmes.

5. The non-formal education components of the scheme should be thought out in detail so that ICDS can function reasonably satisfactorily in all areas and all AWs.
6. Refresher courses, short-term courses and in-service training for all AW functionaries should be intensified.
7. The scheme should be subjected to systematic and closer monitoring; intensive evaluation and action research should be incorporated.
8. Greater community involvement should be encouraged and assured.
9. Frequent regional meetings of 3-4 states at a time should be a regular feature of the plans so that the Central Task Force of the scheme can obtain feedback and thus make further improvements in the scheme.
10. The scheme should be extended in coverage. A *cluster approach* to involve remote and small villages, which are neglected at the moment, is very necessary.
11. Cost efficiency should be stressed at all stages, while ensuring the development of the overall project. The long-term effects of the scheme should be clearly identified.

SUMMARY

The ICDS scheme in India marks a watershed in the child welfare movement in India. It recognizes children as a nation's most important asset. For proper nurture, care and understanding of children as well as the wellbeing of nursing and expectant mothers, it aims at providing an integrated package of six services - immunization, health check-up, referral services, supplementary nutrition, nutrition and health education and, lastly, pre-school education. Services are provided with the help of ICDS functionaries, supplemented by referral services and community involvement. Assessments made by the Department of Women's Welfare, Ministry of Human Resources Development, Government of India, after a decade of ICDS have measured decreases in malnutrition and anaemia, a drop in infant mortality and child mortality rates, significant decreases in preventable diseases, improved nutritional status, plus beneficial effects on the psychological, physical, social and emotional development of children, thus affecting the quality of life of children belonging to the deprived sections of the society.

The ICDS scheme also reduces the developmental deficits of children from 0 to 6 years. Research evidence has confirmed the utility of Portage Training, which can be effectively used at national level by para-professionals and parents, resulting in early detection and prevention of disabilities and developmental delays. Early and systematic stimulation, as well as cost effective intervention by these change-agents, can reduce the deficits and enhance the quality of life of the children. In fact ICDS is a gift to the children of India - a gift to India itself.

REFERENCES

Abu Ghazaleh, H. (1986) 'A Review of the Pre-School Project, Gaza,' Unpublished report.

Bronfenbrenner, U. (1974) *A Report of Longitudinal Evaluations of Pre-school Programmes*, Volume II, Early Intervention, DHEW Publications.

Brown, R. I. & Hughson, E. A. (1987) *Behavioural and Social Rehabilitation and Training*, Wiley, Chichester and New York.

Datta, R. (1986) 'Effect of Different Portage Training Intervention Models on Motor Development of Pre-school Mentally Retarded Children,' Unpublished Ph.D. Thesis, Panjab University, Chandigarh.

Grewal, S. (1984) 'Language Acquisition Programme for Mentally Retarded Young Children,' Unpublished M.A. Dissertation, Panjab University, Chandigarh.

Khosla, R. (1986) *Impact of Pre-school Education in ICDS*, NIPCCD, New Delhi.

Kohli, T. (1983) 'Feasibility of Portage Training to Reduce Developmental Handicaps of MR Young Children in India,' Paper presented at the Ninth All India Conference on Mental Retardation, Saugar University, Sagar.

Kohli, T. (1985a) 'Parents as Non-professional Therapists to Enhance Development of Mentally Retarded Young Children,' Paper presented at All India Seminar, Federation of Welfare of Children in India, New Delhi.

Kohli, T. (1985b) 'Role of Anganwadi Workers in Prevention and Early Detection of Developmentally Deficit Children and Training of Mothers in Reducing Their Deficits,' Paper presented at the First Workshop for AW Functionaries on Portage Training for Developmentally Delayed Children, UNICEF.

Kohli, T. (1986) 'Portage: Progress, Problems and Possibilities in India,' Paper presented at the National Portage Conference, United Kingdom.

Kohli, T. & Saggar, K. (1985) 'Effect of Early Stimulation on Developmental Deficits of Infants Under ICDS Scheme,' Paper presented at 7th International Association for the Scientific Study of Mental Deficiency.

Krishna, K. G. & Nadkarni, M. V. (1983) *Integrated Child Development Services: An Assessment*, UNICEF, New Delhi.

Lal, S. & Wati, R. (1986) *Early Childhood Education - An Effect to Enhance School Enrolment*, Abstract, Conference ICDS, New Delhi.

Loewy, H. (1955) *Training the Backward Child*, Staples Press Ltd, London.

Ministry of Human Resource Development (1985) *A Decade of ICDS*, Government of India, New Delhi.

Ministry of Human Resource Development (1986) *National Policy on Education: Programme of Action*, Government of India, New Delhi.

Ministry of Social Welfare (1974) 'National Policy for Children,' Government of India, New Delhi.

Muralidharan, R. & Kaur, B. (1986) 'A Study of the Relationship Between Physical Development and Language and Cognitive Development of Tribal Pre-school Children,' Paper presented at the National Conference on Research on ICDS.

National Institute of Public Cooperation and Child Development (1983) *National Conference on Non-formal Pre-school Education in ICDS*, New Delhi.

National Institute of Public Cooperation and Child Development (1984) *Manual on ICDS* (1st edn.) NIPCCD, New Delhi.

National Institute of Public Cooperation and Child Development (1986) *A Guide Book for Anganwadi Workers Training Centres*, NIPCCD, New Delhi.

Prakasha, V. (1983) *Zero through Six: Learning and Growing; What We Know of the Very Young Child* (Digest III), UNESCO, Paris.

Prakasha, V. (1984) *Towards an Open Learning Environment for the Young Child: Some Principles, Practices and Issues in Curriculum Planning* (Digest IV), UNESCO, Paris.

Sadka, N. L. (1984) *ICDS: Integrated Child Development Services in India*, UNICEF, New Delhi.

Sahai, A. & Mahajan, B. K. (1986) 'Review of Research on the Health Check-up and Referral Services in ICDS,' Paper presented at the National Conference on Research in ICDS, New Delhi.

Tandon, B. N. & Sahai, A. (1984) 'Management of Severally Malnourished Children by Village Workers in Integrated Child Development Service in India,' *Journal of Topical Paediatrics, 30*(5), 374–379.

UNESCO (1976) *The Child and His Development from Birth to Six Years Old: Better Understanding for Better Child Rearing*, UNESCO, Paris.

Vasundhra, M. K. & Srinivasan, B. S. (1985) *Impact of ICDS on Fertility Regulation - Phase II*, Proceedings of Fifteenth National IAPSM Conference.

Worell, J. & Nelson, C. M. (1974) *Managing Instructional Problems: A Case Study Work Book*, McGraw Hill, New York.

FOOTNOTE

1. The Department of Women and Child Development was carved out of the erstwhile 'Ministry of Social Welfare' with effect from September 25, 1985, and placed under the newly created Ministry of Human Resource Development in 1985.

Chapter Five

LIFESTYLE AND SATISFACTION IN FAMILIES OF
CHILDREN WITH DOWN'S SYNDROME[1]

E. A. Byrne and C. C. Cunningham

INTRODUCTION

> *It has become increasingly clear that an
> understanding of the stress experienced by
> the families of handicapped children requires
> much more than a focus on the way in which
> individual members react to the occurrence of
> a single event. Rather, it involves an
> understanding of the process by which this
> complex system responds to an ever-changing
> set of circumstances.* (Beckman, 1984)

In this chapter, we describe some of the findings
from interviews with the mothers of children in
the Manchester Down's Syndrome Cohort. The cohort
consists of 85-90 per cent of the children with
Down's Syndrome in Greater Manchester born between
August 1973 and August 1980. All of the families
took part in a home based early intervention
project for the first two years of the child's
life and have been visited regularly since then.
The impetus for this study came from the
families themselves during their regular contact
with team members. Despite the fact that all had
received similar early intervention, there appeared to be many differences between them in how
they adapted. Some appeared stressed, describing
relationship problems, difficulties with the
children, feelings of restriction and isolation.
Other families, who objectively did not appear to
be very different, described no problems and
appeared to be getting on well. We decided that
an overview of all of the families in the cohort
was required in order to examine some of the
possible reasons for these differences.

The next section will describe and evaluate recent changing views of the family, with particular reference to families with mentally handicapped children. The model which we used to design our study and understand its findings will be the main focus of this. This will be followed by an account of the methodology. The results of the interviews will then be described in terms of family relationships, family activities, satisfaction and stress. Finally, implications and recommendations resulting from this study will be discussed.

VIEWS OF THE FAMILY

As indicated in the quotation from Beckman (1984), researchers and clinicians are beginning to view families of mentally handicapped children differently. Early studies tended to regard families as a collection of individuals, passively reacting to the birth of a handicapped member (e.g. Evans & Carter, 1954; Schonell & Watts, 1957; Holt, 1958). Such a pathological view assumed that families are subject to high levels of stress and sought to find psychological impairment in family members, often with inconsistent and contradictory findings (see reviews by Crnic, Friedrich & Greenberg, 1983; Byrne & Cunningham, 1985). As this research began to adopt a broader view, it became clear that stress is not an inevitable consequence for families of mentally handicapped children. A combination of factors such as the presence of multiple stressors, the life-cycle stage of the family, the family's interpretation of their situation and the integration of the family prior to the birth of the child appear to be related to outcome in terms of stress and anxiety for individual family members (Gath, 1974; Bradshaw, 1980; Burden, 1980; Beckman, 1983).

More recently, families have been regarded by researchers as consumers of services. This view, exemplified by Wilkin (1979) suggests that it is not the presence of a mentally handicapped child which leads to stress, but the unmet service needs of families. It explores the material and practical problems which families experience and suggests how services might be organized to overcome them. There seems to be a consensus about which problems and needs are most important to families. The most widely felt needs for

additional support include: day provision during
school holidays and at weekends; babysitting
services; financial help; and help with transport
(Lonsdale, 1978; Wilkin, 1979; Carey, 1982).
However, this research ignores the emotional and
psychological needs of families, which may
conflict with their requests for service
provision. For example, families support the
provision of services for integration and normalization, yet may resist this in relation to their
own children (Ferrara, 1979; Card, 1983).

The most comprehensive and meaningful view of
families is one which acknowledges the competence
of families, recognizing that many cope with and
adapt to the stresses they experience. Such a
view, in seeking to explain why families are so
different, emphasizes the complexity of the
family. The family is a system in which all the
elements interact with and influence all other
elements. This system functions as part of a much
wider system (Bronfenbrenner, 1977) and manages
its resources to control and direct change, to
accomplish the developmental tasks common to all
families, and to accomplish the tasks which are
specifically related to families with handicapped
members (Simeonsson & Simeonsson, 1981).

A number of models have been developed to
describe the family as a system (Crnic et al.,
1983; Bubolz & Whiren, 1984; Turnbull, Brotherson
& Summers, 1984). Each of these models considers
the structure of the family unit, relationships
within the family, and the material, psychological
and social resources available to the family in
order to evolve its own *structure for living*
(Bayley, 1973). Each model also describes the
interactions between the family and the wider
social, cultural and economic environment. An
understanding of how the family system functions
requires description of the structural characteristics of the family and their resources at each
level of organization, i.e. individual, family
group, extended family, community and society.

The study described here presents some of
these characteristics and resources for families
of children with Down's Syndrome. The aim was to
describe the lifestyles of the families and their
perceptions of the impact of the child with Down's
Syndrome upon family life. By exploring the
differences between families in terms of their
characteristics and resources, we hoped to be able

to understand how they differed in the ways they coped with and adapted to stresses.

METHODOLOGY

> *The interview seems to give exceptionally good value in terms of detailed data on both behaviour and the attitudes underlying behaviour. In any human activity, the factual event and its associated feeling are of equal importance for our understanding.*
> (Newson & Newson, 1968)

For this reason and because we wished to overview all of the families in the cohort and cover a very broad and detailed range of issues, we decided that an interview would be the most appropriate means of collecting data. Using the interviews of Carr (1975), Gath (1978), Hewett (1970), Waisbren (1980), Wilkin (1979), Wing and Gould (1978) and Wishart, Bidder and Gray (1980) as guidelines, we devised an interview schedule which covered each of the issues raised by team visits to the families, and emphasized by the models outlined above.

Two standardized instruments were used - the Vineland Scale of Social Maturity (Doll, 1965) and the Malaise Inventory (Rutter, Tizard & Whitmore, 1970). We required a measure of the child's ability in order to compare children at similar stages and also to examine the influence of ability on family adaptation. We felt that a measure of social competence was more appropriate and more likely to influence the child's integration into his/her social world. The Malaise Inventory was included as a measure of stress, and to allow comparison with other studies (Byrne & Cunningham, 1985).

The interview began with neutral questions about family size and composition, followed by factual questions about the child. Areas which we felt might be sensitive or difficult for families were introduced later. The sections of the interview were ordered in such a way that each followed on naturally from the one preceding it. The aim was that the interview should be free-flowing, flexible and as much like a conversation as possible.

Of the 134 cohort families who remained in the area when the study commenced, 124 (93%) were

interviewed. Five families refused to participate, and it was not possible to organize
interviews with the remaining five in the time
available. The interviews took place in the
family home and varied in length between one and a
half and five hours, with a mean length of two and
a half hours. Mothers were interviewed, as they
were more likely to be in the home during the day
and were more involved in day-to-day child care.

RESULTS

The findings from the interviews will be presented
in two different forms. First, the answers given
to key questions will be described, illustrated by
quotations from the mothers. Where possible,
comparisons will be made with other interview
studies of families with mentally handicapped and
with non-handicapped children. Second, the
relationships between family characteristics and
resources and certain outcome measures such as
satisfaction and stress, will be explored. In
order to derive measures of resources and outcome
measures, the answers to different, but related
questions were grouped together to give an accum-
ulation of information on a given theme. For
example, the answers to every question related to
support from friends and relatives were combined
to give an index called *Informal Support*.

The results will be described in four sections: 1) The Families; 2) Family Relationships;
3) Family Activities; and 4) Satisfaction and
Stress.

It is important to state here that all of the
results described in sections 1) to 4) are based
on mothers' views and perceptions. It is arguable
whether these would correspond to the perceptions
of other family members, or indeed to observations
made by a researcher. However, this does not mean
that the perceptions of individual family members
are not important and valid sources of data,
especially when the aim of the research is to make
recommendations for service provision to families.
A number of studies have found that stress
experienced by mothers of mentally handicapped
children is more directly related to subjective
factors than to directly measurable features
(Bradshaw & Lawton, 1978; Butler, Gill, Pomeroy &
Fewtrell, 1978,; Beckman, 1983). For example,
Bradshaw (1980) found that stress scores were

related to satisfaction with housing, but not to actual housing standards. In order to gain a full picture of family needs, it is important to interview all family members.

THE FAMILIES

Before considering family relationships and activities, it is important to have a description of the children and the families in terms of characteristics such as age, sex, employment, health, etc. Such characteristics can have an important effect on activities and relationships. Details of this information are presented in Tables 1 and 2. In the case of children who were fostered or adopted, the figures refer to their adoptive or foster families. Severe medical problems include severe cardiac problems, partial sight or blindness, partial hearing or deafness, and epilepsy. The sample is biased towards social classes I and II and there are more boys than girls.

It is relevant to compare some of these distributions with the figures applying to the United Kingdom as a whole. In 1983, when this data was collected, the unemployment rate for men in the United Kingdom was 13 per cent (Central Statistical Office, 1983). The figure of 8 per cent for this sample compares favourably with this. As far as the mothers in the sample were concerned, 6 per cent were in full-time paid employment and 38 per cent were in part-time paid employment. This was at a time when 59 per cent of married women aged 25-44, and 69 per cent of those aged 45-54 were in paid employment (Central Statistical Office, 1983). The figure of 44 per cent for the current sample is somewhat lower than this. Fifty-three per cent of the mothers interviewed said they would like more paid employment. In terms of house ownership, 68 per cent of the current sample owned their own homes. This is similar to the figures for Britain as a whole - 67 per cent (Central Statistical Office, 1983).

The figures presented in Table 2 indicate that patterns of male employment and house ownership are similar for the families considered here and families in Britain as a whole. The women in the current sample, however, had less paid employment than the figures for the country as a whole.

TABLE 1: Child Characteristics

Age %	2:5-3:6	3:7-4:6	4:7-5:6	5:7-6:6	6:7-9:11
	29	20	23	11	16

Sex %	Male	Female
	61	39

Placement %	Natural parents	Fostered/Adopted
	94	6

Position in Family %	Only child	Youngest	Oldest	Middle
	10	53	18	19

Medical problems %	Severe problem/s	Minor problem/s only	No problem/s
	32	38	30

Social Quotient* %	20-50	51-60	61-70	70+	Missing
	11	23	31	23	12

Social Age %	0-2:0	2:1-3:0	3:1-4:6	4:7-7:0	Missing
	21	31	25	11	12

*Social Age is derived from the Vineland and the method for calculating social quotient is equivalent to that for calculating IQ, i.e. Soc. Age/C. Age x 100.

TABLE 2: Parent and Family Characteristics

Marital Status %	Married (1st marriage) 81	Married (2nd marriage) 15		Single 4
Mean Parental Age at Birth of Child %	15–24 19	25–29 19	30–34 32	35+ 27	not known 2
Parents' Education* %	1 27	2 31	3 38	Missing 4	
Father's Employment %	Working 88	Not working 8		No father 4
Mother's Employment %	Not working 56	Part-time 38	Full-time 6
Social Class %	I + II 40	III 41	IV + V 19
Number of Children %	1 10	2 39	3 30	4+ 21

*1. Neither parent has further education (i.e. post 16 years)
 2. One parent has further education
 3. Both parents have further education

FAMILY RELATIONSHIPS

The families in the sample and their children varied widely in terms of their descriptive characteristics (Tables 1 and 2). There was an equal spread in terms of relationships and activities. The relationship which will be considered first is that between the parents and the child with Down's Syndrome, followed by the relationship between the child with Down's Syndrome and his/her brothers and sisters. Finally, the relationship between the child's parents will be described.

Parent-Child Relationships

Just over half of the mothers in the sample felt that they treated the child with Down's Syndrome differently from his/her siblings. Forty-four per cent felt that they made more allowances for the handicapped child. This figure is slightly lower than that quoted by Hewett (1970), for mothers of children with cerebral palsy. A similar proportion of mothers in both samples were unhappy with some aspects of their management of their children (46% in this sample, 40% in Hewett's sample). Of those in the current sample who expressed worries, 20 per cent felt that they sometimes over-reacted or were impatient, and 26 per cent felt that they were not strict enough. It is important to note however, that 54 per cent of the mothers of non-handicapped four-year-old children expressed similar worries about child management (Newson & Newson, 1968).

Eighteen per cent of the mothers in the current sample said that they had slammed the door and walked out because of management difficulties, 48 per cent said they sometimes felt like it and 33 per cent never felt like it. For this reason, it seems important to describe the children's behaviour. When we asked mothers if any aspects of their children's behaviour caused problems or difficulties, 30 per cent said there were no problems, 53 per cent mentioned one or two problems, and 17 per cent three or more problems. It was not the case, however, that mothers who said that they had slammed the door and walked out were those whose children caused most problems (X^2 = 5.2, df = 6, n.s.). The number of behaviour problems shown by the children was significantly greater for those mothers who were unhappy with their child management (X^2 = 26.6, df = 8, p = 0.0008) and in those families where mothers and fathers disagreed about child management (X^2 = 14.7, df = 6, p = 0.02).

The specific behaviours which occurred are listed in Table 3, together with frequencies from the study conducted by Richman, Stevenson and Graham (1982) of a sample of non-handicapped four-year-old children. The most frequently occurring difficulties appeared to be those of the child wandering or running off, not understanding danger, and being difficult to manage because of stubbornness. Each of these occurred in over 50 per cent of the sample.

> *She runs off as soon as your back is turned, straight into danger. You can't take your eyes off her. We have to keep all the doors and windows locked and can't leave anyone to mind her. It means that we can't let her out to play with other children.* (Age 6:2)

When we asked what they found hardest to cope with, 44 per cent of mothers said it was the child's behaviour. The replies given to this question are shown in Table 4. Sixteen per cent said that there was nothing they found hard to deal with. We combined all of the behaviour problems listed by mothers to form an index of Child Behaviour Problems. This is one of the measures we include when we examine the factors related to satisfaction and stress in the final section of the results.

In contrast, when we asked what pleased mothers most about their child, only 2 per cent said that they could think of nothing which pleased them. Replies to this question are also shown in Table 4. Under the heading of achievements, mothers mentioned both general and specific achievements. Personality or manner included how happy or loving the child was and his/her sense of humour and mischievousness.

> *He's a lovable person...a person in his own right. He's coming on better than we ever imagined he would.* (Age 5:3)

> *That in so many ways she can just mix in with others. She has a tremendous enjoyment of life.* (Age 4:3)

TABLE 3: Behaviour Problems

	This Sample %	Richman et al. (1982) %	
		no problem gp	problem gp
Sleeping			
Reluctant to go to bed, won't remain	29	15	26
Wakes at night, cries or screams	8	12	19
Wakes at night, gets up	24		
Wakes early and cries or gets up	29	--	--
Eating			
Refuses food, is reluctant to eat	18	20	39
Will only eat a limited range of food	28	24	44
Throws food	19	--	--
Pesters for food	25	--	--
Management			
Tantrums	18	6	28
Stubborn, disobedient	51	10	39
Pesters for attention	34	10	23
Relationship with other children			
Bossy	25	19	38
Rough, aggressive	28		
Habits			
Rocks	7		
Grinds teeth	27		
Bangs head	6		
Bites self, clothes, furniture	18		
General			
Too friendly with strangers	22		
Wanders, runs off	65		
Doesn't understand danger	66		

TABLE 4: Mother's Greatest Concern and Greatest Pleasure with Regard to the Child with Down's Syndrome

Concern	%
Behaviour problem	44
Developmental delay	18
Nothing	16
Language/speech problem	9
The future	5
Physical/health problem	4
Attitude of others	4

Pleasure	%
Achievements	35.5
Personality or manner	35.5
Everything	16
Acceptance by community	1
Other	10
Can't think of anything	2

> *Just Paul...everything really. He's a little tinker but he's lovely...I wouldn't swap him.* (Age 4:5)

Almost half of the mothers we interviewed were concerned about the way they handled their child and were worried about behaviour problems.

> *It's like acting in a play without knowing the words, or adding up a sum and not knowing if it's the right answer. Your child is different and you're not sure how to deal with him.* (Age 4:6)

Most mothers used similar strategies with the child with Down's Syndrome as with his/her siblings, although almost half of the sample described themselves as being more lenient than they were with siblings. This is similar to Carr (1975), who found that 45 per cent of the mothers of pre-school children with Down's Syndrome in her study never punished their children, whereas the figure for the non-handicapped control group was 17 per cent. The feeling expressed by many mothers in the current sample was that it was necessary to take the differences into account.

> *We take the handicap into consideration...*
> *speak to her more slowly and tell her more*
> *often.* (Age 4:11)

The frequency of behaviour problems does seem to be higher in this sample than in comparable groups of non-handicapped children. The types of behaviours which most frequently cause problems are also somewhat different (Richman et al., 1982).

Sibling Relationships

Eighty-nine per cent of the children in the sample had at least one sibling, and the vast majority played regularly with their siblings, both when the children were alone together (92%), and when the siblings had brought friends home (83%).

> *They all get on smashing.* (Age 4:8)

> *I was really surprised...all the kids are*
> *great with him.* (Age 4:1)

This is similar to the figures given by Newson and Newson (1968, 1976) for their four-year-old (81%) and seven-year-old (85%) samples of non-handicapped children. The reason most frequently given by mothers for siblings not playing with the child with Down's Syndrome was the he/she could not follow or disrupted the siblings' games.

A lower proportion of children were regularly taken out to play by their siblings (60%). The reason given by the majority of mothers when this did not occur was that the child needed more supervision than the sibling could provide. A number (14) also said that they felt it was unfair to expect siblings to take on this extra responsibility. Only one mother said that the sibling was embarrassed. In general, 72 per cent of mothers felt that the children got on well together. Table 5 lists the problems mentioned by the remaining 28 per cent.

When we asked whether or not the siblings ever felt left out, 42 per cent of the mothers thought that this happened. Both Hewett (1970) and Newson and Newson (1968) report figures of 33 per cent for siblings of children with cerebral palsy and for non-handicapped children respectively. All of the answers to questions about the relationship between the child with Down's

Syndrome and his/her siblings were combined to form an index of Sibling Relationships. This index is another of the factors we include when we discuss the factors related to stress and satisfaction.

TABLE 5: Problems Described by Mothers in Sibling Relationships

	Frequency (N=32)	%
Child is aggressive	13	45
Siblings jealous	7	24
Child disturbs siblings at night	6	21
Child disrupts siblings' games	5	17
Child damages siblings' possessions	4	14

It is important to stress that these results describe mothers' views of the sibling relationship. Hart and Walters (1979), on the basis of their interview study of siblings and parents from 27 families with handicapped children, concluded that siblings described more difficulties than parents were aware of. Although the siblings in the current sample were younger than those interviewed by Hart and Walters (1979), the findings described here may still underestimate the difficulties they experienced.

Relationships Between the Parents

The marital relationship was examined in three ways during the course of the interview. Firstly, mothers were asked about the process of decision making with regard to the child with Down's Syndrome. Secondly, we explored how household and child care tasks were shared and mothers' satisfaction with these arrangements. Thirdly, we asked directly about the impact of the child on the marital relationship. These topics will be presented in turn.

In most families, there were some differences in child management between mothers and fathers. Once again, it is important to stress that these were mothers' views. In 40 per cent of families, mothers felt they were more strict, and in 27 per cent they felt that the fathers were more strict. Lytton (1980) in his observational study of parents and their young non-handicapped sons, concluded that mothers play a more prominent role than fathers in trying to change the child's behaviour. They are more likely to use verbal explanations and justifications, whereas fathers are more inclined to use commands. These differences could partly account for the views of mothers expressed here.

In contrast to this, decisions about the child were mostly shared (61% of families). Where one person tended to make the decisions, it was more often the mother (32% of families) than the father (3%). The proportion who tended to agree on most decisions (61%) is similar to the 67 per cent reported by Hewett (1970) and by Carr (1975). Where there were disagreements, they were most frequently about discipline (61%), followed by decisions about schooling (12%), followed by views on short-term care (10%). Two per cent of mothers reported that fathers took no part in decisions about the child, and 4 per cent were single parents.

In order to explore how tasks were carried out within the family, we identified 32 separate household and child-related tasks and asked mothers who did these and who helped. In each case we asked about the extent of help. The results may be summarized as follows:

- mothers are involved at some level in most tasks and perform a large portion of them alone;
- they receive more help with child-related tasks than with household tasks;
- with child-related tasks, more help is given with aspects of playing with and entertaining the children than with dressing, feeding, etc. Least help is given with visits to the doctor, hospital or school;
- more help is given with care of the child with Down's Syndrome than with care of his/her siblings;
- the majority of mothers perform most household tasks alone, with the exception of dishwashing and shopping. The only tasks where mothers are minimally involved are gardening, decorating and repairs;

- fathers help much more than any other family member or anyone outside the home. However, the only tasks in which more than 50 per cent of fathers share are helping with homework, attending parents' evenings at school, gardening, decorating and repairs;
- the support from siblings is much smaller, although it is important to remember that many families did not include siblings who were old enough to help;
- support available from outside the home constitutes a negligible fraction of the total work load.

This picture replicates that described by Wilkin (1979) who used a similar detailed questionnaire to document exactly how much help of different types was received from various sources.

Given the relatively low level of sharing of tasks, we explored mothers' satisfaction with this. Forty-nine per cent said they would like more help in the home - 19 per cent from the family and 30 per cent from some other source. Similarly, 47 per cent of mothers said they would like more time to themselves - although 32 per cent of these said it was not solely the child with Down's Syndrome who prevented them having time to themselves.

> *The children are always around, the housework is never-ending and there's no money to escape from it. I can't even have a bath without the kids coming in. I walk around the block at night to get away from it all.*
> (Age 6:5)

Most mothers did not express a desire for more help from their families (80%). Rather more said they would like more help from services, as they felt their husbands helped as much as they could. All of the information presented in this section was combined to form an index of sharing within the family. The influence of this index on the outcome measures of satisfaction and stress is discussed in the last section of the results.

When we asked about the impact of the child with Down's Syndrome on the parents' marriage most replied that the relationship was unchanged or had improved (67%). The replies are shown in Table 6.

*It's drawn us together...Bob comes first.
Arguments are forgotten for him.* (Age 3:0)

*She helped us a lot in our marriage. It
didn't start properly until we had Jane.*
(Age 9:7)

*When he was first born there was something
between us, 'cause Jim took it badly. I felt
more optimistic. It's OK now though... I'd
say it helped rather than otherwise.* (Age
3:5)

TABLE 6: Influence of the Child with Down's
Syndrome on the Parents' Marital
Relationship

	%
No change	37
Better	30
Worse	14
Better in some ways, worse in others	15
Single parent family	4

These figures are in marked contrast to other
studies, where a greater proportion of marriages
were said to have deteriorated (Lonsdale, 1978;
Pahl & Quine, 1984). There is some evidence that
marital satisfaction may decrease disproportion-
ately over time in families with handicapped
children (Byrne & Cunningham, 1985). The difference between this study and others may be due to
the fact that this was a sample of relatively
young children, or that this was a sample of
families with children with Down's Syndrome. It
is possible that marital stress is different in
families where the aetiology of the handicap is
different. It is unlikely that these differences
are due to the support received by this sample.
In a recent study in which this sample was compared to a matched group of families of children
with Down's syndrome who did not receive early
intervention, but who received similar support and
services otherwise, there were no differences in
marital satisfaction (Cunningham, 1985).
    These findings indicate that decision making
is shared by most parents in the sample interviewed; that most mothers are content with the
help they receive from their husbands in the home,

although they do most of the work themselves; and
that most mothers felt that their marriages had
either improved or remained unchanged.

FAMILY ACTIVITIES

In this section, we examine the frequency of
different family activities and we explore the
extent to which mothers felt these activities were
restricted by the child with Down's Syndrome.

TABLE 7: Frequency of Parental Outings
          (without the children)

	This Sample	Newson & Newson (1968)	Hewett (1970)
Weekly or more	36%	25%	18%
Monthly or more	24%	16%	19%
Every 2/3 months	15%	26%	23%
Less or never	25%	33%	40%

The frequency of parental outings is described in Table 7, together with data from other
studies. These occurred much more frequently for
this sample than for the sample of non-handicapped
four-year-old children studied by Newson and
Newson (1968) and the sample of children with
cerebral palsy studied by Hewett (1970), but these
differences could be due to changing patterns of
family life over time. Of rather more relevance
is parental satisfaction with the frequency of
outings. The majority were content (62%).

> *There's no problem - if we want to go out, we
> go out.* (Age 3:0)

Of the 38 per cent who said they would like to go
out more often, 15 per cent felt that the child
with Down's Syndrome prevented this and 23 per
cent cited other reasons. The majority who felt
the child prevented them going out mentioned
finding sufficiently good babysitters as the
reason.

> *Who will babysit - will they cope in an*
> *emergency - what if Susan gets in a bad*
> *temper and they can't cope?* (Age 6:6)

> *We have to watch Sheila very carefully*
> *because of her heart. She doesn't sleep well*
> *and is often ill, so the family goes out in*
> *relays usually.* (Age 5:6)

These findings are very different from those of Lonsdale (1978) and Butler et al. (1978), where 50 per cent of parents reported that their social activities were severely restricted by the presence of a mentally handicapped child.

A larger proportion of mothers described difficulties with family outings than with outings alone with their husbands (52% versus 38%). For 45 (36%) of these there were minor difficulties, and 20 (16%) described major difficulties. When asked the cause of the difficulties, the majority mentioned some aspect of the child's behaviour, only two cited the child's health problems, and one the reaction of others. Six mothers mentioned problems unrelated to the child.

> *Shopping is a pain - she runs off and it*
> *takes ten times longer. I end up with things*
> *in the basket I don't want or with a tantrum*
> *to deal with. I feel uneasy and don't take*
> *her.* (Age 6:6)

We asked about family holidays next. Sixty-nine per cent of the sample went on holiday at least once a year. Of the nine families who had never been on holiday, all mentioned reasons unrelated to the child, such as lack of money. The majority who had been on holiday described these as successful (77%). Only eight mentioned the child's behaviour as contributing to the lack of success of a holiday. Sixteen families had been on holiday at least once without the child with Down's Syndrome, 11 of them so that the whole family could have a break.

> *We go for the sake of the other children, so*
> *we can spend time with them.* (Age 3:1)

As part of our exploration of family activities, we asked mothers about their use of short-term care. Sixty-one per cent of the sample never used this. Twenty-five per cent used informal sources of care (friends or relatives), and 14 per cent used formal short-term care facilities - mostly residential units (7) or short-term foster families (6). When we asked whether parents would like to be able to use these facilities more, 66 per cent said no - the majority because they felt there was no need, with the next most frequent reason being that they would miss the child. These findings are similar to those of Carey (1982), where 31 per cent of mothers expressed a need for short-term care facilities.

SATISFACTION AND STRESS

The previous sections have presented some information on the different lifestyles of the families we interviewed. It is important now to try to understand what effects these differences have. In order to do this, we needed some measures of family outcome, two of which will be considered here.

The first outcome measure we derived from the interview data was maternal satisfaction. We combined together the answers to all those questions which asked how happy mothers were or whether they wished to change various aspects of their lives. Most of this information has been presented in preceding sections. The index of maternal satisfaction included mothers' satisfaction with: work outside the home; their relationships with partners, friends and relatives; family activities; help in the home; time to themselves; and their plans for themselves. Using this index, 5 mothers could be described as highly satisfied (4%), 90 as moderately satisfied (73%), and 29 as dissatisfied (23%).

We examined the relationship between all of the measures which we had derived from the interviews, and which we felt might be important predictors, and the outcome measure of maternal satisfaction. Predictor measures included child characteristics, parent characteristics, family characteristics and family resources, and are listed in Table 8.

Initially, we looked separately at the relationship between each predictor measure and the outcome measure, using univariate analyses of variance. Five of these appeared to be strongly related to maternal satisfaction. These were:

Age of Child; Child Social Quotient; Number of Behaviour Problems; Mother's Employment; and Family Sharing. All of these measures were combined in a multivariate analysis of variance, in order to examine which variables were most closely related to the outcome measure when all others were controlled for. This analysis indicated that Family Sharing was significantly related to maternal satisfaction ($p < 0.05$, $F = 4.2$, df = 1,13) with satisfaction being highest in those families where tasks and decisions were shared.

TABLE 8: Predictor Measures Used in the Analysis

Child Characteristics

Age
Sex
Family position
Placement
Medical problems
Social quotient
Social age
Number of behaviour
   problems

Parent Characteristics

Age of parents
Parental education
Mother's employment
Father's employment

Family Characteristics

Number of parents
Number of children
Social class
Religion
House ownership
Health of siblings

Family Resources

Importance of religion
Siblings' relationship
   with child
Family sharing
Informal support
Number of profes-
   sionals seen
Number of profes-
   sionals helpful
Membership of
   societies
Criticism of inter-
   vention

We also wished to use an outcome measure which was separate from the interview data, and which had been standardized and used in other studies. We chose to measure maternal stress, in contrast to satisfaction, using the Malaise Inventory (Rutter et al., 1970). This is a 24 item Yes/No inventory which has been widely used as a measure of stress (Gath, 1978; Burden, 1980; Quine & Pahl, 1985). Rutter considered that a score of 5 or above, is outside the normal range and is indicative of depression. The mean score of the mothers we interviewed was 4.46 (SD = 4.07). Thirty per cent of the sample scored above the cut-off point. In Table 9, the mean Malaise scores of mothers in the current study is compared to other studies. The score is lower than that found in most other studies of mothers of mentally handicapped children (e.g. Bradshaw & Lawton, 1978; Quine & Pahl, 1984), and is more similar to mothers of non-handicapped children (e.g. Rutter et al., 1970; Richman et al., 1982).

TABLE 9: Comparisons of Malaise Scores

		Mean	SD	N
This study		4.46	4.07	103
Pahl & Quine (1984)		5.8	4.1	200
Bradshaw & Lawton (1978)		9.0	5.2	303
Bradshaw et al. (1982)		5.7	5.1	78
Burden (1980)	(pre-intervention)	6.1	5.1	25
	(post-intervention)	2.95	2.67	20
Rutter et al. (1970)	(Isle of Wight)	3.22	--	--
	(London)	4.15	--	--

These results indicate that stress, as measured by the Malaise Inventory, is by no means an inevitable outcome for mothers of children with Down's Syndrome.

In order to see which mothers experienced high stress, we examined the relationship between maternal stress and each predictor measure. Six of the measures listed in Table 8 were closely related to stress. These were: Number of Behaviour Problems; Parental Education; Health of Siblings; Sibling Relationship with Child; and Informal Support. Two multivariate analyses of variance were run. The first analysis included only those variables which did not relate to siblings in order that families with only children might not be excluded. The results of this indicated that Mother's Malaise Score was significantly related to Child Behaviour Problems (p < 0.01, F = 4.3, df = 3,7) and Parental Education (p < 0.05, F = 3.5, df = 3,7). The Malaise Score was higher where children exhibited a high number of behaviour problems and was lower in those families where both parents had further education.

These findings were confirmed by the analysis which included the measures related to siblings. There was also a weak association between Sibling Relationships and Malaise Score (p < 0.1, F = 2.6, df = 2,10) with higher maternal stress scores in those families with poor sibling relationships. The indices of satisfaction and of stress were closely associated, as shown by their significant negative correlation (Pearson corr. = -0.37, p = 0.001), although they were related to different predictor measures.

SUMMARY AND CONCLUSIONS

The aim of this chapter was to describe the lifestyles of the families we interviewed, and to explore the ways in which they differed. We hoped that, by focusing on the whole family system and its interaction with the wider environment, we would be able to understand which families experienced difficulties. We chose to examine the factors related to maternal satisfaction and stress as a way of exploring family difficulties. The findings of the study and the conclusions which can be drawn from them are as follows:

1. For most of the families we interviewed, their relationships and activities were no different from those of families of non-handicapped children.
2. For a sizeable minority of families (30%-40%) there were problems. In these families mothers' scores on the Malaise Inventory indicated depression, and maternal satisfaction with many aspects of family life was low. As these two measures incorporate some of the dimensions which are included in measures of quality of life (Flanagan, 1978; Ferrans & Powers, 1985), it is possible to conclude that for at least two-thirds of the sample their quality of life was reasonable

105

in their own estimation. Between one quarter and one third estimated their quality of life as low.

3. The factors which were related to these outcome measures included - a low level of sharing of tasks and decisions within the family; behaviour problems in the child with Down's Syndrome; poor sibling relationships; and low parental education.

4. These factors could serve as important markers to those who are providing services to the family.

5. These findings suggest that simply providing financial and/or practical services is not sufficient. Previous research has indicated that families' practical needs include: day provision during school holidays and at weekends; babysitting services; financial help; and help with transport (Lonsdale, 1978; Wilkin, 1979; Ayer & Alaszewski, 1984; Carey, 1982). However, the findings of this research show that, in addition, in order to alleviate stress and enhance quality of life, interventions must enhance family cohesiveness and encourage the inclusion of all family members in activities and decisions. Resources must be provided for those families where the child is exhibiting behaviour problems by enhancing management skills of all family members. Service providers require training in interventions which focus on the relationships between family members (Affleck et al., 1982).

6. Finally, it is important to recognize that stress and dissatisfaction are not inevitable outcomes for families with handicapped members. Families evolve their own coping strategies using their own resources. We need to be able to recognize which families need support. In families whose estimation of their own quality of life is low, we must remember that the importance of the different dimensions varies and does not impact equally on quality of life (Ferrans & Powers, 1985). Where support is needed, we must provide the type of support which the family needs, in a way which the family can use and which complements their own coping strategies.

REFERENCES

Affleck, G., McGrade, B. J., McQueeney, M., &
  Allen, D. (1982) 'Relationship-focused Early
  Intervention in Developmental Disabilities,'
  Exceptional Children, 49, 259-261.
Ayer, S. & Alaszewski, A. (1984) *Community Care
  and the Mentally Handicapped: Services for
  Mothers and their Mentally Handicapped
  Children,* Croom Helm, London and New York.
Bayley, M. (1973) *Mental Handicap and Community
  Care: A Study of Mentally Handicapped People
  in Sheffield,* Routledge and Kegan Paul,
  London and New York.
Beckman, P. J. (1983) 'Influence of Selected
  Child Characteristics on Stress in Families
  of Handicapped Children,' *American Journal of
  Mental Deficiency, 88*(2), 150-156.
Beckman, P. J. (1984) 'A Transactional View of
  Stress in Families of Handicapped Children,'
  in M. Lewis (ed.), *Beyond the Dyad,* Plenum
  Press, New York.
Bradshaw, J. (1980) *The Family Fund,* Routledge
  and Kegan Paul, London and New York.
Bradshaw, J., Cooke, K., Gledinning, C., Baldwin,
  S., Lawton, D., & Staden, F. (1982) *1970
  Cohort: Ten Year Follow-up Study,* Interim
  Report to the DHSS; 108/6.82., University of
  York.
Bradshaw, J. & Lawton, D. (1978) *Tracing the
  Causes of Stress in Families with Handicapped
  Children,* University of York Publications,
  York.
Bronfenbrenner, U. (1977) 'Towards an Experi-
  mental Ecology of Human Development,'
  American Psychologist, 32, 514-531.
Bubolz, M. M. & Whiren, A. P. (1984) 'The Family
  of the Handicapped: An Ecological Model for
  Policy and Practice,' *Family Relations, 33,*
  5-12.
Burden, R. L. (1980) 'Measuring the Effects of
  Stress on Mothers of Handicapped Children:
  Must Depression Always Follow?' *Child: Care,
  Health and Development, 6,* 111-125.
Butler, N., Gill, R., Pomeroy, D., & Fewtrell, J.
  (1978) *Handicapped Children - Their Homes
  and Life Styles,* Department of Child Health,
  University of Bristol.

Byrne, E. & Cunningham, C. C. (1985) 'The Effects of Mentally Handicapped Children on Families - A Conceptual Review,' *Journal of Child Psychology and Psychiatry, 26*(6), 847-864.

Card, H. (1983) 'What Will Happen When We've Gone?' *Community Care,* 28 July.

Carey, G. E. (1982) 'Community Care - Care By Whom? Mentally Handicapped Children Living at Home,' *Public Health, 96,* 269-278.

Carr, J. (1975) *Young Children with Down's Syndrome,* IRMMH Monograph No. 4, Butterworth, Sevenoaks.

Central Statistical Office (1983) *Social Trends,* HMSO, London.

Crnic, K. A., Friedrich, W. N., & Greenberg, M. T. (1983) 'Adaptation of Families with Mentally Retarded Children: A Model of Stress, Coping and Family Ecology,' *American Journal of Mental Deficiency, 88,* 125-138.

Cunningham, C. C. (1985) *The Effects of Early Intervention on the Occurrence and Nature of Behaviour Problems in Children with Down's Syndrome,* Final Report to The Department of Health and Social Security, London.

Doll, E. A. (1965) *Vineland Social Maturity Scale,* American Guidance Service, Minnesota.

Evans, K. & Carter, C. O. (1954) 'Care and Disposal of Mongolian Defectives,' *Lancet, 2,* 960-963.

Ferrans, C. E. & Powers, M. J. (1985) 'Quality of Life Index: Development and Psychometric Properties,' *Advances in Nursing Science, 8*(1), 15-24.

Ferrara, D. M. (1979) 'Attitudes of Parents of Mentally Retarded Children Towards Normalization Activities,' *American Journal of Mental Deficiency, 84,* 145-151.

Flanagan, J. C. (1978) 'A Research Approach to Improving Our Quality of Life,' *American Psychologist, 33*(2), 138-147.

Gath, A. (1974) 'Siblings' Reactions to Mental Handicap: A Comparison of the Brothers and Sisters of Mongol Children,' *Journal of Child Psychology and Psychiatry, 15,* 187-198.

Gath, A. (1978) *Down's Syndrome and the Family: The Early Years,* Academic Press, London and New York.

Hart, D. & Walters, J. (1979) *Brothers and Sisters of Mentally Handicapped Children, Family Involvement with Services in Haringey,* Thomas Coram Research Unit, University of London Institute of Education.

Hewett, S. (1970) *The Family and the Handicapped Child,* George Allen and Unwin, London and Boston.

Holt, K. S. (1958) 'The Home Care of the Severely Mentally Retarded,' *Paediatrics, 22,* 744-755.

Lonsdale, G. (1978) 'Family Life with a Handicapped Child: The Parents Speak,' *Child: Care, Health and Development, 4,* 99-120.

Lytton, H. (1980) *Parent-Child Interaction: The Socialization Process Observed in Twin and Singleton Families,* Plenum Press, New York.

Newson, J. & Newson, E. (1968) *Four Years Old in an Urban Community,* George Allen & Unwin, London and Boston.

Newson, J. & Newson, E. (1976) *Seven Years Old in the Home Environment,* George Allen & Unwin, London and Boston.

Pahl, J. & Quine, L. (1984) *Families with Mentally Handicapped Children: A Study of Stress and of Service Response,* Health Services Research Unit, University of Kent, Canterbury.

Quine, L. & Pahl, J. (1985) 'Examining the Causes of Stress in Families with Severely Mentally Handicapped Children,' *British Journal of Social Work, 15,* 501-517.

Richman, N., Stevenson, J., & Graham, P. (1982) *Preschool to School - A Behavioural Study,* Academic Press, London and New York.

Rutter, M., Tizard, J., & Whitmore, K. (eds.) (1970) *Education, Health and Behaviour,* Longman, Harlow.

Schonell, F. J. & Watts, B. J. (1957) 'A First Survey of the Effects of a Subnormal Child on the Family Unit,' *American Journal of Mental Deficiency, 61,* 210-219.

Simeonsson, R. J. & Simeonsson, N. E. (1981) 'Parenting Handicapped Children: Psychological Perspectives,' in J. Paul (ed.), *Understanding and Working with Parents of Children with Special Needs,* Holt, Rinehart & Winston, New York.

Turnbull, A. P., Brotherson, M. J., & Summers, J. A. (1984) 'The Impact of Deinstitutionalisation on Families: A Family Systems Approach,' in R. H. Bruininks (ed), *Living and Learning in the Least Restrictive Environment*, Paul H. Brookes, Baltimore, Maryland.

Waisbren, S. E. (1980) 'Parents' Reactions After the Birth of a Developmentally Disabled Child,' *American Journal of Mental Deficiency*, *84*, 345-351.

Wilkin, D. (1979) *Caring for the Mentally Handicapped Child*, Croom Helm, London and New York.

Wing, L. & Gould, J. (1978) 'Systematic Recording of Behaviors and Skills of Retarded and Psychotic Children,' *Journal of Autism and Childhood Schizophrenia*, *8*(1), 79-97.

Wishart, M. C., Bidder, R. T., & Gray, O. P. (1980) 'Parental Responses to Their Developmentally Disabled Children and the South Glamorgan Home Advisory Service,' *Child: Care, Health and Development*, *6*(6), 361-376.

FOOTNOTE

1. This study was funded by a grant from the Department of Health and Social Security.

Chapter Six

QUALITY OF LIFE AMONGST HANDICAPPED ADULTS[1,2]

R. I. Brown, M. B. Bayer & C. MacFarlane

INTRODUCTION

This chapter reports aspects of a quality of life study currently being carried out in Canada in three western provinces. Five agencies are involved whose stated goal is the community rehabilitation of developmentally handicapped adolescents and adults. The study is longitudinal, and is taking place over a six-year period, but, for the purposes of this chapter, only the first three years of the study are the basis for discussion.

The aim of the study is to examine the performance of developmentally handicapped adults in relation to work and to social, home living and allied skill areas, and to gain some knowledge about their own and sponsor's perceptions of their living conditions and their needs, aspirations and concerns. The study took into account the nature of the training agencies they attended and the time and availability of personnel working with the clients.

Although one aim was to observe the effectiveness of rehabilitation programmes, recognizing that no absolute criterion of placement in the community would be very helpful, a major concern was the standards of quality of life of the individuals concerned.

DEFINITION OF QUALITY OF LIFE

Quality of life can be viewed as the discrepancy between a person's achieved and their unmet needs and desires. The larger the gap between what people have and what they need and want, the poorer their quality of life (MacFarlane, 1985). Quality of life can also be viewed as the degree to which an individual has control over his or her environment, while a further reflection is the extent to which individuals increase personal control of their environment regardless of baseline.

In a similar fashion to other researchers (Goodale, et al., 1975; Rodgers & Converse, 1975), it is our contention that both subjective and objective measures are valuable in determining one's quality of life.

Subjective measures are those that deal with the patterns and settings of personal relationships (Bateson, 1972) and the expectations, attitudes and behaviours of individuals (Kennedy et al., 1977). In the case of disabled persons the philosophy of agencies and staff that serve them are particularly important contributors to quality of life. Objective measures include those that assess such elements as the person's living conditions, e.g. noise level, neighbourhood crime rate, educational level, and income.

The measurement of quality of life is, therefore, multidimensional across various life domains. Quality of life includes, but is not equivalent to, people's life satisfaction, their happiness or their sense of control.

Since cultural background, age, religion, sex, experience and training may all influence a person's concept of what constitutes a quality lifestyle (Robinson & Shaver, 1973; Denham, 1983), these and similar variables may be used to group individuals so that the quality of life for a population may be addressed.

METHOD OF STUDY

In this study, client behaviour, social and economic data, and training conditions were collected on an annual basis. The data provided information from which to gauge the effects of the rehabilitation programmes as clients were trained and placed in the community. Both subjective and objective measures of quality of life of the developmentally handicapped persons were obtained.

The following criteria were used in the selection of the agencies:

a) each agency was an adult vocational training centre that emphasized placement and follow-up of trainees in the community,
b) each agency had a comprehensive range of clients which included mildly to moderately mentally or multiply handicapped adults,
c) selected clients and their guardians, separately, agreed to participate in the study.

A range of agencies were consulted about their involvement in the study, and eventually five were selected. These included three agencies in major cities, one agency in a fairly small urban setting, and another agency which was in a rural setting. In order to include a representative range of agencies, two of those selected had residential training components in addition to formal day programmes.

TEST MATERIALS

The following tests were given:

1) The Adaptive Functioning Index (AFI) (Marlett, 1971), which is a standardized and practical measure of behaviours considered necessary for independent functioning in the community. Three scales are present: The Social Educational AFI, which is an objective test, and two behaviour checklists, one in vocational and the other in home living skills. The reliability coefficients for these tests are deemed to be reasonably high as indicated by the test manual.
2) Level of Handicap Grid (Marlett, 1978) was completed by agency staff on each subject during the sample identification stage of the study. This grid provides a description of the subject's functional ability in supervision and care, motor control, mobility, socialization, communication, developmental skills and behaviour.
3) A shortened version of the Weschler Adult Intelligence Scale, as suggested by Maxwell (1960), was carried out. The intelligence quotients provided are a reflection of this scale and are not necessarily equivalent to

113

the full-scale version. Indeed, one advantage of this version is that verbal and non-verbal skills are separated out more clearly than in the full test: an important characteristic in relation to this particular population.

4) A quality of life questionnaire was developed and represented a slightly modified version of that piloted by Brown and Bayer (1979). Subjects were asked to evaluate their lives in a number of domains including residential, health, leisure, self image, financial management, marriage, interpersonal and legal involvements. An equivalent questionnaire was given to sponsors who were largely (81%) parents or other close relatives. These questionnaires were filled in for each of the three years.

5) A range of other tests were also carried out, but for purposes of this report only two additional tests are relevant: frontline supervisor questionnaire carried out each year requesting staff to evaluate their training environments and to describe themselves and their philosophy; more detailed data on staff programme philosophy were obtained through the Marlett and Hughson (1978) Value Priority and Needs Analysis Scale, which requests the rating of 20 personal priorities for rehabilitation. (Full details on tests and procedures can be obtained from the researchers' report to Health and Welfare, Canada, 1985.)

SUBJECTS

The clients selected from the agencies were rated in the first three levels of handicap (i.e. minor to major handicaps - but not profound) on motor control and mobility, socialization and communication, developmental skills and behaviour on the Level of Handicap Grid (Marlett, 1978). Levels 1 or 2 on supervision and care were also included. This indicated that the individuals would be either of a mild or moderate level of developmental handicap in one or more of these areas. While they might have no problems in a particular area, in most cases several areas of deficit were noted. In no case were individuals with severe handicaps involved. All clients in the study were initial placements within each agency, i.e. they had not attended other adult rehabilitation agencies. At the commencement of the study, clients were currently attending the agency, or were accepted into the agency during the first year of the study. Within the two smaller agencies all eligible clients were encouraged to be in the study. In the two large agencies, a sample size of at least 100 clients was selected and these individuals were randomly chosen within a stratified system relating to the number of years they had attended the agency. Thus a scatter of clients was accepted, which was proportionate to the total number of eligible clients in a particular 'agency duration' category, i.e. number of years they had attended the agency.

The most common age grouping was 18 to 30 years, which accounted for 67 per cent of the sample. It is perhaps of interest that there was a slight tendency in the lower age groups for more males than females to be represented, with slightly more females than males in the higher age groups.

TABLE 1: Description of Total Sample in the Study

		AGE	IQ VERBAL (WAIS Maxwell)	IQ PERFORMANCE (WAIS Maxwell)
MALE	mean	28.0 years	62	64
	range	18-63+ years	46-106	47-114
	n	130	121	126
FEMALE	mean	28.8 years	62	62
	range	18-55+ years	46-106	47-104
	n	110	107	107
TOTAL*		240	228	233

CLIENT QUESTIONNAIRE RETURNS	Year 1		Year 3	
	n	%	n	%
	235/240	97.9%	214/234	91.5%

PARENT/SPONSOR QUESTIONNAIRE RETURNS	Year 1		Year 3	
	n	%	n	%
	174/240	72.5%	148/234	63.2%

*Differences in sample size due to untestable subjects.

RESULTS

The major results are presented for discussion purposes. Full data may be obtained from the authors' report to Health and Welfare, and other published or to-be-published records of the study. The results are divided into sections relating to various aspects of lifestyle.

Agency Philosophy and Individual Needs

An examination of the Value Priority Scale results show that, although there is some correlation between the different agencies in terms of their staff's perception of priorities, there is also considerable variation, particularly between staff in the same agency. Some staff believe *independence of the client* and *training through normal means* are extremely important, whereas for others *safety and health* and *clean and sanitary environments* were rated as the most important characteristics.

Despite the selection of agencies partly on the basis of philosophy, there was considerable variation in agency philosophy. In one case, no written philosophy was in existence at the start of the study. One agency believed in a business-like approach to vocational rehabilitation using principles of applied behavioural analysis. This agency supported the inclusion of a sheltered industry alongside their training programme. The agency did not provide agency placement procedures, but referred clients to outside counsellors. They believed that persons with mental handicap should work alongside those with mental illness. The agency did not advocate integrated programming, nor a continuum approach (i.e. a series of specified steps within the training system). They had not developed leisure programmes, residential services or allied programmes. Vocational training and occupation was the main philosophy with a requirement that everybody in training should leave the programme within a two-year period. Another agency had an integrated rehabilitation programme philosophy with social-academic as well as vocational programmes, together with some limited leisure time training on site. There was recognition of allied programme needs such as a sexuality programme. Mentally ill and mentally handicapped were trained

alongside one another. There was a businesslike
atmosphere mixed with training. A training
continuum model was employed. Another agency had
a limited amount of work and espoused a charity
model. There was no philosophy relating to any
service continuum, nor were social, educational or
leisure training components seen as viable or
necessary. The programme was strictly vocationally oriented. Two larger urban agencies had a
continuum model, but with accent on vocational
work. There was some leisure time training, but
not integrated within the model. Residential
training on a continuum of service and training
existed for some clients, but this was not closely
integrated with overall programme planning. Some
social training occurred and was supported, though
for funding reasons this planning could not be at
an advanced level. Thus, in these two agencies
training continua exist, but there was no or
little integration across continua. All agencies
believed in the rehabilitation of individuals into
the community.

Amongst frontline personnel there was enormous variation in the amount of time spent in
training clients, but in all cases the amount of
time spent with clients appears very low. Data in
Year 1 from 97 frontline staff show a mean client
training time of 40 per cent of total time. In
Year 3 the percentage drops to 32 per cent. Less
than half their time was on individual training.
In one agency individual training time was placed
at 7 per cent. The remaining hours were divided
between maintenance, conferencing, cleaning and
record keeping.

From the point of view of individuals
participating within these agencies, a number of
quality of life concerns emerge. An individual
attending a training programme may do so without
the parent or guardian, or the client himself/
herself, knowing much about the aims, objectives,
philosophy or approach of the training system
involved. Furthermore, the goals and philosophy
may differ considerably amongst staff. Yet all
the agencies aimed to place individuals in the
community.

It should be noted that only two of the
agencies had residential programmes, thus raising
a further question about integration of programme
strategy between home and community and vocational
training programmes. As suggested elsewhere
(Brown & Hughson, 1987), it may be extremely

important to ensure that there is an integrated philosophy between different aspects of programming and, wherever possible, there should be a recognition of the importance of each aspect of the individual's life in terms of learning and performance. Quality of training is dependent on all parties knowing and agreeing on the general philosophy and goals and their expression for the programme of a specific individual.

Yet such an integrated philosophy cannot become effective unless frontline staff are able to carry out training. Although there are many Canadian centres which purport to carry out rehabilitation and maintain that their direction is towards training and placement, the actual package received may deviate from this due to unclear philosophy of the agency, divergent views of staff, and inadequate time to deliver individualized or group training. This would be of perhaps little concern if either placement and community integration were effective, or if the perceived needs of clients and sponsors were met. The remaining sections attempt to deal with these issues, but, first, other results which reflect further on these initial comments about quality of training are discussed. We believe, from clinical contact with other programmes, many of these issues are probably reflected in most agencies in the Western world.

Client Performance Levels

Although there are some differences between agencies in terms of client scores on the Adaptive Functioning Index, the variation between clients within agencies seems more significant, underlining the importance of individualized programming and training. One of the major characteristics associated with quality of life is the ability to meet an individual recipient's needs, which suggests individualized programming. An analysis of the Adaptive Functioning Index scores between Years 1 and 3 of the study is particularly relevant. Measures of Social Education levels indicate no significant changes from years 1 to 3 (Table 2), with the exception of writing skills, which deteriorated. In the case of work skills (strengths), significant increases in performance were recorded.

TABLE 2: Comparison of Year 1 and Year 3 Social Education AFI Scores on the Same Sample

VARIABLE	N	T*	YEAR 1 Mean	YEAR 1 Standard Deviation	YEAR 3 Mean	YEAR 3 Standard Deviation	t	p
Reading	188	20	6.93	5.87	6.80	5.68	1.09	0.28
Writing	188	20	6.56	6.12	6.14	6.09	2.59	0.01
Communication	188	20	12.74	4.99	12.70	4.58	0.16	0.88
Concept Attainment	188	20	9.95	5.27	10.07	5.38	0.64	0.52
Number Concepts	188	20	5.82	5.54	6.04	5.59	1.51	0.13
Time Concepts	188	20	7.49	5.88	7.68	5.80	1.35	0.18
Money Concepts	188	20	7.80	5.93	7.76	5.98	0.25	0.80
Community Awareness	188	20	5.84	4.82	5.92	4.77	0.44	0.66
Motor Skills	188	20	11.66	4.58	11.82	4.67	0.78	0.44

* Total Possible Score

TABLE 3: Comparison of Year 1 and Year 3 Vocational AFI Scores on the Same Sample

VARIABLE	N	T*	YEAR 1		YEAR 3		t	p
			Mean	Standard Deviation	Mean	Standard Deviation		
Strengths								
Basic Work Habits	163	40	25.97	7.50	28.20	7.50	3.45	0.001
Work Skills	163	20	17.29	6.54	18.55	6.25	2.55	0.01
Acceptance Skills	163	40	27.69	6.68	29.10	6.58	2.45	0.02
TOTAL STRENGTHS	163	100	70.95	18.56	75.85	17.54	3.31	0.001
Difficulties								
Basic Work Habits	163	24	3.31	2.97	3.11	2.76	0.85	NS
Work Skills	163	14	1.52	1.70	1.45	1.70	0.47	NS
Acceptance Skills	163	24	2.96	2.52	2.98	2.38	0.12	NS
TOTAL DIFFICULTIES	163	62	7.79	5.96	7.55	5.60	0.51	NS

* Total Possible Score

Work skill difficulties, such as forgetting to return items or fooling around in the workshop, showed no significant change (see Table 3). An examination of standard deviation suggests that some clients were near the ceiling in terms of strengths, while some had numerical work difficulties. Thus, from a work skill perspective, placement might be expected.

The data concerning vocational placement complicate the picture (see Table 4).

TABLE 4: Total Type of Day Placement for Year 1, 2, 3 and Overall Average for 3-year Duration

TYPE OF DAY PLACEMENT	TOTAL YEAR 1 N=240	TOTAL YEAR 2 N=239	TOTAL YEAR 3 N=234	TOTAL FOR 3 YEARS
Vocational Training Host Agency	2,798	2,594	2,354	7,746
Vocational Training Alternate Programme	0	53	72	125
Sheltered Industry	2	27	45	74
Part-time Employment	10	28	45	83
Full-time Employment	20	45	76	141
Part-time Volunteer	18	9	5	32
Full-time Volunteer	0	12	13	25
Part-time Alternate Programme*	5	55	6	66
No Day Programme	13	101	192	306

*Alternate day programmes include: community college courses, recreation programmes.

	Year 1	Year 2	Year 3	3 Years
1. People Monthly Placements	1.9%	8.0%	9.3%	6.4%
2. People Monthly Placements in Employment	1.1%	2.5%	4.3%	2.6%
3. People Monthly Placements in Volunteer Situations	0.6%	0.7%	0.6%	0.7%

TABLE 4 cont'd

CALCULATION FORMULA:

People Monthly Placements = $\dfrac{\text{Sum of people in a placement each mth for every mth}}{\text{Sum of total no. of people in the study each mth for every mth}}$

People Monthly Placements in Employment = $\dfrac{\text{Sum of people placed in employment situations each mth for every mth}}{\text{Sum of total number of people in the study each mth for every mth}}$

People Monthly Placements in Volunteer Situations = $\dfrac{\text{Sum of people placed in volunteer situations each mth for every mth}}{\text{Sum of total number of people in the study each mth for every mth}}$

Information is available over the three years in terms of placement into community work. In order to develop a more reliable measure of placement than the usual statistic of being placed in a job, details were accumulated on the number of placements made each month for every month during the period of one year. This was done for part-time and full-time employment and for other types of community 'work' activity. For the first year of the study, 1.1 per cent monthly placements in full or part-time employment were made with equivalent data for Years 2 and 3 being 2.5 and 3.8 per cent respectively. Approximately one third of the placements were in part-time employment.

It is apparent that, although most individuals remained in their original agency and few obtained employment, other types of placement increased and some use was made of community college and allied courses, although other vocational training or sheltered industry was also utilized. However, by Year 3 the total placement rate (i.e. removal from agency) had only risen to 8.8 per cent. A majority of placements concerned individuals who had been in the agency a relatively short time (72 months or less). This was partly due to a policy in one of the agencies which required removal of a client after 24 months in the programme. The results suggest that in four of the agencies a new form of institutionalization is building up, which is of considerable concern at a time when Canadian rehabilitation espouses the cause of normalization with its accent on integration in the community.

It appears that the large traditional institutions are reducing in size only to be replaced by a large number of smaller agencies which are not effectively integrating clients into the community. This is not an argument for returning to institutions, but a concern directed towards challenging and changing the direction of the smaller agency.

Questions regarding quality of life arise. Although a goal of each of these agencies was vocational training and placement in the community, employment was rarely achieved within the first three years of the study despite improvement in work skills. It seems unlikely that many of the individuals can expect employment. This difference between stated goals and what can be reasonably expected is of paramount importance. It may be a feature of the current economic situation, as clinical records for at least one of the agencies show a fairly high placement rate in the 1970s. But it could also be argued from that agency's data that the clients as a group at that stage were probably rather less handicapped.

One of the changes resulting from a deinstitutional policy is that many people are becoming institutionalized in many small agencies rather than a few large agencies. This issue is a complex one, for it may be true that fewer people are being institutionalized than previously, yet there can be little doubt that for people who go to adult rehabilitation agencies for developmentally handicapped persons the chances of vocational rehabilitation at the present time are slim.

The concern is a critical one for agencies within Canada, for it suggests that, if we pursue the rationale of vocational training with the hope of vocational employment, this realization may not occur, undermining philosophy and training, as well as client and, possibly, sponsor expectations. This suggests in terms of our definitions a poor level of quality of life.

Many parents stated they were concerned that, with the present recession, workshops would be either closed or become 'holding tanks' rather than stimulating and challenging environments leading to competitive employment. Coupled with this, parents expressed concern for the future of their children. Many do not expect them to be independent and note the need for residential care when they, the parents, die. These concerns seem to be valid for they are supported by the data,

123

since there are low employment placement rates,
and unclear or inappropriate goals in the context
of unstated or unattainable though laudable philosophies linked to low incidence of individualized
or group training.

Training for Other Aspects of Community Living

Most of the agencies had some involvement in
social competence training, either through classes
or through specific training units. In some cases
residential components involved such training. It
is appropriate to ask to what extent individuals
progressed or had their needs met in these areas.
It has already been noted that no significant
group changes were made in Social Educational or
Residential AFI scores, although many of the
clients perceived themselves as having progressed
at the agency. Perceived improvement on various
skills is noted in Figure 1. The greatest
improvement is seen in the area of work skills,
which is reasonable, since agencies directed their
major programmes to this end, while much lower
incidence of improvement is seen in relation to
social and community items such as buying clothes
and groceries. The percentage showing improvement
is slightly higher in females than males in 18 of
the 19 categories. An analysis of individual
categories shows significant differences in
reading, buying clothes, leisure time and making
decisions. In all these cases, the females
perceived greater improvement than males, but in
the majority of areas less than 50 per cent of the
subjects noted improvement, a factor which may
have considerable relevance to self image.

For males, the lowest improvement is seen in
reading, buying of clothes and groceries, playing
sports, and looking after medications. For
females, the most improvements are perceived to be
in buying groceries, looking after medications,
writing, and playing sports. Ability to use bus
services is also seen as limited improvement for
both groups. This data is based on Year 1 of the
study. These perceptions of improvement seem a
positive contribution to quality of life for some
subjects, but the results are not supported by the
data on performance or by the perception of
sponsors, which are significantly less optimistic.

FIGURE 1: Individual Perception of Skill Improvement Since Coming to the Agency, in Percentage of Total Male and Female Groups (Year 1)

Skill	Males	Females
READING	26.5	50.0
WRITING	33.3	36.1
MAKING CHANGE	33.0	44.2
BUYING CLOTHES	28.6	42.3
BUYING GROCERIES	24.5	31.1
PLAYING SPORTS	27.7	39.1
COOKING	41.2	44.6
LAUNDRY	43.2	50.5
KEEPING CLEAN	32.8	41.1
MAKING FRIENDS	37.9	47.8
GETTING ALONG	44.0	56.5
LOOKING AFTER MEDS	12.0	23.1
WAY AROUND COMMUNITY	48.4	47.7
USING BUS	32.8	42.5
LEISURE TIME	47.3	63.6
MAKING DECISIONS	39.5	58.8
BEING HAPPY	61.5	67.4
WORK SKILLS	74.7	80.0
CO-WORKER RELATIONS	56.0	59.8

MALES ☐   FEMALES ▨

It is of interest that overall there are positive and significant Spearman rho correlations between client and sponsor perceived needs ranging between 0.6 and 0.9, depending on year and sex. Sponsors stated a much higher need for help, largely in social and community areas, but also recognized the need for emotional support of the clients.

The high correlations between sponsor and client's responses suggest that clinicians can rely on client rank order of difficulties or improvements as indicating a hierarchy of training requirements. The magnitude of the needs is often seen as much smaller by the client compared with the parent. Some of the major areas of client and sponsor concern relate to such items as ability to carry out minor equipment repairs, such as replacing a light bulb, budgeting money, buying groceries and planning menus. Less frequently, but still of concern were skills relating to house cleaning and laundry (see Figure 2). These perceptions appear to be consistent with findings relating to AFI scores on client performance.

Despite this, in Year 1 of the study, about 74 per cent of the parents saw the individual moving to an ideal situation at some point. Yet 96 per cent of the clients were seen as usually enjoying where they were living. Reasons for enjoyment provided by the clients included privacy, companionship, ability of near relatives to provide support if necessary, the availability of gardens where produce could be picked, and the availability of pets. Even in cases where the individual liked the environment, there were a number of qualifications. Sometimes there were some qualification or dislike of the place where the individual lived. Reasons included were a lack of friends, people looking into belongings and banning the individual from the kitchen, the lack of privacy, plus a lack of things to do at night.

FIGURE 2: Responses from Sponsor and Client
Questionnaires - Year 1 'Client Needs
Supervision' Combined with 'Client Not
Responsible for Activity', in
Percentages: -

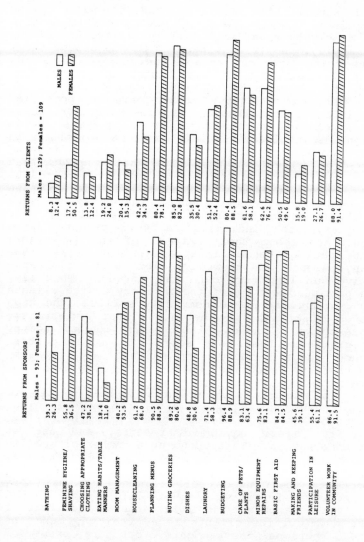

The importance of family activity or involvement and support comes through frequently as a positive element. Even when the individuals are not living with their parents, the close availability of parents or brothers and sisters seems relevant. Quietness, the ability to provide help and support to relatives and friends, having access to films, theatres, pubs and friends seem to be highly regarded. Ability to move around the community, the friendliness of people around them, and being able to regard the place as 'a fun learning experience' were noted by clients as important aspects to quality living.

All of the above areas represent potential training areas, although, for the most part, these were not seen as the major training areas of the agencies involved. In some cases no programmes in these areas applied. An examination of funding from government sources does not suggest that funding is primarily given to support such training, yet, in terms of quality of life and the development of independence, these may be very critical areas for education to be carried out. Further, as indicated above, parents were concerned about the placement of their children once parents become incapacitated or died. Thus many parents saw themselves left with no alternative but long term care and support. This may, in part, be because of inefficiency of the clients in terms of home and community skills. The high level of reliability between client and sponsor assessment of needs, the examination of agency programme content, and scores of actual performance suggest that both clients and sponsors accurately recognize where there is need for training.

To summarize, it would seem that there are major concerns in areas such as house cleaning, planning menus, buying groceries, budgeting, laundry, minor equipment repairs, and use of transportation. This opens up a number of quality of life and training issues. For example, agencies should seek the opinion of clients in terms of their needs for training and what they perceive as important in their life.

It is apparent that, in terms of magnitude of the difficulties clients face, they may make the wrong personal assessments, but, in terms of relative skill or lack of skill, they appear to know where they are weakest and strongest. Sponsors likewise have a very clear impression of

128

where needs lie. Within the programmes examined, individual needs are not being met in many instances, particularly within the home and community areas. This suggests that the philosophy, goals and general direction of training services need to be re-examined and that governments should look carefully at why they are giving money for particular types of services (e.g. vocational employment) when those goals may not be directly achievable. Other goals may be seen as of equal importance and may be a major way for providing a means of attaining a much better outcome to rehabilitation in the long run.

Although we are not denying the importance of vocational training programmes, we are stressing the importance of other aspects of rehabilitation which are, we suggest, fundamental to effective performance.

The quality of rehabilitation programming cannot be seen for adults in terms of employment alone, but should be qualified and clarified in terms of performance in other areas, and include the perception of the client and sponsor in evaluating the effectiveness of service.

The results raise some further questions. For example, why, since in most agencies clients lived at home, were many family members not taking responsibility for much of the home and community living training? Possibly many parents and allied family supporters had attempted such training without success. Possibly some found it quicker and more effective to carry out necessary home and community activities themselves. In any case, it is suggested that it is the responsibility of social and allied authorities to provide training where it is needed, and furthermore they should recognize the skilled nature of such training.

It seems likely that agency services will not greatly enhance quality of life unless they become directly involved in individual clients' lives on a much more comprehensive and personal basis and that this involvement includes more than time in a day programme.

Generality of Findings

The material that has been discussed above raises some important philosophical and practical questions in relation to quality of life of developmentally handicapped persons. From our clinical data we do not see these agencies as atypical, and furthermore would like to suggest that the issues are worthy of examination within a range of other and allied disabilities, for the data represent an inability by many disabled persons to control the quality of their environment. Philosophy and programming within many agencies does not seem directed towards some of the major needs.

Much more attention should be given to the delivery of services within the home and community environment, and this raises the importance of more knowledge being in the hands of frontline practitioners, with an opportunity for these practitioners to spend most of their time in individual and group training. However, this training should be directed towards the needs as noted by clients and sponsors, in order to raise the quality of lifestyle and thus the effectiveness of rehabilitation.

The above entails a different approach to funding on the part of government agencies, and a different perspective on what is and what is not a measure of success within rehabilitation. As implied above, quality of life must be represented in all aspects of lifestyle. It implies improvement and greater control of one's environment and this primarily means home, community and vocational environments. The first two aspects can be effectively improved if adequate skills are developed, and this reflects on the quality and nature of rehabilitation training.

Vocational training may not result in employment, but individuals who master home and community skills possibly have greater prospects for employment. But even more critical is the question whether a vocational training centre should be a primary placement for an individual. It is not a normalized or integrated facility but a means to an end, frequently permanent placement. We suggest an alternative training environment(s) may be more appropriate.

Paradoxically, these arguments for the improvement of quality of life initially assume much greater involvement of services within home environments. They recognize the importance of parental and other sponsor comment and knowledge about needs, but at the same time recognize some of the important characteristics noted by clients. This, in many people's terms, will be seen as greater interference by services in family life, and yet it may be important to do this, with the agreement of the sponsor and client, if rehabilitation is to be more effective. In the long run, it may be the means by which clients are no longer perceived by parents, who are themselves aging, as in need of total support.

Quality of life, then, does not just simply reflect an improvement in terms of what one can handle, and the needs which one can attain. It assumes, in the first place, responsible cooperation and coordination between the parties involved, with a recognition that agency authority and practitioner involvement should be lessened as the individual becomes in greater command of his or her lifestyle.

Life Satisfaction and Quality of Life

However, there is one other aspect to quality of life which cannot be overlooked, and that is the perception by the vast majority of our clients that they are basically happy in the types of situations in which they are functioning. Should this perception not be of overriding value in deciding whether further services are required? Obviously it must play an important role, and here we would expect there to be some major differences between individuals who are developmentally handicapped and have not had opportunities for a more free lifestyle, and individuals who suddenly, at later stages in life, find that they have lost the quality of life that they formerly enjoyed. The argument is a complex one and by the very nature of quality of life is riddled with subjective judgments.

We suggest that quality of life must reflect a number of factors; which ones dominate will depend on the ability and experience of the individual client. The more experienced and the more independent he or she has become, the more he or she is able to provide opinions on life quality which should carry heavy weight in any decisions that are made in service delivery. In many circumstances the individual should be the final authority. But in situations where there is less experience, less ability to judge, then the opinions of others should also be involved to a greater degree. The key word is 'also', because at no stage do we suggest the individual client should not be involved in the decision making process regarding quality of life.

Service providers have a responsibility to ensure that the delivery of services matches the need, as perceived by sponsor and client. This means a dramatic change in service delivery and a dramatic change in the attitude of government departments towards the funding that they provide. No longer is it satisfactory that governments determine that vocational training is the major route for training centres. There are, in terms of life, many other values and skills which must be looked to if an individual is going to have an effective lifestyle.

Furthermore, the incidence of other problems, particularly in relation to physical health, raises social and quality of life issues including matters relating to nutrition. There is some preliminary evidence to suggest that persons in the study are not being exposed to a balanced diet as suggested by *Canada's Food Guide* (Government of Canada, 1983). Results of a two-day nutrition diary completed by subjects during Year 1 of the study showed that at least one third of the subjects did not eat the suggested daily number of servings in each of the four food categories (milk and milk products, fruit and vegetables, meat and fish, breads and cereals).

Quality of Life as an Holistic Concept

The areas noted indicate that quality of life is a holistic concept which requires interdisciplinary programming. Sponsor responses underline that it is in the areas where clients have the least skills where other individuals in society take greatest advantage of them. For example, problems relating to the lending of money and personal belongings were noted in approximately 50 per cent of the sample. Consistent with this is the type of assistance required by the individual. On the basis of Year 1 data, the highest need was found in the areas of emotional support (86.8%), assertiveness training (48.3%), preparation of meals (64%), housekeeping (55%), leisure skill development (60%), leisure time organization (56%), budgeting (69%).

The majority of sponsors who returned questionnaires expressed a concern over the future of their son or daughter. These sponsors noted that due to their own increased age and eventual death they will be unable to advocate for or provide support for their son or daughter. Decreased support systems have been shown to have a negative effect on successful community adjustment (Jackson, 1984). This, coupled with the finding that the necessary social and community skills have not been taught, furthers a dependency relationship and increases the likelihood of developmentally handicapped persons living in institutions as they and their parents age. Maintenance of good nutritional and health habits and weight control were concerns expressed by parents, yet none of the five agencies provided training in weight control on a regular basis, or provided detailed guidance in terms of proper nutrition. One agency did provide such services but had to discontinue this due to lack of funding and reallocation of staffing resources.

Parents were concerned with the medical complications associated with their sons' and daughters' handicapping conditions. Jacobson, Sutton and Janicki (1985) have indicated that the chances of institutionalization increase as the handicapped person ages, especially if they are multiply handicapped, which was the case in a large number of this sample. Parents were also concerned that their son or daughter will be lonely or that advantage will be taken of them.

Although efforts are often made for social interaction with developmentally handicapped persons, these arrangements involving visits by friends to the homes of handicapped persons often result in some preliminary interaction followed by conversation taking place between other non-handicapped adults who are present. The friendship levels appear to be those of exposure rather than self-actualization or true social competency. This is consistent with other data found within the leisure time areas, which underline some of the major difficulties in this area of performance. According to questionnaire results, most leisure activities participated in by the individual are spectator such as watching television and listening to records. Social and physical activities occur much less frequently, raising issues about motivation and competence in the physical and social domains (Brown et al., 1987), while self-actualizing activities are even less common. These results are, to some degree, consistent with Nash's (1953) work on the general population yet we must be concerned that the more advanced activities are not participated in by our

sample because they have never gained more
advanced skills. Many of the more advanced
activities are associated with motivation,
positive self image and competent social skills.
For example, in the five-agency sample, social
skills as measured by the AFI were positively and
significantly correlated with level of leisure
activity (Brown et al., 1987). Although this
cannot necessarily be regarded as a causal
relationship, it does underline the possible
importance of leisure activity and training to
broader needs of rehabilitation.

Programme Costs

We were interested in the costs associated with
delivery of rehabilitation services and how these
costs varied with the size of agency, measured by
the number of clients served, the number of
service units in each agency, and the level of
performance of clients in the rehabilitation
programmes. Total costs varied directly with the
number of clients and the number of service units.
Salaries and staff benefits, the largest portion
of direct programme costs, ranged from 50 per cent
to 80 per cent of total costs and the costs for
agency administration ranged from 4 per cent to 15
per cent of total costs. This variability
appeared to be related to the administrative
structure rather than agency size, which may have
a bearing on the concerns raised about philosophy
and agency goals, the low involvement in social
and leisure training, and the limited availability
of frontline staff for training. All agencies
depended upon government grants, which ranged from
73 per cent to 93 per cent of total revenues.
Revenues raised through contracts ranged from 5
per cent to 24 per cent of total revenues.
Residential costs are not included in these
figures.
    The measure adopted for comparing the costs
of rehabilitation among agencies was the average
cost per client-day. Daily attendance was
collected in each programme of each agency to
obtain the proportion of programme costs attribut-
able to the clients participating in the study,
enabling us to calculate the per client-day costs.
The direct costs for delivery of services ranged
from $15.00 per client-day for the smallest agency
to $45.00 for the largest agency, and the largest

agency had the highest costs for administration while the second largest agency had the lowest costs.

The two large agencies, which were in urban settings and provided some additional services, such as in leisure and social education, had higher costs than the agencies offering fewer services but which were located in smaller cities and towns. However, there is much variability in programme costs and client performance among the agencies, part of which may be due to salary differentials.

There are interesting correlations between costs, client performance and the amount of time staff spend on direct client training. In the agency which had the lowest average client-day programme costs, staff spent the least amount of time on client training, the clients scored highest (i.e. greatest handicap) on the Socialization/Communication and Developmental Skills of the Levels of Handicap Grid (Marlett, 1978) and scored lowest (i.e. poorest) on the Social Educational and Vocational scales of the Adaptive Functioning Index (AFI). In the agency which had the highest average client-day programme costs, staff spent the second highest amount of time on client training and the clients scored second highest on the Social Educational AFI scale. As one would expect, there are positive correlations between the amount of time staff spend on client training activities and client functioning, and between programme costs and client training activities. However, there are anomalies for two agencies in which staff spent above average time on client training returned below average programme costs. The agency with the highest client-staff ratio had lower than average programme costs.

The variability in client training costs is related to the amount of time an agency devotes to vocational rehabilitation versus social rehabilitation, with higher costs associated with more emphasis on social rehabilitation. However, the fact that placement rates of clients into the community are very low for those agencies spending the vast majority of training time in the vocational area questions the appropriateness of these programmes. The cost data suggest that the poorest client performance is associated with less training and therefore lower cost. However, it is also evident that increased expenditures on training, or the diversification of training programmes, may not be necessarily associated with better client performance. The implication of these findings is that the solution is not simply more funding for existing programmes, but different, more effective, use of present funding. Furthermore, the lack of placement means that funding continues to be expended on the same clients. Thus, if diversification of training results in more effective rehabilitation, the same amount of funds can be used to rehabilitate a larger number of persons.

SUMMARY AND GENERAL CONCLUSIONS

1. Some of the recommendations drawn from the above material apply, we suggest, not just to programmes with developmentally handicapped adolescents and adults, but they may be raised as pertinent questions in a wide range of rehabilitation programmes. The definitions of quality of life given in this chapter underline the importance of subjective, as well as objective, measures. For quality of life is seen as discrepancy between a person's achieved and his or her unmet needs and desires.

2. One aspect of quality of life is expressed through the design and application of programmes within the rehabilitation field. It is apparent that in some agencies there are major variations between staff within the agency regarding the important aspects of the programme. It is suggested here that the sponsor and client needs are extremely important ones to take into account and that an examination of perception of each individual's quality of life leads to a very broad view of holistic programming. It further underlines the need for individualization of programmes. It is recommended that agencies should look very carefully at their programme structure from this perspective.

3. Quality of training is likely to be related to the amount of time frontline staff can spend on individual or group training with their clients. This study suggests that a very low proportion of time is spent in these areas and that again this requires careful

monitoring and direction within rehabilitation programmes.

4. Measures of vocational and social educational levels suggested significant improvements in the former but none in the latter. A number of reasons are advanced for this, but in particular it is suggested that other aspects of programming need to be developed further before vocational rehabilitation may become effective in terms of employment.

5. Part of the above concern relates to the very low level of employment placement either on a full or part time basis within the community, which raises whether at this present time philosophy of agencies and stated goals clearly matches with the actual programme effectiveness. Indeed it is suggested that many small 'institutions' may be replacing the larger institutions of a previous decade and that these new agencies are becoming holding tanks for a large number of clients.

6. The above concern probably is associated with parents' and sponsors' view that long term provision must be made for their offspring or wards.

7. Parents see fairly minimal changes taking place within the area of community and leisure time skill areas and note major needs in these areas. Clients' views match the sponsors' in order of need, if not in degree. Thus there is a match between perceived need by client and sponsor and lack of progress and skill in particular areas of programming. A list of some of the areas in which help is perceived as being required is put forward, and there is considerable accent on the development of leisure time and allied skills which do appear to be correlated with social education and vocational level of performance.

8. Some discussion is provided on clients' perceptions of need and aspects of quality of life which they deem to be important. The importance of worries and concerns and the relevance of these to programming areas are raised.

9. The importance of friends and relatives and the support they supply in terms of involvement with them seem to be perceived as highly critical.

10. Although we are not denying the importance of vocational training programmes, we are stressing the importance of other aspects of rehabilitation which involve a much greater association and interaction with the community. This may have fundamental implications for budgeting and for training of staff as well as mode of delivery of programmes. Despite all these concerns, the majority of clients appear basically satisfied with their situations, though this should give no reason for undue complacency in view of the concrete concerns and recommendation for programming coming from clients and sponsors. The authors provide some indication of the extent to which personal advocacy and involvement in programme development and administration should be provided, though accenting the importance of consulting the client and sponsor in terms of programme need.

11. A final area looks at programming costs and notes that, though there are associations between amount of cost and number of front-line staff, it is apparent that cost and programming effectiveness do not necessarily go hand in hand. It is recommended that governments and agencies could in fact modify their programmes considerably in a number of instances without adding additional costs to programme application. Reallocation of funds and duties of staff would seem to be major possibilities.

REFERENCES

Bateson, G. (1972) *Steps to an Ecology of Mind*, Chandler Publishing Co, San Francisco.

Brown, R. I. & Bayer, M. B. (1979) *Research, Demonstration and Practice: 10 Years of Progress*, Vocational and Rehabilitation Research Institute, Calgary, Alberta.

Brown, R. I., Bayer, M. B., & MacFarlane, C. (1985) *Rehabilitation Programs Study*. Report to Health and Welfare (Project No. #4558-29-4) Canada.

Brown, R. I., Bayer, M. B., & MacFarlane, C. (1987) 'Perception of Leisure Activities and Needs Amongst Developmentally Handicapped Adults', *Rehabilitation Research Canada*, (in press).

Brown, R. I. & Hughson, E. A. (1987) *Behavioural and Social Rehabilitation and Training*, Wiley & Sons, Chichester and New York.

Denham, M. J. (1983) 'Assessment of Quality of Life,' in M. J. Denham, *Care of the Long Stay Elderly Patient*, Croom Helm, London/Sheridan House, Dobbs Ferry, NY.

Goodale, J. G., Hall, D. T., Burke, R. J., & Joyner, R. C. (1975) 'Some Significant Contexts and Components of Individual Quality of Life', in L. E. Davis, A. B. Cherns & Assoc. (eds.), *The Quality of Working Life*, (Vol. I), The Free Press, New York.

Government of Canada (1983) *Canada's Food Guide*, Health and Welfare, Canada.

Jackson, R. (1984) 'Transition from School to Adult Life,' in R. I. Brown (ed.), *Integrated Programmes for Handicapped Adults and Adolescents*, Croom Helm, London/Nichols, New York.

Jacobson, J. W., Sutton, M. S., & Janicki, M. P. (1985) 'Demography and Characteristics of Aging and Aged Mentally Disabled Persons,' in M. P. Janicki & H. M. Wisniewski (eds.), *Aging and Developmental Disabilities: Issues and Approaches*, Paul H. Brookes, Baltimore.

Kennedy, L. W., Northcott, H. C., & Kinzel, C. (1977) *Quality of Life in Edmonton: Initial Findings from the 1977 Edmonton Area Study*, Edmonton Area Series Report #1, Department of Sociology, University of Alberta, Edmonton.

MacFarlane, C. (1985) 'Measuring Quality of Life in a Rehabilitation Program,' Paper presented to the International Association for the Scientific Study of Mental Deficiency Conference, New Delhi.

Marlett, N. J. (1971) *Adaptive Functioning Index Social, Education and Administrative Manual*, Vocational and Rehabilitation Research Institute, Calgary, Alberta.

Marlett, N. J. (1978) 'Levels of Handicap Grid,' in *Feasibility Study, Resources for Handicapped People*, WIRTC, Edmonton.

Marlett, N. J. & Hughson, E. A. (1978) *Rehabilitation Programs Manual*, Vocational and Rehabilitation Research Institute, Calgary, Alberta.

Maxwell, A. E. (1960) 'Obtaining Factor Scores on the Wechsler Adult Intelligence Scale,' *Journal of Mental Science*, 106, 1060-1062.

Nash, J. B. (1953) *Philosophy of Recreation and Leisure*, William C. Brown Co., Dubuque, Iowa.

Robinson, J. P. & Shaver, P. R. (1973) *'Measures of Social Psychological Attitude*, Institute for Social Research, Michigan.

Rodgers, W. L. & Converse, P. E. (1975) Measures of the Perceived Overall Quality of Life,' *Social Indicators Research*, *2*, 127-152.

FOOTNOTES

1. The authors gratefully acknowledge the support provided by Health and Welfare, Canada, in funding the Rehabilitation Programmes Study, Grant No. 4558-29-4, through the Vocational and Rehabilitation Research Institute. The material represents the work of the authors and does not necessarily represent the views of the funding agent.

2. We acknowledge with gratitude the time and support given by agency boards, staff, clients and their parents.

Chapter Seven

APPROACHES TO TRAINING: THE SOCIAL SKILLS NEEDED FOR QUALITY OF LIFE

Daniel W. Close and Gilbert Foss

INTRODUCTION

The community adjustment of persons with mental retardation is largely dependent on their competence in interpersonal affairs. Research studies from the 1930s (Baller, 1936) demonstrated that persons with mild mental retardation were roughly equivalent to their non-disabled peers on a variety of indices. Great discrepancies, however, were reported on their abilities to manage social and interpersonal relations. Likewise, Edgerton's (1967) study of the post-institutional adjustment of a group of adults with mild and borderline mental retardation indicated that their ability to maintain positive relationships with others was highly correlated with overall success in the community.

The literature on vocational adjustment also demonstrates the crucial role social competence plays in the successful vocational adjustment of persons with mental retardation (Foss & Bostwick, 1981; Greenspan & Shoultz, 1981; Chadsey-Rusch, 1986). Typically those individuals who are selected for jobs in the competitive employment sector possess adequate social competence (Gold, 1973). Conversely, deficits in social competence exclude many persons with retardation from gaining and/or maintaining competitive employment (Chadsey-Rusch, 1986; Foss, Walker, Todis, Lyman & Smith, 1986; Rusch, 1986).

A major problem that has hindered habilitation efforts in the social competence area is the lack of agreement among professionals concerning the proper focus of instruction. In a recent review of the literature on social skills training, McFall (1982) notes the major conflicts between the competing theoretical models in this area. In particular, he notes that certain theorists focus exclusively on skills needed by the individual, while others note the imperfect or inconsistent cues provided by the environment. McFall concludes his review with the recommendation to clearly identify the social tasks needed for social competence, and to translate those tasks into specific skills for remediation. The result of this activity is an instructional system that is both functional and socially valid. While this social validation approach to identification of the skills needed for social competence in a wide range of adult tasks is a major innovation, additional work is needed to teach the identified skills in a manner which promotes independent, competent performance.

The specific purpose of this chapter is to provide information on teaching social competence skills needed by mildly retarded persons in community settings. Specifically, information will be provided on an instructional system for teaching social and interpersonal skills to persons with mental retardation. Specific emphasis will be placed on teaching skills in community, residential, school and employment settings. In addition, information will be provided on a model service programme developed to teach these skills to adolescents and young adults with mild retardation in a community college setting.

CONTENT DEVELOPMENT

Social validation is a process where researchers identify skills and behaviours that are socially relevant and important for a given client. The use of this procedure has become widely accepted by many researchers in the social sciences in recent years. White (1986) notes that social validation has involved assessment of the social acceptability of interventions regarding:

1) the content of instructional programmes;
2) methods used to teach new behaviours or change existing behaviour; and
3) effectiveness of instructional programmes.

Regarding the first area, social validation procedures typically seek to determine which behaviours are necessary to perform a given role. For example, asking employers which work behaviours are needed to gain and maintain successful employment is a useful social validation procedure. Likewise, assessing the performance demands required to use a bank to deposit money is another example of social validation.

One of the main techniques used in social validation research is to solicit the opinions of individuals who are capable of identifying aspects of social behaviours required for competent performance. Typically a questionnaire is used to identify the skills needed. The results of this method provide important information to begin the process of developing instructional procedures. Social validation procedures are valuable only to the extent that they measure the precise behaviours required for competent performance in a given domain.

In the next section of this chapter, a series of studies will be described which were used to identify a range of social skills needed by persons with disabilities in the employment and independent living domains. The subjective evaluation method was used to solicit the opinions of employers, supervisors, co-workers, teachers and friends regarding the focus of instructional programmes.

Social Skills for Employment

Eight behavioural areas were initially identified as domains relevant to job tenure for mentally retarded adults (Foss & Peterson, 1981). These were:

1) following supervisor instructions,
2) responding to supervisor criticism or correction,
3) requesting assistance,
4) accepting a new supervisor,
5) disruptive behaviour,
6) being distracted by other people,
7) aggressive behaviour, and
8) bizarre or irritating behaviour.

To understand the content of problems in these eight areas, 18 production supervisors and 18 mildly retarded work trainees in nine vocational training facilities in one northwest state reported problems in these eight areas through week-long observation (Cheney & Foss, 1984). Also, 18 competitive employers reported problems they had observed in these behavioural areas through structured interviews with project staff.

The above procedures produced nearly 250 problematic interpersonal situations that mentally retarded workers encountered in vocational settings. A brief description of these problematic situations was sent to a regional sample of 111 vocational training facilities in 12 western states to verify their occurrence in a broad geographical area. Table 1 shows the types of interpersonal problems discovered in terms of six major categories. These categories provided the content for the assessment and training efforts which followed, and each is briefly described below.

TABLE 1:   Content of Problematic Interpersonal Situations

			Number
I.	Problems with Supervisor		
	A.	Handling Criticism and Correction	71
	B.	Requesting Assistance	35
	C.	Following Instructions	26
		Total	132
II.	Problems Among Co-Workers		
	A.	Cooperative Work Behaviour	68
	B.	Handling Teasing and Provocation	30
	C.	Resolving Personal Concerns	16
		Total	114
		Grand Total	246

Problems with supervisor. As shown in Table 1, the problems reported between supervisors and workers consisted of three major types:

1)   handling criticism and correction,
2)   requesting assistance, and
3)   following instructions.

The problem most frequently reported by supervisors involved inappropriate worker responses to criticism or correction. These inappropriate responses usually occurred when the work-trainee was corrected for doing the job wrong or criticized for breaking a work rule.

Problematic situations concerning *requesting assistance* occurred because the work-trainee did not know when to ask for help, asked for help in an unacceptable manner, or did not understand who to ask for help. For example, a number of assistance problems occurred because a work-trainee's regular supervisor was unavailable and the trainee did not know who to ask for help. Finally, problematic situations concerning *following instructions* generally occurred when the work-trainee was given instructions that he/she did not understand or an instruction with which he/she disagreed.

<u>Problems among co-workers</u>. Three primary categories emerged from the reporting of these problematic situations:

1) cooperative work behaviour,
2) handling teasing and provocation, and
3) resolving personal concerns.

The first area, 'cooperative work behaviour', contains three types of problematic situations, including disagreements, conflicts, and distractions between co-workers. All of the interpersonal problems in this category occurred between co-workers assigned to a task which they were to complete cooperatively.

The second category, 'handling teaching and provocation', includes situations wherein one worker was verbally or physically provoked by another. These situations generally were not related to the actual completion of a task but instead seemed to occur between workers while they were working. An example here is one worker teasing another about the way he/she is dressed.

The final category in the co-worker area, 'resolving personal concerns', contains problematic interpersonal situations which generally occurred during breaks or lunch, or at quitting time. These situations can be characterized as ones which require a worker to be able to effectively make or refuse personal requests. For example, a common problem in this area concerned borrowing and loaning things.

After the content for training was identified through the research described above, an employer evaluation procedure was used to develop the standards of effective and appropriate behaviour to be assessed and taught in the curriculum. Approximately 500 employers throughout 12 western states were contacted in this project (Foss, Bullis & Vilhauer, 1984). The employers represented five Dictionary of Occupational Titles categories which accounted for over 75% of the jobs in which mentally retarded people were placed by the state-federal Vocational Rehabilitation programme during the period from 1975-1980. These occupations are:

(a) service,
(b) processing,
(c) machine trades,
(d) benchwork, and
(e) structural work.

Approximately 120 of the 500 employers surveyed completed and returned a questionnaire.

Employers were asked to rate the effectiveness of alternative solutions to the interpersonal problematic situations described above (see Table 1). The interpersonal behaviours assessed and taught in the curriculum, then, are based on the consensual judgment of a sizeable number of the employers in the Western United States.

Social Skills for Independent Living

A recent study by Wells and Close (1986) used the subjective evaluation approach to determine the content of social survival skills curriculum for persons with mild/moderate mental retardation. The authors administered a questionnaire that included the key skills and competencies needed for social survival in integrated residential settings. The questionnaire was designed to acquire information on the importance and relevance of a range of social skills. The respondents were a sample of 150 secondary level special education teachers and 43 skill trainers employed by programmes offering semi-independent living services. Respondents were asked to rate the importance a given skill had for their students or clients. In addition, respondents were asked to rank the social skills in order of importance for sustaining independent living for individuals with mild/moderate mental retardation.

TABLE 2:   Rankings of Top Ten Social Skills

> Taking Responsibility
> Solving Problems
> Controlling Feelings/Emotions
> Saying No
> Willingness to Negotiate
> Being Nice with Others
> Being Intimate
> Communicating with Words
> Asking for Help
> Communicating Without Words

As Table 2 indicates, the skills most highly rated relate to issues of initiation, motivation, self-improvement, negotiation, assertiveness and communication. While these skills are highly valued by teachers and skill trainers, they are not totally consistent with data from the students and clients themselves. Halpern, Close and Nelson (1986) asked clients of semi-independent living programmes which social skills they thought were most important and they responded that making friends, getting along with others and feeling good about myself were the most highly rated.

Thus, the results of the two studies indicate that skills needed for social survival include a large measure of motivation, self-direction, interpersonal flexibility and feeling good about one's self. In the next section of the paper, a set of procedures developed to teach these skills will be presented. Finally, a description of a service setting to teach social skills will be presented.

DEVELOPMENT OF INSTRUCTIONAL METHODS AND MATERIALS

Social Skills for Employment

The vast majority of social skill instructional programmes developed for mildly and moderately retarded persons are composed of one or more of the following instructional techniques: modelling, behaviour rehearsal, or verbal instruction, including problem solving. Jackson, King and

Heller (1981) reviewed 11 published studies on social skill training with mentally retarded persons conducted to that date, and noted that all had used some combination of modeling, behaviour rehearsal, or verbal instruction and the primary instructional method or methods. In spite of the frequency of use of these methods of social skills instruction, however, little is known about which of these methods, or combination of methods, is most effective or feasible for classroom instruction in special education programmes at the secondary level. Yet a recent study by Vale (1978) concluded that curriculum materials in this area were sorely needed by secondary special education teachers.

Consequently, the Oregon Research and Training Center conducted research to examine both the comparative impact and the utility of four different-but-related curricular formats for teaching employment-related interpersonal skills to mildly mentally handicapped secondary students. These four instructional formats were used to compare and contrast the instructional effects of:

a) two types of modeling (teacher modeling and videotape modeling by non-handicapped peers);

b) behavioural rehearsal by student groups of three; and

c) problem solving, a technique in which students discuss a problem from a work situation, generate alternative responses and discuss the consequences of these alternatives.

Each of these instructional approaches are briefly described below.

Modelling, as described by social learning theorists such as Bandura (1977), has long been acknowledged as an effective means of teaching social behaviour. In this method, called observational learning, a model demonstrates the skill to be learned, and the observers are then able to reproduce the behaviours. Goldstein, Sprafkin, Gershaw and Klein (1980) state that the power of modeling lies in its ability to communicate to students *what* they are supposed to do in a given social situation. They also suggest that modeling is not sufficient by itself and other methods must be used to teach students *how* to perform the desired behaviour and *why* they should do so.

A major factor in the effectiveness of modelling is the characteristics of the model (Bandura, 1977). The social power of the model (which may be based, for example, on the model's control of reinforcers, assigned authority, personal attractiveness or similarity to the subject) is positively correlated with the strength of modelling. In social skills training the model is usually an instructor who has both legitimate authority and control of reinforcers for students. In videotape modelling, it is usually peers who model and are effective due to their similarity to students in the class. Videotape modelling differs from teacher modelling both in the characteristics of the model and in the method of presentation (i.e. videotape vs. live). There are also other differences such as the cost of videotape curricula and teacher preference for one method or the other that distinguish the methods. Both types of modelling have been shown to be effective in separate studies (Martin, Rusch & Heal, 1982) however, a direct comparison of methods with mildly retarded high school students has not been conducted.

<u>Behavioural rehearsal</u> is an instructional method common to a number of effective social skills training packages (e.g. Bates, 1980; Filipczak, Archer & Friedman, 1980; Foxx, McMorrow & Schloss, 1983; LaGreca, Stone & Bell, 1983). Behaviour rehearsal is a form of role playing which has been used in a great variety of ways to achieve different goals. In behaviour rehearsal, the responses of the students are constrained through instruction and feedback so that only correct behaviours are practised. Unlike psychodrama, another form of role playing, the student is not asked to take on a role and then behave as someone in that role would behave. Behaviour rehearsal allows students to practise social skills in a supportive environment thereby gaining proficiency and confidence before facing real-life situations.

Senatore, Matson and Kazdib (1982) point out that behaviour rehearsal, when added to other instructional methods, increases student ability. It is also a central component of Goldstein's (1973) Structured Learning Therapy. However, there are costs included in the use of this method. Behaviour rehearsal can take a great deal of class time, perhaps more than is available given the limits of a high school schedule. In addition, variation in teacher's ability to lead behaviour rehearsal activities and provide adequate feedback may mean that the effectiveness of this method depends on the skill of, or the specialized training received by, teachers. Therefore, the examination of alternative strategies seems warranted.

<u>Problem solving</u> is a method of teaching social skills that has been employed successfully with a number of groups of people; however, its use has not often been applied to the instruction of handicapped students (Bullis, 1983). Spivak, Platt and Shure (1976) suggest that problem solving ability is itself a component of social competence. Implied here is the idea that training in the skills of social problem solving will result in improved social competence. Therefore, one advantage of using problem solving as an instructional method for teaching social skills may be an increased generalization of learned skills to real-life social situations.

Ostby (1982), in a study based on the work of D'Zurilla and Goldfried (1971), demonstrated that the social problem solving skills of mildly and moderately retarded adults could be improved using a videotape-based curriculum. Hazel, Schumaker, Sherman and Sheldon (1982) found that a social skills curriculum, including problem solving, was, in most respects, equally effective with learning disabled high school students as with their non-handicapped peers. Thus, although the number of experimental studies is low, there is support for the need to examine problem solving as a method of teaching social skills.

A total of 150 mildly retarded secondary students and 25 teachers participated in this research on instructional methods, including 24 students and 4 teachers who served as the control subjects. The results of the study led to four major conclusions. First, all of the methods were effective in increasing student knowledge of the content. Second, the problem solving approach was more effective than behaviour rehearsal in terms of increasing student knowledge of effective solutions to interpersonal problems. Third, videotape modelling and problem solving were the most effective combination of teaching methods. The final conclusion concerns the relationships between effectiveness of method and time spent teaching. The results of this analysis indicated that the curricula found to be most effective (videotape modelling combined with problem solving) also required the least class time.

Teacher satisfaction with the curriculum each used in the project was assessed on a ten-point scale, with ten meaning highly satisfied and one meaning highly dissatisfied. The vast majority of the teachers (80%) marked a seven or higher. When asked, 94 per cent of the students receiving training said that they were somewhat or very satisfied with the course, and 99 per cent of the students found the training to be helpful or very helpful at work.

Based on the findings of the research summarized above, the *Working II* programme was developed and published. In Working II, the *Test of Interpersonal Competence for Employment* (TICE: Foss, Cheney and Bullis, 1986), and the *Interpersonal Skills Training for Employment* (ISTE: Foss and Vilhauer, 1986) curricula are focused on skills which have been empirically identified as important for job tenure. The focus of both assessment and training is on developing strategies for effective interactions with supervisors and co-workers. Within the area of supervisor-worker relationships, the areas covered are:

1) responding to criticism and correction,
2) following instructions, and
3) requesting assistance.

In the co-worker area, topics covered are:

1) cooperative work behaviour,
2) responding to teasing and provocation, and
3) resolving personal concerns.

TICE is a 61-item test designed to be orally administered in small groups. It was standardized on over 400 mildly retarded adolescents and adults in the United States and Canada (Bullis & Foss, 1986). ISTE provides training methods and materials in the areas measured by TICE. It is a scripted curriculum, using videotape modelling, problem solving, behaviour rehearsal and homework as instructional methods. ISTE was field tested with approximately 150 mildly and moderately retarded young adults in special education classes and rehabilitation facilities. Inquiries regarding either the test or the curriculum should be directed to Dr. Gilbert Foss at the University of Oregon.

Social Skills for Independent Living

The basic premise underlying instruction in social survival skills is that persons with mild/moderate mental retardation need to learn to function in adult roles with significant deviations from the norm. Historically, there has been much confusion and disagreement regarding the nature of these roles and how best to prepare students and adults for them. A major reason for much of this confusion is the lack of sophistication in instructional procedures for teaching social survival skills. A key problem in many instructional programmes for persons with mild/moderate retardation is a lack of attention to specific programming and planning for generalization and maintenance of skills. Typically, an assumption is made that any instruction, no matter how relevant, well designed or implemented, will automatically transfer from the instructional setting to the home, community or work setting. This overall lack of attention to the problems of generalization and maintenance of skills has led to the notion that much instruction is like a *train of hope* method of teaching (Stokes & Baer, 1977).

A recent curriculum has been developed to teach social survival skills to adolescents and young adults with mild/moderate mental retardation (Wells, Keating, Close, Flecker, Auty & McKinney, 1986). Utilizing the skills identified in the Wells and Close (1986) study, the format of the curriculum emphasized teaching for acquisition, generalization and maintenance of skills. Each lesson in the curriculum is designed to ensure clear presentation of concepts, skills and practice activities.

Each lesson in the curriculum follows an instructional format designed to facilitate the acquisition of concepts and skills, and the generalization and maintenance of these skills to non-trained settings. In the following section, the key elements of the instructional format will be presented. Each element will be discussed

using an example from the 'Saying No' module of
the curriculum.

Review of Basic Concepts

This section is designed to ensure that students
are knowledgeable about the requisite skills
needed for instruction. It is imperative to cover
these requisite skills prior to teaching so as not
to make any erroneous assumptions about the
students' knowledge or skills. This review section specifies the concepts, skills and instructional strategies to be used in this lesson. In
the review, emphasis is placed on ensuring that
the students understand the purpose of the lesson
and are committed to participating in the process.
In addition, this section includes general words
which are essential to understanding the lesson.
Frequently the review will use a brief sequence of
examples and require the student to demonstrate
knowledge about a concept. For example, prior to
the lesson on 'Saying No to Strangers', the students should be able to demonstrate knowledge
about the differences between friends and
strangers. The demonstration can occur using the
small group response procedures specified in the
instructional format. Thus, during the 'Review'
section, students receive knowledge about the
essential content and procedures included in the
lesson. Progress toward other components of the
lesson occurs when all students demonstrate
knowledge or competency in these requisite skills.
See example below:

Module 1:   Saying No

Lesson 6:   Saying No to Strangers - At the Door

Objective: Students will be able to say no to
            strangers who come to their door.

Review: To begin here:
            1. students should be able to dis-
               criminate between strangers and
               friends, and
            2. students should know how to ask who
               it is when someone knocks on the
               door.

Discussion of the Context of the Lesson

The purpose of the Discussion section is to provide a context for the skills to be taught. In this section the counselor/leader either reads a prepared script included in the lesson, or summarizes the main points of the lesson in a conversational manner. It is important that the discussion is brief and informative, and related exclusively to the focus of the lesson. A related purpose of the Discussion is to engage students in a directed conversation on the purpose of the lesson. This Discussion also provides the basis for the delineation of the specific *Rule* that will serve as the focal point of any given lesson. See example below:

Discussion:

Never let strangers into your apartment. When someone comes to the door, always ask who is there. If it is a stranger, do not open the door. It may be a salesman, someone collecting money for a charity, or someone who wants to ask questions. Sometimes it may be someone who is just pretending to do one of those things, when they really just want to rob or hurt you. The best thing is to keep the door closed. If it is already open, close and lock the door. If you have a peephole or a window, always look out first before opening the door.

Ask: Why is it important to say no to strangers at the door?

(Encourage responses)

Say: Because they might want to take advantage of you in some way (e.g. sell you something you do not need, collect money you cannot afford to donate, or pretend to do these things to try to hurt you in other ways).

Rule-Based Instructional Sequence

The curriculum employs a rule-based instructional format. Gagne (1977) defines a rule as *'an inferred capability that enabled the individual to respond to a class of stimulus situations with a class of performance'*. In regard to social skills, a rule is an internal state that governs one's behaviour and allows one to reliably perform within a code of standard conduct.

In the present curriculum, rules of conduct are stated and defined according to both purpose and function. For example, saying no to a stranger means we do two things:

1.   You tell the person *no*; and
2.   You do something to show you mean it.

The purpose of the rule is to be able to express yourself in an assertive manner to reach a personal goal. To accomplish this purpose, one must perform certain acts of community (e.g. say no, let them know you mean it).

In teaching social skills two main devices are utilized to aid in teaching. The first, visual-spatial displays (Engelmann & Carnine, 1982), is a method of organizing complex information into simple visual formats. See example below:

Rule: WHEN SOMEONE COMES TO YOUR DOOR, ASK WHO IT IS. IF IT IS A STRANGER, DO NOT OPEN THE DOOR.

Show visual/spatial display:

Traditionally, pictures and symbols have been used successfully to teach a range of complex skills to sophisticated learners. Bourbeau, Sowers and Close (1986) recently adapted these procedures to teach banking skills to persons with mild retardation with great success. In the current curriculum complex social interactions are summarized via black line drawings. Each display measures 21½" x 14" and is large enough to accurately present the rule and performance demands.

A second technique is the use of instructional sequences designed to teach complex discriminations and responses. A discrimination sequence is used to help students learn the rule or concept. Likewise, a response sequence is utilized in teaching students how to apply a rule and respond appropriately to a situation. When sequencing examples, it is important to provide both positive and negative instances of the rule, to ensure that students discriminate between the right way and the wrong way to perform the skills. For example:

1. A stranger asked you if you'd like a ride home. You said, "No", and you walked away.

   Did you say no the right way? (Yes!) How can you tell? (Because I did two things. I said no and walked away.)

2. A stranger said he wanted to be your friend and asked you to come with him. You said, "Well, where are we going?"

   Did you say no the right way? How can you tell? (Because I didn't do two things. I didn't say no and do something to let him know I meant it.)

3. A stranger asked you if you'd like a ride home. You said,"No", and walked away.

   Did you say no the right way? (Yes!) How can you tell? (Because I did two things. I said no and walked away.)

4. A stranger asked you to come and help him find a store you have been to many times. You said "Well, I know that store but I'm on my way to the bank, so I can't show you where it is."

   Did you say no the right way? (No!) How can you tell? (Because I didn't say no and do something to let him know I meant it.)

5. A stranger sat down next to you and asked for a drink of your soda pop. You said "No" and you moved away.

   Did you say no the right way? (Yes!) How can you tell? (Because I did two things. I said no and moved away.)

In discrimination sequences, attempts are made to use relevant situations to teach the rule. In the discrimination sequence, the response required is to determine whether the example presented is consistent with the rule. The teacher will read the example and ask a student whether the correct response was given. If the student responds as indicated in the parentheses, verbal encouragement is provided. If the student responds incorrectly, the teacher provides the appropriate answer and asks the student to repeat it.

The response sequence follows a similar pattern. Unlike the discrimination sequence, however, the teacher only provides the example. The student then must provide the appropriate response. For example:

You are walking along the street. A stranger pulls up next to you in a car and asks if you want a ride.	What should you do? (Say no and keep walking). Right. Why? (Because you always say no to strangers by doing two things. You say no and keep walking.)

In most cases in the curriculum, the discrimination sequences precede response sequences. The exception to this rule is the use of extremely complex discriminations which may confuse the student. It is important to build a solid background of discrimination and response on simpler concepts prior to presenting these very difficult examples.

Behavioural Rehearsal

After the student has acquired the proper discriminations and responses described in the previous section, a series of practice activities commences. In the curriculum, the students rehearse all facets of the lesson in the classroom setting. In this situation, the teacher plays the role of the stranger and requires the student to rehearse the proper responses. Each student has the opportunity to practice many examples in the simulated classroom environment, with feedback provided by the teacher and other students. In addition, each student is required to practise the correct responses whenever the situation arises in the natural environment. Students report all instances of practice to the group during the next teaching session.

AN INTEGRATED SETTING FOR TEACHING SOCIAL SKILLS

Both of the instructional systems described in this chapter are currently being implemented as part of the curriculum in an adult education programme in community colleges in the Western United States. The Adult Skills Development Program (ASDP) (Close, Auty & Keating, 1986) is designed to assist community colleges to teach functional independent skills to adults with mild disabilities. The ASDP curriculum includes course work in the following areas:

1. <u>Money Management</u>, including budgeting, banking, bill paying, and managing spending money;
2. <u>Food Management</u>, including meal planning, grocery shopping, nutrition and cooking;
3. <u>Job Search</u>, including applying for and interviewing for work;
4. <u>Developing Interpersonal Skills for Employment</u>; and
5. <u>Survival Skills for Apartment Living</u>.

The five courses vary in format to meet the specific requirement of the content, but a consistent instructional approach employing effective teaching techniques is maintained throughout the curriculum.

The ASDP curriculum was designed for adolescents and adults who are or will be living in independent living settings. In three years we have served approximately 300 people. The students' ages have ranged from 16 to 74. Using traditional scales of adaptive behaviour, the students fit categories ranging from moderately mentally retarded learning disabilities. Approximately 25 per cent of the students work in competitive jobs, about 60 per cent in sheltered workshops, and the remainder are unemployed. All students reside in community-based settings, either on their own, in group care or foster homes, or with their families. The primary characteristics associated with the students is their desire and motivation to become more independent. A related characteristic is that all students are able to learn using instructional materials which use a variety of teaching strategies in small group settings.

The Adult Skills Development Program is located at the downtown branch of Lane Community College. Course offerings are administered by the Coordinator of Adult Education at the college. Each course is organized into a 10-week module, following the regular college schedule.

Instruction occurs in classroom and other community-based settings such as banks, bus transit stations and the student's own apartment. A combination of small group and individualized instruction is provided to each student. Class size is typically limited to ten students per course. Each class is instructed by a lead teacher with part-time instructors providing additional assistance when needed.

SUMMARY

Information on teaching skills for social competence was presented. The content areas of employment and independent living were selected for emphasis because of the close relationship between these skills and quality of life. The process of social validation was highlighted as an effective manner to determine which skills are relevant for inclusion in training programmes. In addition, detailed examples of instructional procedures derived from research activities at the University of Oregon Research and Training Center in Mental Retardation were presented. Specific emphasis was placed on teaching skills in the community settings where the actual skills would ultimately be used. Finally, a model service programme which teaches social and interpersonal skills for employment and independent living was described.

REFERENCES

Baller, W. R. (1936) 'A Study of the Present Social Status of a Group of Adults Who, When They were in Elementary School, were Classified as Mentally Deficient,' *Genetic Psychology Monographs, 18,* 165-244.
Bandura, A. (1977) *Social Learning Theory,* Prentice-Hall, Englewood Cliffs, New Jersey.
Bates, P. (1980) 'The Effectiveness of Interpersonal Skills Training on the Social Skill Acquisition of Moderately and Mildly Retarded Adults,' *Journal of Applied Behavioral Analysis, 13*(2), 237-248.

Bourbeau, P. E., Sowers, J. A., & Close, D. W. (1986) 'An Experimental Analysis of the Generalization of Banking Skills from Classroom to Trained and Untrained Bank Settings in the Community,' *Education and Training of the Mentally Retarded, 21*(2), 170-178.

Bullis, M. (1983) 'A Construct Validity Study of the Test of Interpersonal Competence for Employment,' unpublished Doctoral Dissertation, University of Oregon.

Bullis, M. & Foss, G. (1986) 'Assessing the Employment-related Interpersonal Competence of Mildly Mentally Retarded Workers,' *American Journal of Mental Deficiency, 91*(1), 43-50.

Chadsey-Rusch, J. (1986) 'Identifying and Teaching Valued Social Behaviors,' in F. R. Rusch (ed.), *Competitive Employment Issues and Strategies,* Paul H. Brookes, Baltimore.

Cheney, D. & Foss, G. (1984) 'An Examination of the Social Behavior of Mentally Retarded Workers,' *Education and Training of the Mentally Retarded, 19*(3), 216-221.

Close, D. W., Auty, W. I., & Keating, T. K. (1986) *The Adult Skills Development Program,* University of Oregon Press, Eugene, Oregon.

D'Zurilla, T. & Goldfried, M. (1971) 'Problem-solving and Behavior Modification,' *Journal of Abnormal Psychology, 78*(1), 107-126.

Edgerton, R. B. (1967) *The Cloak of Competence: Stigma in the Lives of the Mentally Retarded,* University of California Press, Berkeley, California.

Engelmann, S. & Carnine, D. (1982) *Theory of Instruction: Principles and Applications,* Irvington Press, New York.

Filipczak, J., Archer, M., & Friedman, R. M. (1980) 'In-school Social Skills Training,' *Behavior Modification, 4,* 243-264.

Foss, G. & Bostwick, D. (1981) 'Problems of Mentally Retarded Adults: A Study of Rehabilitation Service Consumers and Providers,' *Rehabilitation Counseling Bulletin, 25*(2), 66-73.

Foss, G., Bullis, M., & Vilhauer, D. (1984) 'Assessment and Training of Job Related Social Competence for Mentally Retarded Adolescents and Adults,' in A. Halpern & M. Fuhrer (eds.), *Functional Assessment in Rehabilitation,* Paul H. Brookes, Baltimore.

Foss, G., Cheney, D., & Bullis, M. (1986) *Test of Interpersonal Competence for Employment: Working II,* James Stanfield & Company, Santa Monica, California.

Foss, G. & Peterson, S. (1981) 'An Identification of Social/Interpersonal Skills Relevant to Job Tenure for Mentally Retarded Adults,' *Mental Retardation, 19*(3), 103-106.

Foss, G. & Vilhauer, D. (1986) *Interpersonal Skills Training for Employment: Working II,* James Stanfield & Company, Santa Monica, California.

Foss, G., Walker, H., Todis, B., Lyman, G., & Smith, C. (1986) 'A Social Competence Model for Community Employment Settings,' in P. Ferguson & G. T. Bellamy (eds.), *Transition from School to Work and Adult Life* (Vol. 2) (Reports from the consortium for youth with disability), University of Oregon, Rehabilitation Research and Training Center in Mental Retardation, Eugene, Oregon.

Foxx, R. M., McMorrow, M. J., & Schloss, C. N. (1983) 'Stacking the Deck: Teaching Social Skills to Retarded Adults with a Modified Table Game,' *Journal of Applied Behavior Analysis, 16,* 157-170.

Gagne, R. M. (1977) *The Conditions of Learning,* (3rd edn) , Holt, Rinehart & Winston, New York.

Gold, M. (1973) *Some Thoughts on Training,* University of Illinois Press, Champaign, Illinois.

Goldstein, A. P. (1973) *Structured Learning Therapy: Toward a Psychotherapy for the Poor,* Academic Press, New York.

Goldstein, A. P., Sprafkin, R. P., Gershaw, N. J., & Klein, P. (1980) *Skill Streaming the Adolescent,* Research Press, Champaign, Illinois.

Greenspan, S. & Shoultz, B. (1981) 'Why Mentally Retarded Adults Lose their Jobs: Social Competence as a Factor in Work Adjustment,' *Applied Research in Mental Retardation, 2,* 23-38.

Halpern, A. S., Close, D. W., & Nelson, D. J. (1986) *On My Own: The Impact of Semi-independent Living Programs for Adults with Mental Retardation,* Paul H. Brookes, Baltimore, Maryland.

Hazel, S. J., Schumaker, J. B., Sherman, J. A., & Sheldon, J. (1982) 'Application of a Group Training Program in Social Skills and Problem Solving to Learning Disabled and Non-learning Disabled Youth,' *Learning Disability Quarterly*, 5, 398-408.

Jackson, H. J., King, N. J., & Heller, V. R. (1981) 'Social Skills Assessment and Training for Mentally Retarded Persons: A Review of Research,' *Australian Journal of Developmental Disabilities*, 7(3), 113-123.

LaGreca, A. M., Stone, W. L., & Bell, C. R. (1983) 'Facilitating the Vocational-interpersonal Skills of Mentally Retarded Individuals,' *American Journal of Mental Deficiency*, 88, 270-278.

Martin, J. E., Rusch, F. R., & Heal, L. W. (1982) 'Teaching Community Survival Skills to Mentally Retarded Adults: A Review and Analysis,' *The Journal of Special Education*, 16, 243-268.

McFall, R. M. (1982) 'A Review and Reformulation of the Concept of Social Skills,' *Behavioral Assessment*, 4, 1-33.

Ostby, S. S. (1982) 'Social Problem-solving Training with Mildly and Moderately Retarded Individuals,' unpublished Doctoral Dissertation, University of Wisconsin, Madison.

Rusch, F. R. (1986) *Competitive Employment*, Paul H. Brookes, Baltimore, Maryland.

Senatore, V., Matson, J. L., & Kazdib, A. E. (1982) 'A Comparison of Behavioral Methods to Train Social Skills to Mentally Retarded Adults,' *Behavior Therapy*, 13, 313-324.

Spivak, G., Platt, J., & Shure, M. (1976) *The Problem-solving Approach to Adjustment*, Jossey-Bass, San Francisco.

Stokes, T. F. & Baer, D. M. (1977) 'An Implicit Technology of Generalization,' *Journal of Applied Behavior Analysis*, 10, 349-367.

Vale, C. A. (1978) *National Needs Assessment of Educational Media and Materials for the Handicapped*, Educational Testing Service.

Wells, R. L. & Close, D. W. (1986) 'Social Validation of Social Skills for Persons with Mild Handicaps,' *Education and Training of the Mentally Retarded*.

Wells, R. L., Keating, T. K., Close, D. W., Flecker, S., Auty, W. I., & McKinney, L. L. (1986) *Social Skills for Apartment Living*, University of Oregon Press, Eugene, Oregon.

White, D. M. (1986)   'Social Validation,' in F. R.
    Rusch (ed.), *Competitive Employment*, Paul H.
    Brookes, Baltimore, Maryland.

Chapter Eight

ENVIRONMENTAL DESIGN FOR DISABLED PERSONS

Roy V. Ferguson

ENVIRONMENTAL DESIGN AND HUMAN BEHAVIOUR

Architecture is a discipline which has traditionally not been very concerned with behavioural
considerations while psychology, by contrast, has
tended to overlook the physical aspects of the
environment (Krasner, 1980). A relatively new
field of study, environmental psychology, attempts
to span these two areas by regarding person/
environment as an integral unit in considering the
reciprocal relationships between humans and their
environment (Fisher, Bell & Baum, 1984).
    In emphasizing that design does influence
behaviour, Canter and Craik (1981) point out that
the built environment should not just reflect
principles of construction and aesthetics but also
be designed with a careful view to meeting the
behavioural and psychological needs of the
inhabitants of the buildings. For example, in
considering the behavioural aspects of architectural design, work has been done on the relationship between lighting and task performance (Boyce,
1975), windowless offices and worker dissatisfaction (Ruys, 1970), and the effect of furniture
arrangement on social activity (Holahan, 1972;
Campbell, 1979). It has now been demonstrated
that people feel more comfortable in decorated
spaces (Campbell, 1979) and the good mood created
by pleasant environments seems to increase the
willingness of people to help each other (Sherrod
et al., 1977). It has also been shown that people
feel more like interacting and talking in pleasant
settings (Russell & Mehrabian, 1978) and that
privacy is one of the most important aspects of

the design of interior space (Fisher, Bell & Baum, 1984).

The increasing awareness of the relationship between design and behaviour has resulted in more careful attention being given to behavioural criteria in the planning of primary environments where humans spend large amounts of time. Homes, residential centres, schools and programme set-tings are primary environments for disabled persons where the relationship between design and behaviour is of particular significance.

It should be noted that the terms disability and handicap often are used interchangeably, although a distinction can be made. Harris, Cox and Smith (1971) defined *disability* as the loss or reduction of functional ability, while *handicap* is the disadvantage of restriction of activity caused by disability. One disabled friend of mine out-lined this relationship quite clearly in stating, *'My body makes me disabled, but the environment makes me handicapped'*.

A SHIFTING PARADIGM FOR THE CARE OF DISABLED PEOPLE

Major changes in the philosophy of care for disabled persons have occurred over the past years. Most pronounced was a shift away from a predominately medical model of care towards more of an educational approach. The medical model tended to treat disability as though it were an illness and the majority of care was based in institutions, designed primarily to be 'contain-ers', which effectively removed the disabled from the mainstream of society. The rehabilitation educational approach, by contrast, is predicated on the notion that disabled persons should be integrated into the community and provided with the supports necessary for them to experience an independent, normalized life. As the models of care shift over time, environments must be designed differently to support and reflect these changes.

DESIGN PARAMETERS

Four major parameters have been used to guide the basic design of environments for disabled persons:

GOVERNORS STATE UNIVERSITY
UNIVERSITY PARK
IL 60466

cost, durability, efficiency and aesthetics. More recently, a fifth dimension has been added through the examination of behavioural factors. The psychological impact of the designed environment upon its occupants is now beginning to be considered as an important part of the planning of a new building.

Consideration of the psychological factors in design for disabled persons is a complex process, but one of vital importance. As the general awareness grows that physical and psychological functioning are not mutually exclusive entities, but interdependent phenomena on a shared continuum, more effort is being applied to understanding the psychological effects of physical environments on their inhabitants and the joint effects of physical and social environments on behaviour. The *social environment* is the setting in which these transactions occur (Wachs & Gruen, 1982). In view of this interrelationship between environment and behaviour, physical and social environments must be considered as important factors in rehabilitation programmes for the disabled and can be conceptualized as adaptive or therapeutic to the degree that they facilitate and support the clinical goals of the programme.

Consideration of the effects of the environment on behaviour is a concept or philosophy which must be carefully developed throughout the planning process in designing new buildings. In reality, the physical structures of rehabilitation environments are not often designed with a specific philosophy in mind and the use of space appropriate to the goals of the programme grows out of intuition rather than being based on concrete data (Nellist, 1970; Bayes & Francklin, 1971).

THE DESIGN PROCESS

The planning and design of a specialized environment, such as a rehabilitation centre or school for disabled persons, is a long process involving many persons and input from all of the users of the new structure. Careful consideration must be given to the clinical and administrative objectives, values, priorities and philosophies of the entire organization. Only through this information can a building be designed to clearly reflect the intentions of the users.

One of the initial steps in the design process is the development of goals and objectives which relate to the specific needs of the users of the building. The aim is to achieve the greatest degree of congruence between the needs and preferences of the users and the design features of the building (Fisher, Bell & Baum, 1984). In order to achieve the best matching of form to function in the design of the building, the gap between those who design environments and those who use them must be minimized through the use of multidisciplinary design teams sensitive to a variety of user needs. Carver and Rodda (1978) note that *'it is part of our environmental inheritance that the "normal" environment has been designed in the main by the "normal" man for the "normal" man'*. Involvement, wherever possible, of the primary users in the design process is necessary to offset this tendency. Design criteria which are linked to the developmental and functional needs of disabled persons help to increase the congruence between the built environment and the requirements of the primary users.

PUBLIC ATTITUDES TOWARD DISABLED PERSONS

Before examining the relationship between architecture and disabled persons, it is first necessary to examine some prevailing public attitudes toward disabled persons. Public attitudes toward disabled persons have an effect on rehabilitation and adjustment (Roeher, 1961) and much of the research suggests that these attitudes are in large part negative (Wright, 1983). Also noted is a tendency within the public to classify disabled persons into either inferior or superior status positions. Persons with disabilities who are categorized by others into an inferior status position are generally viewed as being less worthwhile. Conversely, the superior status position reflects the view that disabled persons are more sensitive, kind, courageous, etc. than are ordinary people.

These stereotypic attitudes are perpetuated in part by media portrayals of disabled people. Thurer (1980) argues that the portrayal of disabled persons in art and literature is usually as sinister, evil or monstrous. Similarly, disabled persons are rarely depicted as ordinary persons in

167

comic books (Weinberg & Santana, 1978) or movies (Byrd & Elliot, 1985).

The stereotypic attitudes noted above were undoubtedly reflected in the design of environments for disabled persons. For example, consider the large institutional settings constructed for disabled persons in the past. These buildings were usually large in scale, were designed for efficiency rather than comfort, and were typically isolated from the rest of the community. They were intended to be residential facilities, and yet were totally lacking in any of the design characteristics typically associated with residential dwellings inhabited by the general public. In effect, these residential institutions removed disabled persons from the public eye and served as monuments which contributed to the maintenance of the stereotypic attitudes noted above, and in particular the negative ones. It is as Winston Churchill once said, *'We shape our buildings and then our buildings shape us'*.

In contrast, thoughtful environmental design can encourage greater involvement of disabled people as active participants in society. The development of small residential units integrated into regular communities would reduce much of the unfamiliarity with disabled persons experienced by the general public. A more visible and active role in society would place emphasis on the wide range of things disabled persons can do, rather than on what they cannot do, and have a pronounced effect on public attitudes toward disabled persons. Non-institutional residential units located within the community would help to create a sense of similarity rather than difference in regards to disability. Attempts to develop increased visibility within society were undoubtedly accelerated by the recent high-profile media coverage of disabled athletes such as Terry Fox, Steve Fonyo and Rick Hansen. Certainly this will have a positive influence on public attitudes towards disability, which can be augmented by designing environments that integrate disabled persons into regular society so that they become a more visible element. This continued and regular contact is necessary in order for public attitudes to change.

SELF-CONCEPT AND ADAPTIVE BEHAVIOUR

Vargo (1985) points out that disability can be seen as an assault on a person's self-concept and that successful adjustment *'means not only learning how to best manage one's physical environment, but also developing a new self-concept, one that is cemented in different values regarding what it means to be worthwhile'*. While managing the physical environment effectively is not the only variable in the psychological adjustment to disability, it certainly is central to the development of a positive self-concept. *Self-concept* is broadly defined as a person's perception of self which is formed through experiences with and interpretations of one's environment and is greatly influenced by others (Shavelson & Bolus, 1982). A restricted physical environment will negatively influence the development and maintenance of a good self-concept in a disabled person by limiting the type and number of experiences and people readily available. Again, consider the large and isolated residential institutions which were so typical in the past. These structures were designed in a manner which, because of their scale, fostered inflexible routines, depersonalization and dependency. The negative impact these institutions had on the self-concept development of their residents was tremendous.

Adaptive behaviour, defined as the ability to cope with the physical and social demands of the environment, also contributes to the development of a positive self-concept within disabled persons since a greater degree of adaptive behaviour means that an individual can function more independently within the community. As more adaptive behaviour is developed, greater access to the community is provided which, in turn, provides the needed experiential and social prerequisites for a strong self-concept. Also, increased access to the community will mean greater visibility which should create more familiarity with the disabled on the part of the general public and result in more realistic and positive attitudes.

The development of adaptive behaviours is facilitated in environments which have been modified or adapted to the particular needs of the disabled person. To illustrate, let us consider a person whose legs are paralyzed due to having polio as a child. This person, confined to a wheelchair, is able to live quite independently in a residential unit which is designed with ramps, wide doors, bathroom hoists and modified kitchen appliances. The same person can provide his own transportation in a van which is equipped with hand controls and a hydraulic platform hoist, and is able to work in an office building which has ramp access, elevators and washrooms designed for the disabled. Similar features in shopping centres, theatres and other public buildings extend the ability of this person to be self-sufficient. In other words, some fundamental environmental modifications can enable the person to move from a dependent role in a restrictive institutional setting to an independent and productive role in the community. The adaptive behaviours facilitated by adapted environments have an enormous effect on the self-concept of disabled persons.

ENVIRONMENTAL ADAPTATION, MASTERY AND CHOICE

Adaptations which have been made to the primary environment are often a good indicator of the particular coping style adopted by a disabled person and his or her family. For example, if the coping style is one characterized by denial, the disability may not be accepted and dealt with realistically. Reactions such as depression, hostility, withdrawal and anger predominate and there would be little attempt to seek greater independence through environmental modifications. The view is often held that disability is a sickness from which the individual will eventually recover.

An alternate view is one where the disabled person and his or her family recognize the permanent differences which exist and set out to develop environmental modifications and adjustments which promote adaptive behaviours and increased independence. The occurrence of environmental adaptations are often the earliest indicator of the development of this coping style.

Adaptive environments must be designed for disabled persons so that they can be more independent and achieve a sense of environmental mastery. It is important for disabled persons, as it is with the unimpaired, to be able to exercise environmental choice. Certainly some of the choices available to the unimpaired and mildly impaired are closed to persons with severe disabilities. However, total environmental mastery is not possible for the unimpaired either. Not everyone is capable of skiing, wind surfing or climbing Mt. Robson. Environmental choices are made by unimpaired persons on the basis of need, interest, priority, ability and situational constraint. Carver and Rodda (1978) point out that:

> *Integration does not imply that every conceivable option open to all unimpaired people can be made equally available to every impaired person. It does demand, however, that there should be a sufficient range of options open to any impaired individual to enable him to function as a mature person and pursue a personal lifestyle as satisfying in its own way as his neighbour's.*

The issue, then, is not necessarily to create environmental adaptations which provide every possible option to the disabled person, but, more realistically, to ensure that there are not any environmental barriers to the participation of disabled persons in mainstream society.

Special playgrounds for disabled children are examples of adaptive environments designed to provide opportunities for mastery and choice. Starting with the notion that the physical environment has a rich impact on learning (David & Wright, 1974; Altman & Wohlwill, 1979) and that many of the regular playgrounds are frustrating or impossible for a disabled child, playgrounds with *prosthetic qualities* (Moore, 1980) began to appear. The first of these was the Adventure Playground for Handicapped Children, developed in the mid-1960s. This was a marvellous facility in the Chelsea area of London designed by Lady Allen (1968) to *'insure that the handicapped child can have rich, varied, and spontaneous experiences'*. Through thoughtful design it provided children with a variety of graded challenges and paced alternatives suited to a full range of abilities. The environment provided choice and the opportunity for mastery by children of all disability types. However, the playground was located behind a tall brick wall and was not made available to non-disabled children in the surrounding community. While meeting many of the developmental needs of disabled children admirably, it did not foster integration with regular children. More

171

recently, playgrounds such as the Playground for All Children in New York and the Boundary Park Playground in Vancouver have been designed to provide graded challenges and paced alternatives for disabled children, but in a setting which encourages interaction with non-disabled children. In other words, specific environmental adaptations have been made to provide opportunities for mastery and choice, but within the regular community so that disabled users are not segregated.

DESIGNING FOR THE DISABLED PERSON

There is growing awareness that the physical environment plays an important role in helping individuals compensate for various disabilities so that they can function more independently. However, too often assumptions are made by designers that disabled persons are a homogeneous group, where in actual fact there is probably no other segment of the population which manifests such a broad diversity of individual problems and needs. In order to provide a physical environment which is safe, convenient, flexible and barrier-free, as well as one which enables choice, control and independence, the designer must be sensitive to the various needs of the disabled who will be inhabiting the structures. Through the application of behavioural design criteria, physical environments can be built which assist the disabled in compensating for physical and psychological difficulties.

Let us consider some examples of general behavioural design criteria which would apply to practically any programme setting for all types of disability. The opportunity for involvement in food preparation would represent a typical independence need reflected in most programme residents. Consequently, programme settings should be designed to include small scale food preparation areas which supplement or replace (depending on the scale of the setting) the commercial kitchens which do not provide the opportunity for programme residents to be actively involved in food preparation activities. Small, non-institutional food preparation areas would be analagous to a kitchen in a home where snacks can be prepared at any time. In addition to providing increased choices and alternatives to institutionalized meal time routines, an accessible food preparation area serves as a place where skill training can occur, which helps the resident move towards greater independence. In larger settings where a commercial kitchen is necessary, some of these same developmental needs can be met through the inclusion of lounge areas which contain a refrigerator and microwave oven.

Another example of a general design consideration based upon a primary need would be easy access to the outdoor environment. Regardless of whether the resident of a programme setting is physically, perceptually, emotionally or mentally disabled there exists a need to experience the seasonal changes as well as the sights, sounds, textures and smells of the natural environment. The interactions, stimulation, choice and change afforded by being outdoors are vital to any programme resident and must be readily accessible. For some types of disability this means designing an interface between interior and exterior environments which easily accommodates wheelchairs and other wheeled forms of mobility. For others, it may mean the inclusion of a sunny courtyard or park which can be carefully supervised. The main point is that the design of any programme facility must reflect this need. Too often we are witness to programme buildings for disabled persons which have been located in busy downtown settings which do not readily lend themselves to these considerations.

It must be recognized that disabled persons have the same need as others for personal independence, a choice of housing alternatives, a satisfying job, adequate income, recreational opportunities, etc. Their efforts to address these needs are often frustrated by obstacles within their physical environment. For example, a person with a moderate disability, such as loss of coordination, arthritis or an amputated arm, encounters difficulty in using typical design features like stairs, water taps and door knobs. Persons in wheelchairs are restricted by narrow and/or heavy doors, stairs, small washrooms, inaccessible public transportation and elevator buttons which are placed too high.

Once it is recognized that disabled persons have the same needs as the non-disabled, interesting and creative solutions to environmental barriers begin to emerge. In one instance a tremendously resourceful family, involved in a rehabilitation hospital, had an adolescent son

with a severe physical disability due to a spinal
injury which confined him to a wheelchair. The
boy wanted to live as typical and normal a life as
possible and was encouraged in this goal by his
parents and siblings. He had a number of neighbourhood friends whose company he enjoyed, but
found that he was not able to play with them in
the park in front of their house because there
were no sidewalks and his electric wheelchair
would not operate over rough terrain. The
parents, in consultation with their son and a
local engineer, designed an electric all-terrain
vehicle with low pressure tires which would climb
curbs and negotiate all sorts of irregular top-
ography. Not only did this vehicle, with bucket
seats, racing harness and roll bar, enable him to
navigate the park with his friends, but it allowed
him to offer rides to them in a manner which was
similar to having a first car or motor bike.

In a similar vein, this same family devised
an environmental adaptation which addressed
another typical, adolescent developmental need:
surfing. They rigged up a harness on a small,
rubber dingy which allowed the boy to ride the
waves in Hawaii experiencing the same thrill,
adventure and mastery as his able-bodied counter-
parts. This family was truly remarkable in their
ability to find adaptations for environmental
barriers to the developmental needs of their son.

While it is not possible within the confines
of this chapter to examine the unique environmental needs of each type of disability, there are
some universal ones which apply to all persons
across the broad range of disabilities: the need
for safety, comfort, convenience/accessibility and
the need for control.

Safety, Comfort, Convenience and Accessibility. These are important design features to
incorporate in both short and long-term residential facilities for disabled people. Safety,
comfort and convenience/accessibility are fundamental requirements of all residential facilities
for disabled persons, whether private residences,
group homes or institutions. To promote safety, a
facility (particularly in the case of institutional care) should permit sufficient staff surveil-
lance to prevent accidents or to detect them when
they do occur, while not creating an atmosphere
lacking privacy. It has also been shown that,
when staff and residents in a facility are in

close proximity, staff may behave in ways that encourage dependency (Harris, Lipman & Slater, 1977). Further, design features such as handrails, safety glass and nonslip walking surfaces should be present to prevent accidents as well as mechanisms like call buttons (located at appropriate heights) which enable disabled residents to request assistance if a problem is encountered in a private area such as a bathroom.

The design of environments should also promote comfort and convenience by providing orientation aids such as colour coding or universal pictographs which facilitate wayfinding. While wayfinding aids are absolutely essential in a larger and more complex treatment centre, they might also be considered in the design of smaller group and individual residential settings for residents who have visual problems or who become easily disoriented. Sheltered entrances, adapted toilet facilities, modified kitchen layouts and wide corridors are just a few examples of design elements which promote comfort and convenience for disabled persons. Facilities should be designed to be warm and home-like in appearance with plenty of stimulation throughout. Using bright and warm colours (as opposed to the typical institutional white, beige or pale green) (Mehrabian & Russell, 1974), considering alternatives to standard fluorescent lighting (Wandersman et al., 1985), including plenty of windows (Ruys, 1970) and utilizing less formal furniture arrangements (Holahan, 1972) will have a positive effect on the mood and behaviour of the inhabitants of the environment. It has been shown that environments designed to stimulate the auditory, visual and tactile senses increase appropriate and acceptable behaviours in institutionalized mentally retarded adolescents (Kreger, 1971; Levy, 1974). Levy (1976) describes the physical environment as a catalytic agent in the learning process of mentally retarded persons.

Through the use of modern technology, residential environments can be designed which allow disabled persons to live independently. For example, persons capable only of operating a keyboard or microswitch with a single finger or by blowing into a pneumatic tube can activate electronic mechanisms which dial telephones, turn on lights, operate television sets, open doors, and run computerized communication systems. Perhaps this sort of high-tech environment is what Le

Corbusier had in mind when he defined home as a *machine for living* (Foote, 1977). At any rate, the majority of disabled persons are able to live in their own homes or small, community-based group residences if this type of environmental support is available.

However, most disabled persons do not require environmental modifications as elaborate as this in order to live independently. For many it is only a matter of providing some fundamental modifications to residential structures and public buildings in order to make them accessible and functional. There are many resources which provide guidelines for the planning and design of housing for the disabled. The Central Mortgage and Housing Corporation (Canada) (1974), for example, has produced a manual called *Housing the Handicapped* which provides design criteria for various types of housing alternatives ranging from single family dwellings to integrated apartment buildings. Another factual and comprehensive resource is a book by a British architect, Selwyn Goldsmith, called *Designing for the Disabled* (1967). Still another useful resource on building requirements and anthropometric data for persons with disabilities, which is particularly well illustrated, is *The Section 3.7 Handbook* produced by the Province of British Columbia (1984). Resources such as these and others are instrumental in the design of barrier-free environments.

Control. Settings which are barrier free allow disabled persons to move about independently and, in so doing, foster feelings of personal control. This perception of control is an important factor in preventing feelings of helplessness, both real and learned. Garber and Seligman (1981) describe the ultimate consequence of loss of control as learned helplessness. If repeated efforts at establishing control in a situation result in failure, there is a tendency to stop trying, which becomes a response pattern generalizing to other situations. In effect, the person learns to be helpless even in situations where control is readily available. Disabled persons are particularly vulnerable to the process of learned helplessness because of the many environmental barriers with which they are confronted. Until more environments are designed to be barrier free, it is important to involve the disabled person in finding solutions to aspects of the environment which function as obstacles so that a learned helplessness pattern does not become established.

The design of environments should provide, whenever possible, opportunities for choice which, in turn, enhance feelings of control in the inhabitants. The facility should be located in the community in such a way as to allow residents to choose among a variety of available services such as shopping and recreational facilities. Choice and perceived control are also facilitated through design which enhances privacy and creates a sense of personal space and territory exclusively for the individual's own use.

Personal space is defined as an invisible boundary surrounding us, into which others may not trespass, and regulating how closely individuals will interact (Fisher, Bell & Baum, 1984). It moves with the individual, changing in size according to the situation. Personal space has a protective function serving as a buffer against potential emotional and physical threats such as too much stimulation, stressful over-arousal, insufficient privacy and aggression. It also serves a communication function since the distance maintained from others will indicate the level of intimacy desired in the relationship. It has been noted that non-disabled persons are more comfortable interacting with disabled persons at greater interpersonal distances (Dabbs & Stokes, 1975; Kleck et al., 1968). Research has demonstrated other spatial behaviour differences. For example, Sommer (1969) and Horowitz, Duff and Stratton (1964) found that persons with schizophrenia require more space than 'normals'. Further examination of the proxemics in special needs settings demonstrated that emotionally disturbed children require more personal space than regular children (Weinstein, 1965; Fisher, 1973; Kendall et al., 1976) as do emotionally disturbed adolescents (Newman & Pollack, 1973). Foley and Lacy (1967) suggested that because of the mentally ill patient's vulnerability, the physical environment will have a greater impact, either positively or negatively. Interestingly, Hayduk and Mainprize (1980) found no differences in the spatial behaviour of blind and sighted individuals, although various behavioural and spatial organization differences have been described in other work.

Territory is defined as visible, stationary and home-centered areas regulating who will

177

interact (Sommer, 1969). Territories are places which are owned or controlled by one or more individuals. Neighbourhoods, offices, bedrooms and even particular chairs or tables are examples of territories. The work of Taylor and Strough (1978) demonstrated that defined territories increased feelings of control in subjects. Being on one's own territory or 'turf' has been shown to elicit feelings of control, security and improved performance (Barton, 1966; Holahan & Saegeit, 1973; Holahan, 1972). Consequently, the design of environments for disabled persons should encourage individuals to personalize areas and thus create a sense of personal territory. It is important to note that most of the research on personal space and territory with disabled persons has been done in institutional settings, so that it is not certain whether the findings generalize to home situations. However, because of the pervasiveness of these concepts, spouses and parents of disabled persons residing in their own homes would be advised to organize the physical environment to enhance feelings of personal control.

Personal space, then, is invisible, portable and body-centered, regulating how closely individuals will interact. Territory is visible, stationary, and home-centered, regulating who will interact. Both are key concepts in design for the disabled which is aimed at increasing perceived environmental control.

QUALITY OF LIFE AND ENVIRONMENTS FOR DISABLED PERSONS

The concept of quality of life usually includes considerations such as the freedom of choice, personal life satisfaction, community involvement, and social interaction/support. As outlined earlier, careful environmental design is an important and fundamental factor in creating choices, control, opportunities and independence for disabled persons which, in turn, influences self-concept. Of course, all of these variables contribute to a sense of general life satisfaction.

Environments which are designed to be adaptive and barrier-free allow disabled persons to be more actively involved in the community and to experience greater social interaction and support.

Easy access to public buildings provides opportunities for disabled persons to attend theatres, sports events, concerts, plays, restaurants, libraries, museums and galleries, all of which contribute to their general quality of life. However, environments which facilitate greater participation in the community also create a spiral of change for disabled persons. Increased community involvement means greater visibility for disabled persons which is necessary in the process of changing public attitudes toward them. As public attitudes change, they are reflected in social policies which enable even fuller participation of disabled persons in society. Of course, we still have some way to go, but the main point is that environmental adaptation is a necessary step to activate this spiral process of change in regard to quality of life for disabled persons.

SUMMARY

The following are the main points contained in this chapter:

1. The increasing awareness of the relationship between environment and behaviour has resulted in more careful attention being paid to behavioural criteria in the design of built environments.
2. The shift away from a medical model and towards a rehabilitation educational model of care has influenced the type of environments being designed for disabled persons.
3. Physical environments are an important element in rehabilitation planning and should be designed to support programme philosophies, values and objectives.
4. Environmental design must be congruent with the needs and preferences of the inhabitants. The needs of disabled persons are similar to the non-disabled, but environments must be adapted in different ways for different disabilities so that these needs can be met.
5. Public attitudes toward disabled persons tend to be stereotypic.
6. Environments designed to integrate disabled persons into regular society will facilitate the contact necessary for attitude change.

7. Environments have a direct influence on the self-concept of disabled persons by supporting the development of adaptive behaviours.
8. Special playgrounds have been designed to provide the opportunity for challenge, mastery and choice in disabled children.
9. Although disabled people represent a very heterogeneous group in respect of specific environmental needs, they have universal requirements for safety, comfort, convenience/accessibility and control.
10. Through environmental adaptations and technological support, the majority of disabled persons can live independently within the community.
11. Barrier-free environments foster feelings of involvement, independence and personal control.
12. The concepts of personal space and territory are key elements in design for the disabled which is aimed at increasing perceived environmental control.
13. Environmental adaptation is a necessary first step in activating a spiral process of change in regard to the lifestyle of disabled persons.

REFERENCES

Allen, Lady, of Hurtwood (1968) *Planning for Play*, MIT Press, Cambridge, Massachusetts.

Altman, I. & Wohlwill, J. F. (eds.) (1979) *Human Behavior and Environment: Vol. 3, Children and the Environment*, Plenum, New York.

Barton, R. (1966) 'The Patient's Personal Territory,' *Hospital and Community Psychiatry, 17,* 336.

Bayes, K. & Francklin, S. (eds.) (1971) *Designing for the Handicapped*, George Godwin, London.

Boyce, P. R. (1975) 'The Luminous Environment,' in D. Canter & P. Stringer (eds.), *Environmental Interactions: Psychological Approaches to Our Physical Surroundings*, International Universities Press, New York.

Byrd, E. K. & Elliot, T. R. (1985) 'Feature Films and Disability: A Descriptive Study,' *Rehabilitation Psychology, 30,* 47-51.

Campbell, D. E. (1979) 'Interior Office Design and Visitor Response,' *Journal of Environmental Psychology, 64,* 648-653.

Canter, D. V. & Craik, K. H. (1981) 'Environ-
mental Psychology', *Journal of Environmental
Psychology, 1,* 1-11.
Carver, V. & Rodda, M. (1978) *Disability and the
Environment,* Paul Elek, London.
Central Mortgage and Housing Corporation (1974)
Housing the Handicapped, CMHC, Ottawa.
Dabbs, J. M. & Stokes, N. A. (1975) 'Beauty is
Power: The Use of Space on the Sidewalk,'
Sociometry, 38, 551-557.
David, T. G. & Wright, B. D. (eds.) (1974)
Learning Environments, University of Chicago
Press, Chicago.
Fisher, J. D., Bell, P. A., & Baum, A. (1984)
Environmental Psychology (2nd edition), Holt,
Rinehart & Winston, New York.
Fisher, R. L. (1973) 'Social Schema of Normal and
Disturbed School Children', *Journal of Educa-
tional Psychology, 40,* 122-125.
Foley, A. & Lacy, B. (1967) 'On the Need for
Interprofessional Collaboration: Psychiatry
and Architecture,' *American Journal of
Psychiatry, 123,* 1013-1018.
Foote, S. (1977) *Handicapped at Home,* Quick Fox
Publishers, London.
Garber, J. & Seligman, M. E. P. (eds.) (1981)
Human Helplessness: Theory and Applications,
Academic Press, New York.
Goldsmith, S. (1967) *Designing for the Disabled*
(2nd edition), McGraw-Hill, New York.
Harris, A. I., Cox, E., & Smith, C. R. (1971)
*Handicapped and Impaired in Great Britain,
Part 1,* HMSO, London.
Harris, H., Lipman, A., & Slater, R. (1977)
'Architectural Design: The Spatial Location
and Interactions of Old People,' *Gerontology,
23,* 390-400.
Hayduk, L. A. & Mainprize, S. A. (1980) 'Personal
Space of the Blind,' *Social Psychology
Quarterly, 43,* 216-223.
Holahan, C. J. (1972) 'Seating Patterns and
Patient Behavior in an Experimental Dayroom,'
Journal of Abnormal Psychology, 80, 115-124.
Holahan, C. J. & Saegeit, S. (1973) 'Behavioral
and Attitudinal Effects of Large-Scale
Variation in the Physical Environment of
Psychiatric Wards,' *Journal of Abnormal
Psychology, 83,* 454-462.
Horowitz, M. J., Duff, D. F., & Stratton, L. O.
(1964) 'Body-buffer Zone,' *Archives of
General Psychology, 11,* 651-656.

Kendall, P. C., Deardoff, P. A., Finch, A. J., &
    Graham, L. (1976) 'Proxemics, Locus of
    Control, Anxiety and Type of Movement in
    Emotionally Disturbed and Normal Boys,'
    Journal of Abnormal Child Psychology, *4*(3),
    9-16.

Kleck, R. E., Buck, P. L., Geller, W. C., London,
    P. S., Pfeiffer, J. R., & Vukcevic, D. P.
    (1968) 'Effect of Stigmatizing Conditions on
    the Use of Personal Space,' *Psychological
    Reports*, *23*, 111-118.

Krasner, L. (ed.) (1980) *Environmental Design and
    Human Behavior*, Pergamon Press, New York.

Kreger, K. (1971) 'Compensatory Environment
    Programming for the Severely Retarded
    Behaviorally Disturbed,' *Mental Retardation*,
    9, 29-32.

Levy, E. (1974) *Effects of Environmental Enrich-
    ment on the Behavior of Institutionalized
    Mentally Retarded Adolescents*, Developmental
    Disabilities Office, Department of Health,
    Education and Welfare, Washington, D.C.

Levy, E. (1976) 'Designing Environments for
    Mentally Retarded Clients,' *Hospital and
    Community Psychiatry*, *27*(1), 793-796.

Mehrabian, A. & Russell, J. A. (1974) *An Approach
    to Environmental Psychology*, MIT Press,
    Cambridge.

Ministry of Municipal Affairs (1984) *The Section
    3.7 Handbook*, Province of British Columbia.

Moore, G. (1980) *Designing Environments for
    Handicapped Children*, Educational Facilities
    Laboratories, New York.

Nellist, I. (1970) *Planning Buildings for Handi-
    capped Children*, Crosby Lockwood & Son Ltd.,
    London.

Newman, R. C. & Pollack, D. (1973) 'Proxemics in
    Deviant Adolescents,' *Journal of Consulting
    and Clinical Psychology*, *40*, 148-154.

Roeher, G. A. (1961) 'Significance of Public
    Attitudes in the Rehabilitation of the
    Disabled,' *Rehabilitation Literature*, *22*,
    66-72.

Russell, J. A. & Mehrabian, A. (1978) 'Environ-
    mental Task and Temperamental Effects on Work
    Performance,' *Humanitas*, *14*, 75-95.

Ruys, T. (1970) 'Windowless Offices,' *Man-
    Environment Systems*, *1*, 49.

Shavelson, R. J. & Bolus, R. (1982) 'Self
    Concept: The Interplay of Theory and
    Methods,' *Journal of Educational Psychology,
    74*, 3-17.
Sherrod, D. R., Armstrong, D., Hewitt, J.,
    Madonia, B., Speno, S., & Fenyd, D. (1977)
    'Environmental Attention, Affect and
    Altruism,' *Journal of Applied Social
    Psychology, 7*, 359-371.
Sommer, R. (1969) *Personal Space,* Prentice-Hall,
    Englewood Cliffs, New Jersey.
Taylor, R. B. & Strough, P. R. (1978) 'Territor-
    ial Cognition: Assessing Altman's Typology,'
    *Journal of Personality and Social Psychology,
    36*, 418-423.
Thurer, S. (1980) 'Disability and Monstrosity: A
    Look at Literary Distortions of Handicapping
    Conditions,' *Rehabilitation Literature, 41*,
    12-15.
Vargo, J. W. (1985) 'Attitudes and Adjustment,'
    Alberta Psychology, 14, 5-6.
Wachs, T. D. & Gruen, G. (1982) *Early Experience
    and Human Development,* Plenum, New York.
Wandersman, A., Andrews, A., Riddle, C., &
    Fancett, C. (1985) 'Environmental Psychology
    and Prevention,' in R. Felner, S. Farber, L.
    Jason, & J. Moritsugu (eds.), *Preventive
    Psychology: Theory, Research and Practice,*
    Pergamon, New York.
Weinberg, N. & Santana, R. (1978) 'Comic Books:
    Champions of the Disabled Stereotype,'
    Rehabilitation Literature, 39, 327-331.
Weinstein, L. (1965) 'Social Schemata of Emotion-
    ally Disturbed Boys,' *Journal of Abnormal
    Psychology, 70*, 457-461.
Wright, B. A. (1983) *Physical Disability: A
    Psychological Approach* (2nd edition), Harper
    & Row, New York.

Chapter Nine

ENHANCING THE QUALITY OF LIFE: THE ROLE OF THE
ARTS IN THE PROCESS OF REHABILITATION

Bernie Warren & Roberta Nadeau

INTRODUCTION

> *Art...is one of the major modes of expression*
> *of human thought and has been through the*
> *centuries the most powerful, the most con-*
> *stant, and the most controversial witness to*
> *that thought.* (Parmelin, 1977)

What sets human beings above the other primates is
our ability to communicate not just such basic
needs as hunger or imminent danger, but also the
ability to express complex emotions and ideas both
literally and symbolically. In the arts the use
of symbolic images can enable individuals not only
to express their own personal view of the world to
others but also, through this symbolic
representation, to capture in artistic moments
ideas and feelings which can transcend both the
limitations of their creator and the historical
moment in which they were created. These
milestones of human history do more than simply
record what went before; they represent the
underlying fabric, the mores, beliefs, aspirations
and so on of the culture in which they were
created and, as such, always make an immeasurable
contribution to that and future generations'
quality of life.

Artistic expression has always been one of
the cornerstones of all known human communities.
However, in more recent times participation by
individuals in avenues of cultural and artistic
expression has been seen to be the realm of *THE
ARTIST*. As a result, in modern societies there is
little or no participation in the arts by the rest
of society, who, by definition, view themselves as

NON-ARTISTS. It comes as no surprise therefore to those of us who believe that artistic expression is the birthright of all human beings that a general malaise, a sense of alienation, has occurred in the general population. A feeling, often impossible to substantiate, that somehow in our modern industrialized world, despite all our technological advances, something important is missing from our lives. Nowhere is this apparent lack more obvious than in the lives of people who, by reason of birth, accident, illness or some other trauma, find themselves requiring rehabilitation or therapy in order that they may coexist within or re-enter the normal world.

THE ARTS AND SOCIETY

> *Art is found in all known societies. It is (as) ubiquitous as religion and, ..., no less important as a social phenomenon.* (Lovell, 1980)

The arts have always been a part of human existence; and, while other members of the animal kingdom may dance in courtship or sing to mark territory, it is only human beings who create works of art as a means of conveying ideas and recording these same ideas for posterity. These artefacts, the products of artistic endeavours, are what most people would associate with the word *Art*, because to most people Art is something one hangs on a wall or pays to see at a gallery or a theatre. However, this is but the tip of the iceberg. It is unfortunate that in modern civilizations most people are unable to dissociate the concept Art from the artefacts, the end products of artistic endeavours, which can be bought, sold or paid for in some way or other. While this current conception of art as treasury or commodity is a fairly recent development, it is nevertheless widely held. From the point of view of the rehabilitation practitioner, or the arts therapist, the most disturbing part of this current view of art is that to a great extent the communal, expressive, healing and spiritual functions of artistry have been all but lost to our western technological society. What little of these functions still remains is subservient to the all important rationality of cost effectiveness.

185

Unlike other animal species we do not simply react or respond to external stimuli in a 'knee-jerk' reaction, for we possess the gift of imagination. The ability to think beyond the concrete and the real. This ability to call upon memories, sensations and experiences brings with it the potential to create a bridge between what has been, what is and what might be. Through this ability to imagine we are able to respond to our external world in a variety of ways. Through imagination we can respond to the feelings and actions of others as if they were our own. Most importantly, it is through our ability to imagine that we can manipulate symbols.

It is through the manipulation of symbols, in both literal and metaphoric configurations, that human beings are able to communicate their inner feelings, desires and responses to their outer world. Ultimately, artistic expression is concerned with the manipulation of symbols to communicate emotions, thoughts and ideas. Art in all its forms - dance, drama, music, painting, poetry, sculpture - is thus an expression of the inner world through symbolic means, with the artistic symbols mediating between the inner reality of the individual and the outer reality of the society in which he or she lives. It is through this process of mediation and manipulation that what modern society has come to call ART evolves.

THE MYTH OF 'THE ARTIST'

> *Creativity is for the gifted few; the rest of us are compelled to live in environments constructed by the gifted few, listen to the gifted few's music, use the gifted few's inventions and art, and read the poems, fantasies and plays by the gifted few. This is what our education and culture condition us to believe; and this is a "culturally induced and perpetuated LIE".* (Nicholson, 1974)

Anyone who has seen Woody Allen satirize the New York art world, most notably in *Manhattan* or *Hanna and Her Sisters*, is immediately reminded of the arbitrary, culturally specific and sometimes ludicrous nature of art appreciation. For, while what we refer to as *artistic activity* or *the arts* have always been part of human societies, the concept of *art*, with words to describe, classify and explain it as an activity, is a fairly new one. According to Malraux (1956), for this concept to come into being, what we refer to as works of art had to become isolated from their functions. He goes on to suggest that it was during the Renaissance that there began to emerge that specific value to which we give the name of art. It has only been with the emergence of art as commodity that we have needed to know how to respond to and classify a work of art. Beauty is no longer in the eye of the beholder, but rather it is determined by the eye of the market analyst. The use of words to describe and quantify human expression (in sound, movement, line, colour, etc.) is much more a reflection of economic market forces than it is anything to do with aesthetics. The emergence of the concept of *THE ARTIST* is an extension of this same phenomenon. It is a phenomenon which has had devastating consequences for all those who consider themselves to be without talent, but in particular it has had especially severe effects on the lives of people who for whatever reason require rehabilitation.

Caute (1972) and others have suggested that, as a result of man's inability to humanize, let alone keep up with, scientific and technological innovations, man has become increasingly alienated from his most distinctive faculty, his intelligence. At the same time, the products of this intelligence require greater and more specialized knowledge and skill. Often this leads to narrow specialization, to fragmentation of personality, to the imitation of automata, to worshipping efficiency and ultimately to paying the price with soul-destroying boredom.

However, as society has become more and more complicated, individuals have become increasingly isolated from active participation in artistic experience. Adults in Western industrialized societies rarely engage actively in imaginative pursuits with any degree of comfort. We are not prepared to spend the necessary time and effort which will enable our imaginations to see the light of day. Instead, for the most part, we are satisfied to sit back and allow artists to entertain or stimulate us vicariously.

No longer is it necessary for the entire community to participate in the artistic event. The artist is the community's highly

> *trained delegate, or representative, who
> alone enters the ethereal realms of imagina-
> tion and then returns to recreate that world
> for the community.* (Johnson, 1984)

One result of this current state of affairs
is, as Coles (1981) has pointed out, that, as a
result of the rift which has developed between art
and people, the artist has become isolated from
the society of which he is a part. In our society
we tend to celebrate the artist's work, but not
the artist. We may be prepared to hang a painting
in our living room, but would we invite an artist
into our dining room? Being an *artist* is a dirty
word. Artistry is not encouraged in schools
because it is not seen as a legitimate job. Art
is not seen as work, it is perceived as play, and
in our extremely rational society, with its heavy
emphasis on the work ethic and cost effectiveness,
play is only for kids!
Recently while teaching a course on arts and
rehabilitation in the Gaza Strip we asked the
students, all of whom were Palestinians, a question we often ask of our students at the beginning
of such courses. The question, *'What is Art?'*, is
normally replied to by students in Canada, Europe
and the United States in terms of finished products - paintings, plays, poems, etc. On this
occasion one of the students replied very simply,
but very seriously, *'Art is Life. Art is everything.'*
Unlike many societies where art and life are
perceived as one and the same thing, something
that ALL people take part in, our society has
successfully dissected art from life. One has to
make the choice to be a part of life, viewing
objets d'art from a distance, experiencing the
vicarious titillation that they can create, or one
can choose the *death* of THE ARTIST. The unfortunate result of all of this is that, in the later
part of the twentieth century, modern industrialized man has become alienated from the processes
of artistic experience. In so doing, human beings
have also increasingly isolated themselves from
the processes of life.

THE ARTS, HEALING AND COMMUNITY

> *Historically, healing, community and the arts
> were highly integrative events. Group*

> *singing, dancing, drumming and dramas were the core of the community's identity and basic to its survival.* (Johnson, 1984)

As a result of the great oracle and purveyor of culture, Television, it is often extremely difficult to find cultures untainted by the melting pot of Western industrialized society, from which conclusions about the workings of previous societies can be drawn. Consequently, much of today's supposition concerning the role and value of the arts to previous and simpler societies is still based on field studies done in the early part of the twentieth century. Nevertheless, work done in recent years - by, amongst others, such people as: Sue Jennings (1985), with the Temiar in Malaysia; Paul Spencer (1985), with the Samburu in Northern Kenya; by Schechner and Schuman (1976), with the Tsembago and others in the Highlands of New Guinea; and by Richard Courtney (1980), with the Coast Salish Indians of British Columbia - has not only greatly enhanced our understanding of the relevance of the arts in those societies, but has also shed light on the significant role the arts have to play in all societies, including our own. In particular, it has led many authors to question if so called 'primitive' and 'retarded' cultures, despite being inferior in respect of economic, material and technological considerations, may not have a more mature and healthy attitude to artistic expression than do the 'developed' cultures.

In less complicated societies than our own, the arts often had/have a significant role to play. As Johnson (1984) has suggested, the arts often acted as the common bond through which people joined together and gained a feeling of togetherness, what Turner (1969) has referred to as *Communitas*. Often in these societies one individual would act as the focal point for the community's artistic expression. This person is most usually referred to as a *Shaman*.

According to Halifax (1980), Shamans are not only spiritual leaders, but also food finders, psychologists and entertainers. Often they have sacred and social functions which can cover an extremely diverse range of activities. Not only are they poets and singers, but also they are dancers and visual artists. They lead the people in singing, dancing and enactment both as an exercise in *Communitas* and as a means of maintaining or enhancing the quality of life of the society. Lewis (1971) suggests the power of the Shaman over the audience is a result of the rhythmic music and singing and later the dancing of the Shaman which gradually involves every participant in more and more collective action. Lewis maintains that after a Shaman's performance various moments of the event may be clearly remembered by the audience. He also suggests that, because in shamanizing the audience at the same time acts and participates, they gain an emotional satisfaction greater than that produced by theatrical and musical performances, literature and general artistic phenomena of the European complex.

In our own culture perhaps only the perform-ances of the most charismatic rock performers can achieve the same effect. Yet, with the possible exception of global events such as Bob Geldof's Live Aid Concert, few have such lasting value for the community as a whole. We do not have, as Courtney (1980) has suggested the Coast Salish Indians do, *'a role concept in which everyone "shares" in the total community'*. Most of all, unlike some societies, we do not have in modern Western society a Shaman who, as artist, healer and spiritual leader, acts as Halifax (1980) has suggested *'...(as) the focus of basic human values that define the relationships between human beings, the culture's relationship to the cosmos, and the society's relationship to the environ-ment'*.

Today it is perhaps only in an occupied land, where most freedoms are removed by the occupying forces through oppression or acts of war, that the arts - particularly those referred to disparag-ingly by critics as traditional or folk arts - have great significance to the whole community. It is small wonder that it is often the poet, writer or painter, and not the politician, who is incarcerated first by occupying forces because, like the Shaman, they can act as the focal point for an oppressed society. To those being occu-pied, joining together as a community - be it in Northern Ireland, the Gaza Strip, South Africa, or wherever - to perform tribal songs can help create a sense of belonging, a sense of communitas, and keep cherished hopes of political freedoms alive. For it could be argued that only in the act of joining together in communal artistic expression does the oppressed people's existence have meaning. Singing the traditional songs and dancing the traditional dances reaffirms that they are alive. That, whilst they may be oppressed, no one may take away their heritage or their destiny. No one may take away their right to be *artists*.

ABILITY AND THE ARTS EXPERIENCE

> *Art is not concerned merely with great artists, with genius or with prodigious skills. It is fundamentally, the outward form of an inward search. To participate in the search; on whatever level and with whatever ability, is to be an artist.*
> (Gettings, 1966)

All of the arts consist of two parts: a process - a way of doing, an intangible undefinable essence; and a product - an artefact that can be viewed, heard or felt not only by its maker, but by others. These two parts need each other. They have a symbiotic relationship, they are intertwined. An individual may start the artistic process aimlessly but, because the process evolves from an individual's need to express some thought or feeling and to shape that impulse through his or her medium, as soon as engagement begins, so does the production of an artefact. This product does not ever have to be identified, articulated or completed, but without its presence there can be no shape to the artistic endeavour.

The product exists on its own. An artefact, being the final fruit of an artist's labours, has a life independent of its creator. It is the grown up child well able to leave home and live on its own. Ultimately, it can be sold or paid for. As a result, the product can be subjected to aesthetic, cultural, political, psychological or economic criticism.

The process, on the other hand, can never be captured. Process will always be the individual's personal journey of discovery, and whether or not the final finished product is offered for public consumption or merely serves its creator as a map of his or her journey does not matter. It was the journey itself that was important, not arriving at the final destination. Schechner (1972), talking about theatre performance, explains Process as *'that state of being when the performer does not*

191

care how he looks or sounds, (and) is not even conscious of the effect of his work'. Process is the individual's internal struggle for harmony between the two poles of discipline and spontaneity.

The arts are ultimately a statement of the unique abilities of each individual human being. It is through the arts and perhaps the arts alone that human beings can shape emotions into an artefact - dance, painting, story, song. These can not only serve as a testament to the beauty of the human spirit, but may also help overcome what might otherwise be crippling blocks to normal accomplishment. One can, as Claire Grey, a member of BEYOND ANALYSIS (a theatre company comprised of ex-psychiatric patients), so poignantly expressed it, *'work with pain and turn it into art'* (Thibeau, 1981).

Yet it is perhaps the process by which the emotion is channelled that is of greatest value to each individual human being. As has been suggested previously (Warren, 1983, 1984), each artefact is *'a unique creative thumbprint'* that only one person could ever create in exactly that way, but it is in the act of creation - in the linking of mind, body and soul - that they are truly made aware of their birthright. That as a human being, irrespective of their age or their physical, intellectual, or emotional capabilities, they have the right to make their own unique creative mark. To say *'I am here. I exist'*.

The arts are not a science. They are concerned with the exploration of that most unscientific of concepts, *the soul*, and with the expression of the innermost core of humanness - the communication of emotion through form. Unfortunately, one cannot simply learn the theorems of art and create a 'work of art'. For, no matter how many times the would-be artist has joined up the dots or painted by numbers, something will always be missing. Initially, then, the arts cannot be approached through logic. Nevertheless, the logic of composition, form and style do have a valuable place to play in artistic creation. However, it is only after one has practised and mastered the discipline of technique that logic can be harnessed to emotion. This is the long hard road undertaken only by those whose prime purpose is to make the arts their profession. Few will take this path. Yet, for all, the arts are the language of the soul and, as such, have something of value to be offered. We believe that all people are creative, and agree with Senior (in Coles, 1981) that it is merely a question of finding the appropriate means and the specific techniques that will suit an individual's personality.

THE ARTS AND REHABILITATION

> *Several myths surrounding the severely physically disabled pervade the fabric of our society, affecting the way non-disabled persons view, relate to and treat persons with physical limitations. These myths also affect the way disabled persons view their own disabilities, impeding their adjustment and ability to assume cherished social roles and enjoy life to the fullest.* (De Loach & Greer, 1981)

Disability is a fact of life. In fact we would go so far as to say that all human beings, to greater or lesser extents, cope with states which provide them with challenges to be overcome in their efforts to successfully achieve the normative expectations of their society. However, we also believe that disability is a socially constructed myth, one that is changed by culturally and temporally determined factors beyond the control of individual human beings. As a result, individuals are labelled as being different from the socially accepted norms. This process of identification and classification of differences, with its attendant stigmatization, has profound effects on the individual's quality of life.

In a world which believes incorrectly that art is the domain of THE ARTIST, all people without those two elusive and illusionary traits, skill and ability, are discriminated against. For people who are perceived incorrectly as being *imperfect*, this is doubly so. Yet the artistic process, i.e. the transformation of intangible emotion into tangible form, is, we believe, the birthright of all individuals. If, as is the case in our modern industrial society, people without discernible obstacles to overcome are actively discouraged from participating in the arts, what chance for persons still referred to by many in our culture as the poor cripple?

In modern Western societies art is a spectator sport! Yet, even as a spectator, the disabled person is both actively and passively the recipient of discrimination. In 1982 the British Government produced a major report on *Public and Private Funding of the Arts* which, Attenborough (1985) suggests, shamefully, almost totally, ignored the needs of disabled people. Subsequently Attenborough was invited by the Carnegie United Kingdom Trust to chair a committee of inquiry into the arts and disabled people. The findings of this committee were published in 1985 as *Arts and Disabled People: The Attenborough Report*. Whilst many of the findings in this report related specifically to the United Kingdom, many of them are universal concerning the plight of disabled people's access to the arts both as experience and as artefacts. For example, the report suggests:

> *Some disabled people, who may, for instance, be blind or wheelchair users, can attend arts events only if accompanied by someone else.*

> *Wheelchair users often have only a limited choice of seats in the theatre, perhaps in the dress circle or in a box. Usually the seats are at the side of the auditorium and too often have poor sight lines.*

> *Lack of adequate transport is a major obstacle to the involvement of disabled people in arts activities. For wheelchair users in particular, public transport is usually unsuitable.*

These are just some of the obstacles that act as barriers preventing disabled people from fully spectating.

> *Many of the barriers are attitudinal; fire regulations, insurance liabilities, and preconceived ideas about the safety and desirability of having handicapped people on the premises all serve to inhibit the disabled visitor.* (Fischer, 1978)

In addition, studies carried out by one of the authors as part of the Ludus Special Schools Project (Warren et al., 1981) suggested that where segregation exists, e.g. in special schools and mental subnormality hospitals, performing artists, be they individuals or professional companies, tend to shy away from working in these situations. The overall result of this is that few disabled people, particularly those who for whatever reason have been institutionalized, are exposed to what may be loosely referred to as 'quality' cultural experiences.

Whilst there have been some moves by artists, professional companies, galleries and pressure groups representing the needs of disabled people to change the policy of governments, a number of factors, particularly a downturn in most industrial economies, have made this a very difficult process. Newman (1985) has encapsulated the problem all too clearly when he suggests that *'many people may still regard the arts as an optional extra in life and begrudge any resources other than physical or medical care or social support spent on the handicapped'*. Levete (1982), however, advocates that all disabled, disadvantaged, elderly and isolated people should have the opportunity to participate actively in every aspect of the cultural life of their community.

Gardner (1982) has strongly emphasized that culture (which Read, 1947, describes as *'the end-product of the outstanding personalities of a number of artists'*) is an essential factor in human development. He argues that cultural deprivation has a severe and negative effect on an individual's development.

Extending the arts experience to all members of our society is of value, not because participants may become the bastions of culture - leaving legacies for their children and future generations - but rather for the inherently beneficial effects this engagement brings to personal interaction and to the quality of life itself. As our society has become more complicated, there have been fewer socially acceptable avenues for individuals to express themselves. As we have already suggested, the traditional avenues of self-expression accessible to our ancestors have been denied us. More and more people live in high density urban population centres where a growing number of disorders related to stress and alienation have been reported. Unfortunately, as Fischer (1978) reports, the arts are still perceived by the vast majority of handicapped people as *'an inconvenient obstacle course strewn with rules, regulations, revolving doors and inaccessible opportunities'*. Nevertheless, it is the work that is being done with those

195

deemed in need of rehabilitation, special education or therapy which is alerting the general
population to the value of artistic experience to
everyone.

Human beings have a need to communicate their
existence. To say to others, *'I am here. I
exist.'* More than this, irrespective of our
ability or the number of obstacles we must overcome to coexist successfully with others in our
society, there is a need for each one of us to be
positively acknowledged as unique individuals.
The arts, rather than demanding conformity to a
socially prescribed set of rules, stand apart as a
celebration of the individual as an individual.
Because they are perhaps the most specific expression of their uniqueness, the arts represent one
of the most powerful and different contributions
to the rehabilitation or therapy of disabled
persons. In addition, they have an immense
contribution to make to the quality of life of
people in general.

ART, DISABILITY AND THE QUALITY OF LIFE

> *If one desires to know the spirit and inner
> life of a people, one must look at its art,
> literature, dances and music, where the
> spirit of the whole people is reflected.*
> (Fleming, 1980)

Studies undertaken by the authors (Nadeau, 1965,
1983; Nadeau & Warren, 1984) suggest that there is
a correlation between a society's relationship to
the arts, both as process and product, and the
overall health of the society as shown in such
indices as socio-cultural change and the physical
and mental health of the individual members of
that society. This has led the authors to suggest
that the relationship between arts, artist and
society can be thought of as a barometer of the
health of any given society. The role of the arts
in the lives of individuals in any given culture
can be viewed as an indicator of the quality of
the social, physical, intellectual and artistic
life of that culture.

In industrialized cultures of the later
twentieth century, disabled people are, to greater
or lesser extents, isolated from the mainstream of
society. Likewise the general population is
isolated from the processes of art. Not only do

we believe that these two states are connected, but also that the latter itself compounds the behaviour problems exhibited by individuals in modern society, particularly in those disorders related to stress and alienation. Reacquainting people with the value of artistic endeavours can help reduce communication and behaviour problems exacerbated by stressful conditions and feelings of alienation.

The arts have an important contribution to make to the quality of a disabled person's life and can help them to re-integrate with the rest of society. In fact, Courtney (1983) has gone so far as to suggest that the arts media must be employed if we are to be successful in the war against mental distress and human handicaps. In addition, the work that is currently being carried out by artists, arts educators and arts therapists not only is proving to be beneficial to people facing physical, intellectual or emotional challenges, but a side-effect has been to help reacquaint the general population, to some extent, with the therapeutic power of the arts experience.

As we have consistently argued throughout this work, experience of, exposure to and involvement in the arts should be available to all people, without the need to consider such factors as age, ability or gender. Yet, either deliberately or tacitly, many disabled people are prevented from fully participating in the artistic activities of their society. This is to the general detriment of their overall quality of life. To be barred from engaging as either spectator or participant in the general artistic milieu, whilst defining the status quo for the majority of people in our logico-rational culture, we would argue is doubly damaging to persons already alienated as a result of the challenge(s) they must face simply to coexist with others not similarly encumbered. We strongly believe that all people should have access to the arts because the arts have a major role to play not only in the health and wellbeing of individuals, but in the quality of life experienced by the society as a whole.

THE POWER OF THE ARTS

Historically, the arts and creative expression have challenged individuals to

197

> articulate the substance of life and to
> reaffirm their existence. As octogenarian
> sculptor, Edna Eckert, confined to her home,
> told us, I think creative people are often
> long-lived because we are always re-inventing
> life; what we did yesterday we create anew
> tomorrow. Inherent in this process is hope.
> (Weisberg & Wilder, 1985)

Arts specialists, most notably arts therapists, often make claims about the curative powers of the arts experience. The authors are not convinced that the arts can legitimately claim to be a cure for anything. One major problem is that everything the arts do is virtually impossible to test directly. However, we feel they can claim to be influential in the improvement of the quality of life of all members of society. This improvement in the disabled person's quality of life may in itself act as a catalyst for change. It would probably be fair to suggest then that the arts can act as a catalyst for change - speeding up those therapeutic transformations which may have been imminent given time, but which were nevertheless essential to the disabled individual's re-integration within the society that had stigmatized and alienated him or her.

There are at least three major areas in which the arts help improve the quality of life for people facing obstacles: PERSONAL DEVELOPMENT - elements of the artistic process which relate to a growth of self-concepts; SOCIAL EDUCATION - elements of the arts experience which educate society to the abilities of persons coping with disabling conditions; ENVIRONMENTAL ENRICHMENT - artefacts (dances, poems, etc.) produced by disabled people as the end products of the arts experience which enrich the lives of both the producer and those around them. These three are often closely interlinked, but each has a different part to play in the overall enhancement of the quality of life.

Personal Development

Many people in our society view severely disabled people as being powerless. In addition, many people, either deliberately or otherwise, and sometimes with the best of intentions, act to maintain this *state of grace*. As a general observation, the more severely disabled an individual is, the less power society is willing to grant that individual to determine the course of his or her own life. However, as Charlene De Loach and Bobby Greer (1981) point out, too many people still believe that education or rehabilitation can only be effective when a trained professional does something *TO* or *FOR*, rather than *WITH* an individual who requires his or her services. Disabled persons, like everyone else, are thinking and feeling individuals. The results of their education or rehabilitation are affected by their motivation, degree of self-confidence, and feelings of self-esteem.

By engaging in the artistic experience, the personal development of disabled persons may be enhanced particularly in the areas of motivation, self-confidence and self-esteem. Gibbons (1982), talks about his own experiences as a disabled person. Growing up in a small town in Ontario and being named the *Timmy* for the Easter seals campaign, developing an *'expectation of inability'* as a result of reactions he experienced within his community. He talks of how starting to paint at the age of 17 helped him to think of himself as having a relationship with his environment. He talks about his *'odd relationship'* with his *'unorthodoxly packaged body'*. How he fluctuated between viewing his body as a prison or a burden. At best he viewed it neutrally as being something that was just there. This was his view until 1981 when he attended movement workshops given by Warren and members of LUDUS Dance-in-Education Co. Gibbons talks of how the movement exercises filled him with joy. They showed him he could move and made him realize that he had a *'physical self (which) can do a lot for me and for others'*. As he said, *'that sort of thing is very important, just to change an old way of looking at yourself'*. For him the movement exercises were both enlightening and empowering. As he put it, *'The artistic process forced me to get out of somebody else's picture of me and get back into me and finally to get out of myself again and into the world.'* The arts experience enabled him to integrate himself with his body and within his environment.

So, while some may consider disabled people to be powerless, participation in the artistic process, being a uniquely personal experience, is a means of empowerment. Individuals engaged in the artistic experience have to take sole responsibility for what they feel, what they think and what they make. So while a professional may occasionally work *WITH* an individual, ultimately the arts must be undertaken *BY* that individual; it simply cannot be done *TO* or *FOR* him or her.

Artistic experience, like death, is something that we all must face and comprehend alone. In the arts there are no predetermined right answers. Each individual brings his or her own personal experiences to bear upon the artistic process; this enables the individual participating to make a unique statement about him/herself, one that no other person could ever do in exactly the same way. As a result, artistic experience can continue throughout an individual's lifetime. In fact age, rather than being an impediment, often leads to enriched participation in the arts. In particular, visual artists, like good wines, generally improve with age.

For artists and non-artists alike, the artistic process is a personal journey of discovery and, at least in the initial stages of the journey, no one is able to fail. It is this which enables even the most severely disabled person to experience some success. The enjoyment of success and the laughter that is often attendant upon the arts eventually leads to an increase in self-confidence and self-esteem, and to an increased motivation to participate not just in the arts experience, but in life itself. The artistic process is, in essence, an individualized and largely self-directed course in personal development.

Any person isolated from society must undergo a process of metamorphosis before being able to successfully re-integrate within that society. DeLoach and Greer (1981) suggest that the disabled individual must undergo a gradual transformation in how he or she sees himself or herself. This is primarily an internal process involving a transformation of self-perception. This internal metamorphosis is an essential stage in the disabled person's reawakening as a complete person.

Schechner and Schuman (1976) maintain that at the heart of theatre is the notion of transformation. This notion of transformation is also quintessential to the therapeutic and rehabilitational process. Ultimately, those in need of therapy or rehabilitation seek to, or are required to, change from what they are to what is culturally, temporally and socially acceptable. It is a process of adaptation and transformation which is essential to social survival and peaceful coexistence. The arts enable individuals to work with emotions and/or ideas and give them form. The arts can play a significant role in this process, for inherent in all the arts is an act of transformation.

However, for any person needing to experience this process, for a successful reintegration to occur, a similar metamorphosis must take place in those members of society who initially isolated him or her. It is not sufficient for the stigmatized person simply to say *'I now feel OK about myself. I'm ready to become a full member of society again'*. Before this can occur the attitudes of society, which isolated the individual in the first place, have to change. Society has to accept their 'difference' as being within the socially acceptable norms. If this occurs at all, it happens slowly as a result of personal exposure by members of that society to individuals coping with that difference. The process can be speeded up by an active campaign of social education.

EDUCATION OF SOCIETY

> *The act of putting on shows about disability, performed by disabled people, is in itself an education for the audience.* (Tomlinson, 1982)

Research done by Blacher and Dixon (1982) has suggested that characters with handicaps have appeared on the theatre stage throughout history. For the most part, these characters were included as dramatic elements because they enhanced a play's character, dialogue, mood, plot or theme. They suggest reasons for the use of handicapped characters in dramatic presentations saying that because drama deals with *'characters in conflict'* and because handicaps *'complicate the lives of both characters and individuals in society'* they are therefore *'ideally suited characteristics for playwrights to use'*. However, Shari Thurer (1980) suggests that the use of physical handicaps in literature and art is *'almost never unencumbered by the trappings of metaphor'*. She sees this as a reinforcement of social stereotyping which is both *'blatant and pernicious'*. So while the theatre has had the power to educate society to the problems of the disabled person and thereby improve their quality of life, over the past 25 centuries for the most part it has simply maintained the status quo.

However, in the last ten years companies have come into being whose actors, choreographers, dancers and directors have themselves been coping with physical, intellectual or emotional challenges. In addition, the work of disabled playwrights is reaching the theatres more frequently. This, coupled with a noticeable change in attitudes towards integrating disabled people in society, has led to more and more disabled people using the theatre arts both actively and passively as a vehicle for propaganda and as a weapon in the war of societal education and for social change.

Not only has the work by such companies as Graeae, Theatre Unlimited, Amici, and Dancers of the Third Age and writers such as David Freeman helped improve the awareness of the general population of the obstacles that disabled people have to overcome, but it has also helped to make them aware of their abilities. Films such as *The High Country* and plays such as *Stronger than Superman* have also depicted disability in a positive light, while the play *Children of a Lesser God* provides work for a severely hearing impaired actress and is also signed throughout. This has two effects; firstly, the hearing impaired person may enjoy the performance and, secondly, it forces non-impaired members of the audience to come in contact with the reality of hearing impairment. More importantly actors like Nabil Shaban and Hamish Macdonald are graduating from companies dealing solely with the issues and problems of disability, and are being employed by professional companies on the basis of their ability NOT their disability.

ENVIRONMENTAL ENRICHMENT

> *A man who has attained mastery of an art reveals it in his every action.* (Hyams, 1982)

Throughout the centuries there have been many notable artists who have had a disability. Some are legendary, such as Beethoven who had hearing impairment, Toulouse-Lautrec who had a congenital malformation, and Van Gogh who was mentally unstable. There are also many other artists who struggled with disabilities and chronic, crippling diseases, e.g. Renoir with arthritis, Klee with scleroderma, and Chekov with tuberculosis, who produced rich legacies for the human race in spite of the obstacles they had to overcome to do so. Sandblom (1982) argues that Lord Byron's clubfoot had a large part to play in *his youthful genius*, citing the poet's own words to back his assumption. Similarly, he argues that Paganini's disability (he suffered from Ehlers-Danlos' Syndrome which produces hyperflexibility in the joints) may have played an important role in *his violinistic virtuosity*. In fact the history of artistic production throughout the centuries is full of examples of people who in spite of, and in some instances because of, chronic crippling diseases and disabilities have created artistic masterpieces.

It is clear, then, that disability or chronic disease is not in and of itself sufficient reason to prevent artistic creation. As was suggested earlier, inherent in any artistic exploration is the creation of an artefact; the two are inextricably linked. Whilst the process of artistic exploration is perhaps of greatest value to the individual coping with a physical, intellectual or emotional challenge, the completion of an artefact has in itself great value. Performing a dance, appearing in a play, or creating a painting can be very beneficial, for the completed artefact makes a statement about the uniqueness of the individual who created it. One three-year-old girl coping with severe emotional obstacles picked up a paintbrush in her diminutive hand. She loaded it with red paint. Holding the brush firmly, she commenced gently stabbing the paintbrush onto the paper making a pattern of red splodges. As she did this she sang *'I'm the only one in the whole world who can do this'*. Previously, this young girl had a very low self-esteem, she was powerless and had little that she could call her own; however, in the space of a few short minutes she had created a painting which, though perhaps not meeting the criteria of 'masterpiece', she found pleasing and made her very happy. She had created a piece of work which could enrich her environment, and in the process had started to improve her self-esteem and increase her sense of self-worth.

ARTS FOR ALL - A QUESTION OF ACCESS

> *Active participation in creative activities*
> *like painting, writing and acting...knocks*
> *down presuppositions there may be about*
> *people with disabilities and also leads them*
> *to reappraise their own lives.* (Shaban, 1982)

Throughout this chapter we have been putting forward arguments concerning the value of the arts for persons in need of rehabilitation in its broadest sense. Whether an individual is coping with a physical challenge, such as spina bifida, an intellectual challenge, such as Down's Syndrome, or an emotional challenge, such as sexual abuse, the arts can help individuals come to terms with themselves and the society in which they live. In areas of personal self-concepts, socialization and environmental enrichment, the arts have a great deal to offer both to the process of reintegration and rehabilitation, and to the individual's overall quality of life. Yet too many people are still being denied access to their birthright to be creative, to make that unique creative thumbprint.

Assuming that the reader has followed, and to some extent agreed, with our arguments, many of which require a *leap of faith*, he or she must find themselves facing the question of what steps can be taken to amend the current status quo? How can the arts be made more accessible to persons facing challenges? In this penultimate section we wish to identify some approaches and projects that we feel have been particularly successful.

In Canada, Europe and the United States there have been many different approaches taken to help disabled persons gain access to the arts. Some of these initiatives have been specific to a local area or building, while others have had significant effect throughout the world. The range, scope and number of approaches deserving mention which have been initiated over the last 20 years are far too great to be covered in detail. What we present, then, is no more than a selection of examples, which nevertheless bear testimony to the variety of possibilities available. In doing so we hope to stimulate the reader to contemplate, and hopefully implement, arts provision for people with whom they work. As always, the only limit to creativity is the scope of the human imagination.

Arts provision for disabled people comes in all shapes and sizes. Projects, workshops, exhibitions and so on have been initiated by individuals, small groups, institutions, large agencies and communities, with the reasons for the initiation of arts services being perhaps as diverse as the range of individuals and groups who acted as catalysts. One consequence has been that the structure of the programmes, being extensions of the uniqueness of the people involved, is equally diverse. The only common denominator behind the organization of arts provision would seem to be a love for humanity, and a knowledge that the arts are the most unique expression of that humanity. The only thing that links them together is their use of the arts.

Having made the suggestion that every arts programme is different, we would like to look at a few examples of four different types of approaches to improving the accessibility of the arts for all. We will describe these as FORUMS, REFERRAL SERVICES, PROVISION IN SITU, and PEER DIRECTED INITIATIVES.

Forums

Over the years there have been many forums held on the role of the arts in rehabilitation and therapy. All too often these forums are run by *able-bodied* professionals for other *able-bodied* professionals. The people for whom the services were to be provided were rarely invited to attend. However, more recently forums have been run where disabled persons have had a voice in the proceedings. To give but two examples, in 1981 from 23 to 25 October, a residential seminar was held at Ysgol Erw'r Delyn, Wales, which brought together disabled and able-bodied artists and non-artists to discuss the provision of the arts for disabled people in Wales. As a result of this and a further seminar in 1982, an organization, Arts for Disabled People in Wales, was formed to co-ordinate and foster arts activities for people with disabilities throughout Wales.

As another example, in 1980 and again in 1981, Roberta Nadeau, herself disabled and a visual artist and art therapist, organized two weekend seminars at the Muttart Gallery in Calgary. The seminars, *Beyond Expectations* and *Expectations and Beyond*, brought together disabled and able-bodied

205

artists, arts educators and arts therapists to discuss the nature and importance of the arts experience for people facing physical, intellectual and emotional challenges. In addition the forums provided disabled artists access to information related to pursuing their profession(s), e.g. marketing and agents. Two indirect results of these seminars were: 1) the formation of the Alberta Arts Therapy Association, whose aims are *To improve the quality of human life through the arts (visual arts, dance, drama and music) whether this be part of a therapeutic treatment, or to help individuals overcome a specific handicap or disability, or for people who seek personal growth through the arts;* and 2) the commencement of courses in the arts therapies through the Faculty of Fine Arts and Rehabilitation Studies Programme at The University of Calgary.

Referral Services

Referral services generally seek to act as the liaison between artists, who can provide artistic services, and institutions or individuals who seek these services. As such they have an important role to play in the provision of accessible arts experiences for all people.

SHAPE was formed in 1976 in the United Kingdom by Gina Levete. It is a network of about 14 independently operated but associated agencies located in different parts of the UK which coordinate services and introduce artists of all disciplines to persons with special needs. They also provide a subsidized ticket service to enable institutionalized persons to visit theatres, concerts, galleries, etc.

HAI (Hospital Audiences Inc.), founded by Michael Jon Spencer in 1969, is a similar organization that operates in the United States. Since its inception it has enabled disabled persons in New York to attend Broadway and off-Broadway shows, concerts and dance events. Since 1979 it has also operated a workshop programme with professional performing and visual artists for institutionalized persons.

In 1982 Gina Levete created INTERLINK, whose motto was *Integration through the Arts*, as an international network linking artists and arts companies with organizations and institutions for disabled or disadvantaged people. In its four years of operation INTERLINK helped to support some remarkable initiatives and some excellent projects.

Provision in Situ

Provision of arts service in situ has been one of the trademarks of referral services. However, there have been many examples of arts provision, in institutions such as hospitals, group homes and special schools that have been initiated by individuals and groups working with or within the institution. Two examples are the LUDUS Special Schools Project and the Manchester Hospitals Arts Project.

The Special Schools Project was carried out in 1980-82 as a research/development project in the North-west of England by LUDUS Dance-in-Education company with support and funding from three education authorities, The Schools Council, The Calouste Gulbenkian Foundation, The Arts Council of Great Britain and numerous other arts and educational bodies. It was an extension of work undertaken by Ludus in 100 special schools during the previous five years. The project involved nearly 30 special schools catering for over 2,000 children with a wide range of physical, intellectual and emotional disabilities. The project brought together a professional dance/theatre company with teachers, educational researchers, arts therapists and special school children. The project raised the profile of the arts on the special education curriculum, trained teachers in the use of the arts with special children and made many suggestions about the preparation, development and presentation of professional theatre performances in special schools.

The Manchester Hospitals Arts Project is perhaps the most remarkable example of the changes the arts can make in institutions. Initially started by the vision and initiative of one man, Peter Senior, the MHAP is a shining example to all. The project started in 1973 as a result of Senior, a painter and college lecturer in art, starting to display his own work in the out-patients' waiting area of Withington Psychiatric Hospital near Manchester. The first arts team started work in 1977 with four members. Now 17 artists are employed, and together with students and volunteers, they provide a full range of arts activities and events including textile/fibre arts, paintings, murals, photography, puppetry, music and all kinds of performances. Whilst the development of the team(s) has not been without its problems, the work of the project has led senior health care officials to move from positions of hostility, to accepting grudgingly, to commenting that *'the arts are central not peripheral to the health service'* (Davis, in Coles, 1981).

Peer Directed Initiatives

The number of projects where disabled people are actively involved not only as participants/observers, but also as decision makers, are fewer than those run by able-bodied professionals. However, in recent years arts provision where the recipient is also the manager, organizer or leader has become more common. Here are two brief examples. The National Theatre Workshop of the Handicapped was started by Dr. Rick Curry, himself disabled, in New York in 1977. NTWH offers *'a comprehensive training in theatre arts for disabled people'*. In addition, it *'helps place members of the workshop in auditions and acting jobs'* (Newman, 1985).

In 1971 the Swedish Association of Visually Handicapped Artists and Craftsmen was founded to look after the professional interests of its members. Their membership is currently around 40 and members must demonstrate their skills prior to being accepted. As most information about new techniques, marketing of work and so on are contained in publications written for sighted readers, the association produces cassette tapes containing this information and details of courses for their members. The association also organizes exhibitions of members' work which are *'held each year in different venues in order to enable more of the public to be aware of the SKKF artists' work'* (Newman, 1985).

EDUCATION OF PERSONNEL

If, as we hope, some readers have been stimulated to undertake new initiatives, there are three major factors which need to be considered in the attempt to provide opportunity in the arts for all. First and foremost there is the question of:

Programme Personnel - personnel need to possess the necessary training to design a programme which meets the needs of the participants, and the skill to help individuals facing physical, intellectual or emotional challenges successfully deal with the artistic and creative challenges they will have to face. This requires training in the arts, at the very least a *working knowledge* of the problems participants will be facing and, above all, a sensitive, caring and flexible approach.

Programme Suitability - irrespective of whether the programme is planned for people with specific disabilities or for integrated groups, the programme needs to provide opportunity for individuals facing challenges to express themselves. Ideally, there should be provision for participants to be involved in determining both their needs and specific goals, and at the very least to have some avenue by which they can attest to whether these needs/goals are being met by the programme.

Physical Accessibility - it is absolutely essential that individuals facing challenges can gain access to the building in which the programme, performance or exhibition is to be housed, otherwise the most brilliant personnel and most superbly designed programmes are absolutely wasted.

All of the programmes above, in their own special ways, have taken account of the three basic considerations outlined. For the reader contemplating the initiation of new arts initiatives, remember that all of the above started in a small way and often had many problems along the way which, perhaps unfortunately, are rarely detailed in reports of their success.

As a last thought, a 'taster event' such as an arts awareness weekend or an arts day may be a simple but effective start. To start in a small way by bringing together artists and disabled persons for one day or a weekend where people may explore what the arts have to offer, or by having artists hang their own work in an institution, can open doors to people who often, through no fault of their own, have been isolated and alienated from their right to be creative and have been alienated from the mainstream of life itself. We believe that this not only will start to improve the quality of life of people so isolated, but also has the potential, through their successes, to show the rest of society what they have been missing.

REVIEW

The arts consist of two parts: a process and a product. In the arts there are no predetermined right answers.

1. The arts are the language of the soul and ultimately a statement of the unique abilities of each individual human being.
2. Artistic experience can continue throughout an individual's lifetime. In fact age, rather than being an impediment, often leads to enriched participation in the arts.
3. Artistic expression is concerned with the manipulation of symbols to communicate emotions, thoughts and ideas. It has always been one of the cornerstones of all known communities.
4. None of the arts is a science. They are an expression of an individual's inner world through symbolic means.
5. The role of the arts in the lives of individuals in any given community can be viewed as an indicator of the quality of the social, physical, intellectual and artistic life of that community.
6. Historically, healing, community and the arts were integrally linked.
7. Unfortunately, the communal, expressive, healing and spiritual aspects of the arts have been all but lost in technological societies. This has had devastating effects on the overall quality of life for individuals in industrialized cultures.
8. The emergence of the concept of *THE ARTIST* has had devastating consequences for all those considered to be without talent.
9. Individuals have become increasingly isolated from the arts and have thus lost their primary means of self-expression. One result has been that many disabled people are prevented

from fully participating in the artistic activities of their community.

10. Creativity is not just for the gifted few, and disability or chronic disease is not in and of itself sufficient reason to prevent a person from participating in the arts.

11. Every human being, irrespective of their age or their physical, intellectual, or emotional capabilities, should have the right to make their own unique creative mark and to participate actively in the artistic life of their community.

12. In areas of personal self-concept, socialization and environmental enrichment the arts have a great deal to offer to the individual's overall quality of life.

13. Reacquainting people with the value of artistic endeavours can help reduce communication and behaviour problems exacerbated by stressful conditions and feelings of alienation.

14. The arts can help disabled individuals develop positive self-esteem and feelings of self-worth and help motivate them to improve their own quality of life.

15. Performances realistically presenting disabled persons' abilities can have a positive effect on the quality of a disabled person's life.

16. Artefacts produced by disabled people can enrich their own and others' surroundings and positively affect their quality of life.

17. We described four different approaches to the provision of accessible arts for all: FORUMS, REFERRAL SERVICES, PROVISION IN SITU and PEER DIRECTED INITIATIVES.

16. We suggested three major factors in the provision of accessible arts for all: PROGRAMME PERSONNEL, PROGRAMME SUITABILITY and PHYSICAL ACCESSIBILITY.

REFERENCES

Attenborough, D. (1985) *Arts and Disabled People*, Bedford Square Press, London.
Blacher, J. & Dixon, M. B. (1982) 'A History of the Handicapped on Stage,' *The Journal of Special Education*, 16(1), 21-35.
Caute, D. (1972) *The Illusion*, Harper & Row, New York.

Coles, P. (1981) *Manchester Hospitals' Arts Project*, Calouste Gulbenkian Foundation, London.

Courtney, R. (1980) *The Dramatic Curriculum*, University of Western Ontario Press, London, Ontario.

Courtney, R. (1983) 'The Medium is the Missile: Arts Therapy in the Electric Age,' *Canadian Art Therapy Association Journal, 1*, 3-14.

Davis, N. (1981) in P. Coles, *Manchester Hospitals' Arts Project*, Calouste Gulbenkian Foundation, London.

De Loach, C. & Greer, B. (1981) *Adjustment to Severe Physical Disability - A Metamorphosis*, McGraw Hill, New York.

Fischer, R. (1978) 'Who Cares About the 5%?' Unpublished document prepared for the information department of the Arts Council of Great Britain.

Fleming, W. (1980) *Arts and Ideas*, Holt, Rinehart & Winston, New York.

Gardner, H. (1982) *Art, Mind and Brain*, Basic Books, New York.

Gettings, F. (1966) *You Are An Artist: A Practical Approach to Art*, Hamlyn, London.

Gibbons, D. (1982) 'Art and Personal Growth,' Talk given as part of the seminar, Expectations and Beyond, Muttart Gallery, Calgary, Alberta.

Halifax, J. (1980) *Shamanic Voices*, Penguin, Harmondsworth, England.

Hyams, J. (1982) *Zen in the Martial Arts*, Bantam Books, New York.

Jennings, S. (1985) 'Temiar Dance and the Maintenance of Order', in P. Spencer (ed.), *Society and the Dance*, Cambridge University Press, Cambridge, England.

Johnson, D. R. (1984) 'The Arts and Communitas,' *Design*, No. 86.

Levete, G. (1982) 'The Role of Interlink,' *Positif*, No. 1, p. 3.

Lewis, I. M. (1971) *Ecstatic Religion*, Penguin, Baltimore, Maryland.

Lovell, T. (1980) *Pictures of Reality*, British Film Institute, London.

Malraux, A. (1956) *Voice of Silence: Man and His Art*, Doubleday, Garden City, New York.

Nadeau, R. (1965) 'A Paper With No Name About An Art With No Rules,' Unpublished paper.

Nadeau, R. (1983) 'Mirror of the Self: The Power of the Arts Experience in Expanding Human Horizons,' Keynote Address to Expanding Human Horizons Conference, University of Calgary, Calgary, Alberta.

Nadeau, R. & Warren, B. (1984) 'Partners in Therapy: A Metamorphosis,' Paper presented at 5th Annual Conference, Canadian Art Therapy Association, University of British Columbia, Vancouver, British Columbia.

Newman, C. G. H. (1985) 'Consultant's Viewpoint - Healing Role of the Arts,' *Positif*, No. 12.

Nicholson, S. (1974) *RIBA Journal*, February.

Parmelin, H. (1977) *Art Anti-Art*, Marion Boyars, London.

Read, H. (1947) *The Grass Roots of Art: Four Lectures on Social Aspects of Art in an Industralised Age*, Wittenborn, New York.

Sandblom, P. (1982) *Creativity and Disease*, George F. Stickley, Philadelphia, Pennsylvania.

Schechner, R. (1972) 'Aspects of Training at the Performance Group,' in R. P. Brown (ed.), *Actor Training* (Vol. I), Drama Book Specialists, New York.

Schechner, R. & Schuman, M. (1976) *Ritual, Play and Performance*, The Seabury Press, New York.

Senior (1981) in P. Coles, *Manchester Hospitals' Arts Project*, Calouste Gulbenkian Foundation, London.

Shaban, N. (1982) 'DISCUSSION - Does Creative Participation Prevent Isolation?' *Positif*, No. 1.

Spencer, P. (1985) *Society and the Dance*, Cambridge University Press, Cambridge, England.

Thibeau, A. (1981) 'From Weakness to Strength,' *City Arts*, July.

Thurer, S. (1980) 'Disability and Monstrosity: A Look at Literary Distortions of Handicapping Conditions,' *Rehabilitation Literature, 41*, No. 1-2, 12-15.

Tomlinson, R. (1982) *Disability, Theatre and Education*, Indiana University Press, Bloomington, Illinois.

Turner, V. (1969) *The Ritual Process*, Aldine, Chicago, Illinois.

Warren, B. (1983) 'Experience in the Arts - Therapy for All?' *Alberta Arts Therapy Association Journal, 1, (1)*, 2-3.

Warren, B. (1984) *Using the Creative Arts in Therapy*, Croom Helm, London/Brookline Books, Cambridge, MA.

Warren, B., Thompson, C., Ewert, J., & Merwitzer, M. (1981) 'LUDUS Special Schools Project: Report on Stage One of the Project 1980-81,' Unpublished Report.

Weisberg, N. & Wilder, R. (1985) *Creative Arts with Older Adults*, Human Sciences Press, New York.

Chapter Ten

RELIGION AND REHABILITATION: A PARTICULAR
CHALLENGE FOR CHRISTIANITY

Patrick McGinley

INTRODUCTION

Practitioners in the field of rehabilitation find
it difficult to relate to the idea of miracle
cures. On the one hand, the typical instant
miracle cure seems too quick and too easy and it
is difficult to relate this to the long process of
rehabilitation. On the other hand, the rehabilitation practitioner might well wonder why the
miracle worker who can cure one leper or ten
lepers does not perform that much more fundamental
miracle of wiping out all leprosy, thus relieving
so much human misery.
     Among all the miracles described in the
Gospels, there is at least one which the rehabilitation practitioner will find particularly
compelling reading; a miracle which is attrac-
tively and realistically described and which is
consistent with the experience of people who,
after a period of blindness, are enabled to see
again, following surgery. Here is the account
from Mark (Chapter 8: 22-26):

> They came to Bethsaida, and some people
> brought to Him a blind man whom they begged
> Him to touch. He took the blind man by the
> hand and led him outside the village. Then
> putting spittle on his eyes and laying his
> hands upon him, He asked, 'Can you see
> anything?' The man, who was beginning to
> see, replied, 'I can see people; they look
> like trees to me, but they are walking
> about.' Then He laid his hands upon the
> man's eyes again and he saw clearly; he was
> cured, and he could see everything plainly

> *and distinctly. And Jesus sent him home*
> *saying, 'Do not even go into the village'.*
> (Jones, 1966)

The Gospel accounts of the miracle cures of Jesus are not just so many stories of magical cures making the point that Jesus had special power over evil. The miracles and the consistent attitude of Jesus towards the personal dignity of people who were blind or who suffered from leprosy, paraplegia, or mental illness set out clearly for all Christians the challenge to take seriously the dignity of afflicted people and the challenge of caring for and providing for the rehabilitation and integration of all disabled people.

Christianity is not unique among religions in placing such a significant emphasis on the dignity of the disabled individual. Gold (1981) points out that while, in general, heroes tend to be physically attractive and articulate people, this is not so for the heroes in the Jewish tradition. He gives examples from early Judaism of Moses' severe stutter, Jacob who limped following his encounter with God, Sarah who was barren for most of her life, and Leah, Jacob's wife, who had weak eyes. Gold (1981) points out the concern for the dignity of the diseased person evident in the sections of the Torah which deal with lepers. It was necessary to separate someone with a contagious disease; yet they were not sent away or locked up forever, they did not become non-persons; they were kept in a place on the periphery of the camp, not so far from the others, until they could rejoin the group. Gold points out that priests in the Jewish tradition who were crippled or physically or mentally handicapped could not perform certain of the priestly functions, yet they were not excluded from all the activities, just whichever ones they were unable to perform because of their limitations (Gold, 1981).

Myles (1981) describes the concern for the dignity of disabled persons which may be found in the early writings of Islam and Asian religions. According to Myles, the written revelation of Islam records specific provision for the guardianship of property of feeble-minded people and he describes Islamic schools of legal interpretation discussing the rights of the mentally disabled person as far back as the eighth and ninth centuries AD, nearly four hundred years before the first English legislation and anticipating by a thousand years the current Western debate on the same subject (Myles, 1981).

The following pages look at the challenges and concerns that face religion, particularly Christianity, at a period where the philosophy of normalization sets a pattern for integration of disabled persons into the community.

GREEK AND HEBREW THOUGHT - EASTERN AND WESTERN

In view of the clarity with which the Gospels point the way to Christians regarding the practical nurturing of the dignity, integration, and welfare of disabled people, the question arises as to why religion in the Western world has not had a more succinct focus on this important aspect of its mission? This question will probably never receive a fully satisfactory answer and it is beyond the scope of this chapter; it may be useful, nevertheless, at least to suggest a direction in which one aspect of the solution may be found.

The challenge of Jesus and the Gospel regarding the dignity and status of disabled persons was the practical challenge expressed in and by and for a Hebrew community. One could speculate that the pragmatic outlook of Hebrew thinking would have led the early Christian Church to practical and effective responses to this challenge, if the young Church had developed where it was founded, within the Hebrew culture. But history determined a different course for the early Church, which quickly became immersed in the abstract philosophy of the Greeks. The Greek philosophy which was espoused by the early Church gave it an academic, intellectual and abstract dimension and it was this intellectual legacy which became the focus of religious thinking and religious development. The cost was an underdevelopment of and lack of emphasis upon more pragmatic aspects of worshipping God and service of neighbours. Jones (1961) describes the divergence and also the complementarity of Greek and Hebrew thinking and the reader is referred to that text for a scholarly treatment of the subject. Offner and Van Straelen (1963) give a view of the difference between the manner of thinking of Eastern and Western minds; they characterize Eastern thinking as *broad, general-izing, inclusivistic and syncretistic* and Western thinking as *narrower, particularizing, exclusivistic and discriminating*, and they go on to state, *'the orientals feel a natural repulsion towards all intellectual activity which distinguishes things one from another and opposes them one against the other without ever reuniting them'.*

THE MODERN PERSPECTIVE

It is not possible, here, to attempt even to sketch the outline of the ebb and flow of theological thought from the early writers through Augustine and Aquinas to the present day. Likewise, the thread of philosophical thought through Descartes and Pascal to Wittgenstein and Russell, together with the warp and woof of religious and political history, lies beyond the scope of this short chapter. Kung reviews the complex intertwining of theology, philosophy and history and the reader is referred to his 1980 text.

There are, however, at least two reasons why it would be an error to write off the centuries of growth of religions as not having sufficient relevance to such themes as rehabilitation and integration.

Firstly, the view that the developing Christian religions were entirely dominated by authoritarianism, strict legalistic structures and ritual is not only inaccurate but, more seriously, it is a viewpoint which is damaging to present-day religions. Furthermore, it is a view which contains within it the germ of an unwarranted cultural and religious self-satisfaction and self-complacency. Hauerwas (1974) argued that the portraying of the developing Christian religions as being authoritarian and legalistic not only distorts history but gives *'a disastrously vague character'* to modern moral theology and ethics.

Secondly, and perhaps more pertinent here, this negativistic view of religion may be shown to be inaccurate by the careful documentation of the work of many religious orders and religious groups who were founded by visionaries of their day, often to fulfil specific functions in the area of the care and rehabilitation of disabled people. For example, Reichgelt (1957) gives a detailed account of the life and work of Peter Joseph

Triest (1760-1836). Canon Triest founded the Sisters of Charity of Jesus and Mary in 1804 and he founded the Brothers of Charity in 1807. A quotation from Reichgelt will strike many responsive cords in the rehabilitation practitioner of the late twentieth century:

> *During the summer of 1807... he (Canon Triest) was entrusted by the Civil Alms Commission with the direction of the civil hospital at Byloke. This was a very delicate task, because he had to uphold the Abbess' authority and, at the same time, remedy the existing abuses. Doctors were obliged to make regular and thorough examination of patients; the sick were to be visited at fixed hours... superfluous staff and idlers were dismissed.* (Reichgelt, 1957)

The rehabilitation practitioner, especially one who has been involved in the preparation of evaluative reports on rehabilitation centres, perhaps using such tools as PASS, will be able to identify with several aspects of Canon Triest's work during the summer of 1807, from the delicacy required in preparing an evaluation report which will have the desired effects of combining financial economies with a more effective pattern of service delivery and use of professionals' time, while at the same time carefully avoiding giving counter-productive offence to the administrative structures and, in particular, to the chief executive.

The growth of the Brothers of Charity was such that by 1886 the Order had 397 members of whom 303 were Belgians, 58 were Canadians and Americans, 19 were Dutch, 13 were German, and 4 were English. Working in 22 communities, the Brothers had 24 centres and were caring for more than 2,000 mentally ill, old and infirm people, as well as more than 5,000 poor children among whom were 600 orphans, 200 deaf and dumb, 60 blind and 300 young delinquents (Reichgelt, 1957). Today, the Brothers of Charity are working in rehabilitation, particularly with people who have learning difficulties and mental handicap, on five continents in 16 different countries from Peru to Japan and from Canada to South Africa.

The Order of Sisters founded by Peter Triest, the Sisters of Charity of Jesus and Mary, is likewise involved in rehabilitation work the world over.

The founding of the Irish Sisters of Charity in 1815 by Mary Aikenhead and the subsequent development of the services in the area of education, social work and health services, around the world, is described by Donovan (1979). This religious group has evolved along rather different patterns of development over the past 170 years to arrive at their present level of health services and rehabilitation services, internationally.

The number of religious orders and groups working in the health and rehabilitation area is considerable, certainly in the hundreds. These include such groups as the Franciscan Missionaries of the Divine Motherhood, the Daughters of Charity of St. Vincent de Paul, the St. John of God Brothers and the Bon Secours Sisters, just to name a few.

One of the principal enemies of development and improvement in the rehabilitation area is complacency and certainly religion has no justification to be complacent as regards its record in rehabilitation work. Stubblefield (1975) gives some interesting statistics on an exploratory study which was undertaken to survey the views and behaviour of 220 clergymen in the United States. The denominations surveyed include: Baptists (24%); Methodists (19%); Church of Christ (17%); Presbyterian (9%); Nazarene (7%); and Catholic (5%). While 96 per cent of the clergymen expressed the view that the Church had a responsibility for the religious care and training of retarded children, only 9 per cent reported that their church made any special provision for the retarded and only 4 per cent indicated that they had plans to do so in the near future. But the most disappointing of Stubblefield's findings was the extent to which clergymen viewed understanding as being a critical criterion in determining the acceptability of a mentally handicapped person for church membership. Stubblefield found that there was a consensus that membership of the Church was conditional on the degree of retardation, though he states that the clergymen felt that retardation, *'in and of itself'* should not be a reason for exclusion. Stubblefield found that Baptist and Church of Christ ministers had more definite views about the need for *'responsible religious decision on the part of the retarded'*, but that this presented fewer problems to

Presbyterian, Lutheran and Catholic ministers and priests (Stubblefield, 1975).

There is evidence of a certain internal inconsistency in Stubblefield's findings. The consensus view seemed, on the one hand, to say that retardation in and of itself should not be a reason for excluding someone from church member-ship, yet the individual's understanding the meaning of being a Christian and a church member appear to be the criterion for acceptance or rejection. Wilkie (1980) argued that this kind of inconsistency and ambiguous attitudes on the part of clergymen and church members resulted in handicapped people being too often objects of pity, condescension and charity rather than accepted as colleagues and equals.

Heifetz and Franklin (1982) investigated the involvement of clergy with mentally retarded persons and their families. Forty clergymen (17 Roman Catholic priests, 6 rabbis, and 17 Protes-tant ministers) were given two interviews and completed rating scales on information about their backgrounds and their willingness to provide a variety of services to families with retarded members. The clergymen were shown a list of 40 activities and asked to indicate whether they had carried out the activity or whether they were willing or unwilling to do it. The activities included 'visiting the retarded at home', 'teaching retarded persons to pray', 'giving a talk/sermon to promote community acceptance of retarded people', and 'joining local associations for retarded citizens'. The 40 clergymen interviewed had done an average of 13.6 of the items on the activity list; but the standard deviation, 9.4, indicates the very great differences within the group. One clergyman had done 32 of the activities while another had done none of them.

ARCHITECTURAL ACCESSIBILITY

The most concrete expression of a failure on the part of the Church to take seriously those physi-cally handicapped individuals who are confined to wheelchairs is the architecture of churches of every denomination around the world. Prior to the 1970s, at least, pitiably few churches were designed to allow equal access to handicapped and non-handicapped alike. Sadly, the same phenomenon may still be observed today in the design of churches only very recently opened - and in 1987 no church group can claim that they are unaware of the strong negative message which is taken by disabled people who find themselves physically denied access to a church building. However, there is little doubt that the situation with respect to architectural unsuitability of church buildings has much improved, especially over the last five years. Several major church groupings have made specific recommendations and adopted policies specifying that all new church buildings or major renovations should give access to church buildings by disabled people in wheelchairs. Such a policy was adopted in the United States in 1977 by the United Presbyterian Church, the United Church of Christ, and the United States National Council of Churches (Wilkie, 1980). At least two church groups utilize financial encouragement in their efforts to persuade church congregations to design buildings which admit physically disabled people; the American Lutheran Church levies a financial penalty on churches which do not conform and the Board of Service and Mission in America have agreed that they would ordinarily refuse to grant loans to congregations for church construction unless the plan conformed to standards requiring easy access for physically handicapped people (Wilkie, 1980).

ACCESS IS NOT ENOUGH

Designing church buildings which avoid physical barriers for handicapped and disabled people is, of course, only the tip of the iceberg. It is a minimal step indeed in comparison with the amount of work which remains to be done if religion is to play its role in the complete integration and acceptance of all people regardless of type or level of physical or mental handicap. Indeed, Wilkie (1980) and Lant (1981) referred to a worrying belief, among Christians and Jews, that mental or physical handicap is an indication of impurity or, worse still, an indication of the sins of the father being visited upon the offspring. Beliefs along these lines, although inconsistent to the core of the main religious faiths, need to be recognized and taken seriously by the rehabilitation practitioner and by religions alike because they are often deeply

ingrained and because they are the kinds of belief
which, even in the 1980s, persist in leading
parents to denying the existence of handicap and,
consequently, to failing to seek appropriate
rehabilitation services for their children at an
early age. While the problem of thoughtless
church architecture can be effectively dealt with
by adopting formal resolutions and policies within
the structure of the different religions, the
problem of changing the attitudes and behaviour of
clergymen, of congregations and of individual
church members is a much more complex one.
Indeed, it is a problem which shares many of the
difficulties encountered in the more general task
of the cultural amelioration of physical and
mental handicap in the widest sense. The principal difference is that in the religious sphere
individuals generally share a belief in and an
acceptance of certain fundamental principles.
Furthermore, the Bible or an equivalent is usually
highly respected and given an unequivocal
acceptance. While these considerations should
facilitate the task of changing the attitudes and
behaviour of the religious-affiliated, it would be
unrealistic to suppose that the task is an easy
one or even that it is necessarily a task which is
assured of success. On the contrary, the task
will meet success if and only if it is taken
seriously by committed individuals and only if
these individuals and groups of individuals
utilize appropriate educational strategies.

The Healing Community

Thankfully, the recent past has seen the emergence
of just such outstanding individuals and organizations. One organization, entitled The Healing
Community, under the leadership of Wilkie, himself
a disabled person since birth, offers a nationwide
programme in the United States. The Healing
Community, described by Colston (1978), was
designed to raise the consciousness of the
religious community with respect to handicapped
and alienated persons. It sought to help
religious groups to give a greater social
acceptance to handicapped people and to help them
live more ordinary community lives. The Healing
Community has developed interfaith groups in local
communities and has set up pilot projects as
models showing how people with handicaps may be

successfully involved in the mainstream of ordinary living.

Special Religious Education Division (SPRED)

The Catholic Archdiocese of Chicago initiated a Special Religious Education Division (SPRED) in 1962 in response to the diocesan concern for this ministry. With more than 72 SPRED centres in the Chicago area, religious services are made available to the developmentally disabled of all ages and SPRED, through contacts throughout the United States, provides a national support service for special education programmes and catechesis education. Through SPRED, catechesis trainees can now obtain full university accreditation.

Yad Voezer (Helping Hand)

The Jewish Orthodox Community has given rise to the formation, in the 1970s, of an organization called Yad Voezer (Helping Hand). This group caters for Orthodox members of the Jewish community who have either physical handicaps or mental handicaps. According to Lant, *'Whenever possible, the emphasis has been on drawing the disabled out of isolation and into the community. Typical is the Jewish society for the mentally handicapped 'Home from Hospital' campaign which aims to reintroduce suitable patients from mental handicap institutions into communal life'* (Lant, 1981).

St. Joseph's Centre, London

The Catholic Diocese of Westminster which includes all of London north of the Thames has set up a pastoral office for handicapped people called St. Joseph's Centre. The centre, under the direction of Fr. David Wilson, has three main areas of concern: the spiritual life of people with handicaps; helping parishes to understand and to accept their responsibilities towards handicapped people and their families; and providing the resources, through the centre to do this work. *'The main way parishes are helped is through training lay volunteers who get to know the families with a handicapped member, and also those*

who live in residential facilities of one sort or
another. It is like a befriending scheme'
(Wilson, 1983).

The World Council of Churches

The World Council of Churches has exerted a
significant influence among member churches in the
maintenance of meaningful discussions on the place
of the disabled in the Church. One example of the
recommendations of the World Council was that:

> *The churches should examine their practices
> to ensure that their treatment of the handi-
> capped is such as to manifest the nature of
> the Kingdom to men in the world. And they
> should make sure that it is not only doctrin-
> ally, but also practically possible for the
> handicapped to participate as fully as they
> are able in the life of our congregations.
> They should allow the handicapped and their
> needs to share in setting the tone of church
> life, as they certainly did of Jesus' minis-
> try.* (Moede, 1971)

THE NATURE OF THE CHURCH

At the present time, churches are engaging in
radical thinking concerning the fundamental nature
of religion itself. This rethinking is sometimes
rather too simplistically characterized in terms
of a *return to basics - let's get back to the
Bible.* Certainly this is one aspect of the
rethinking and it is undoubtedly an important
aspect. But in the same way that a driver who
sets out to drive from Vancouver to Toronto
staying overnight at Calgary and Winnipeg would
find it unproductive to imagine on the morning
that he sets out on the last stage of his journey,
from Winnipeg to Toronto, that he is really
starting all over again from Vancouver, it is
counter-productive to expound the view that the
Church should, as it were, start all over again
from the beginning of its historical journey. The
Church must move onwards from where it is, not
from where it was two thousand years ago. Religion, in the 1980s, is a complex multifaceted
aspect of life in Western society and its evolution through the ages, with all the philosophical

and theological strands of which it now comprises, must be taken into account and utilized to the full in the forthcoming development. Indeed, the true nature of the Church as it relates to people with handicaps is already being clearly defined by a number of writers who have a special commitment to people with handicaps. Wilson points out that the Church is not made up of articulate, mature, highly organized people seeking to help others but that it is, instead, a community seeking to integrate within itself the weak and the inadequate as well as the strong and active. Wilson writes, '... *she (the Church) is the gathering together of the competent and the incompetent (and who is to say which is which?), in such a way as to be the sign of unity for mankind as a whole*' (Wilson, 1975).

Bach expressed a similar view somewhat more critically. He describes the Church, the Body of Christ, as being the opposite of the rehabilitation model. Bach sees rehabilitation in terms of incorporating people who are in some sense 'not normal' into ordinary society. He says:

> *The Body of Christ, on the contrary, means this: the blind eight-year-old girl is already a member of the Body of Christ and does not have to become one. The weak members are already members of the Body of Christ. The only question is whether we act accordingly.* (Bach, 1981)

Yet the challenge of normalization (Wolfensberger, 1972) is to ensure that the individual is enabled, as far as possible, to lead as normal a life as possible. That this requires training, adaptation of facilities, and successive attempts to integrate a person into the society in which he wishes to partake sets particular challenges and goals for the Church.

WHETHER WE ACT ACCORDINGLY: RELIGION AND REHABILITATION IN ACTION

In this chapter there has been a review of the commitment to disabled persons which is found in the Gospels and which may be traced in the earliest writings of the principal religions. The impact of some congregations founded early in the last century has been sketched briefly; the educational and pastoral work for the disabled of several present day groups has been sketched in outline. The radical review of the fundamental nature of the Church itself with particular regard to the place of disabled persons within the church brings us to the important question: are there examples of communities which bear witness to the truth that disabled people and those with ability are full equal joint members of the Church with no trace of a spiritual aspect of the doctor and patient relationship?

L'Arche Communities

Jean Vanier founded L'Arche movement in August, 1964, in the village of Trosly-Breuil, in France (Clarke, 1974; Vanier, 1979, 1982a, 1982b; Allier, 1982; Dunne, 1986a). L'Arche is the French word for *The Ark* and its choice as a name for the community and for the movement symbolizes Noah's Ark, a place of refuge, a community of great variety, and the gift of hope (Clarke, 1974). L'Arche Communities exemplify the inspiration of religion leading people to live together, in equality, pursuing the search for healing relationships; some of the people are staff, known as assistants, and some of the people have handicaps. Vanier describes the objective:

> *Our aim is not just to have Christian assistants bound together in Christian love to 'look after' the weak and the poor. Our goal is to live in community with handicapped men and women, to create bonds with them and thus to discover their pathetic call. It is to create a community where handicapped people are fully members ... this unity in community between assistants and handicapped people is the heart and essence of L'Arche.* (Vanier, 1982a)

Among the unique strengths of L'Arche movement must be counted its ecumenical development, for the communities now include Christians of every denomination as well as Hindus, Muslims, and others (Philippe, 1982; Sadler, 1982; Vanier, 1982b); and the depth of the appreciation and expression of the difficulties, struggle and even pain which are necessarily involved for the assistants in their everyday work, sharing intimately

227

with such handicapped and damaged brethren (Mosteller, 1982; Vanier, 1982b).

Therese Vanier makes the following comment on the priorities of the communities:

> *Religious, philosophical and theological reflection and discussion take second place in our communities to the actual business of trying to live together. This order of priorities is not necessarily something to be proud of but it is a fact and, I believe, a fact on which we can build. This is our challenge.* (Vanier, 1982)

Saint-Macary (1982) describes the evolution and development of the administrative and management structures which are utilized by L'Arche Communities. Although he describes the principles underlying the structures and gives useful insights into decision-making strategies, Saint-Macary's work shares with many of L'Arche writers an attractive tentativeness, an appealing openness and an impression of searching rather than that of presenting solutions. He says:

> *We still have a long way to go to find structures that are truly for community living. In my seven years at L'Arche, I have learned that it is better to have imperfect structures that are adapted to reality than to try to apply the perfect plans which are only in our heads. We must strive to remain free, always eager to perfect and adapt structures for they are indispensable instruments of growth in the community. Our search has only begun.* (Saint-Macary, 1982)

The Botton Village Community, North Yorkshire, England

Very different from L'Arche Community, though nonetheless committed to the pursuit of Christian community involving a sharing of the lives of co-workers and villagers, is the Botton Village Community near Danby in North Yorkshire. Founded by Carol Konig in 1955, the village houses 300 people (200 villagers and 100 co-workers and their families). The co-workers subscribe to the ideological motivation of Rudolf Steiner's Anthroposophy, although the many services and seminars

are entirely optional and, indeed, some villagers
and co-workers attend the Church of England church
at Danby. The villagers at Botton have handicaps
such as mongolism, autism, brain damage, mental
handicap, and emotional periods of depression and
rage. The Botton Village Community refuses to
admit people who need constant medical attention.
The twin emphases of the community life of the
village are the religious dimension with its
service entitled the Act of Consecration of Man
with mystical, symbolic Eastern influences
together with a ritualistic attention to particular colours and a special reference to numbers
and numerology; and, secondly, its emphasis on
self-sufficiency, farming being the most important
village industry producing all the meat and dairy
needs and most of its vegetable requirements
(Gaylord, 1974).

The Chemin d'Esperance Community

The Chemin d'Esperance (The Way of Hope) Community, based at Arnes, France, is a non-residential
community serving children and adults with physical disabilities and with mental handicap;
membership is open to non-handicapped people as
well. Founded by Michel Mille in 1965, with a
view to the provision of specialized catechesis
for people with handicaps in the diocese of Arras,
the movement quickly gave rise to the desire to
form a basic Christian community giving priority
to relationships, the welcoming of others, and the
fundamental sharing of the daily experiences of
life within the full meaning of the Christian
faith. According to Devestel:

> *The community sets great store upon a clear
> vision of the human experiences. The small
> daily happenings of people which usually go
> unnoticed are dwelt upon by the community.
> The members are invited to examine these
> events in the light of Christian principles.
> The resulting Christian perceptions and
> attitudes are not confined to the family
> circle but take on a social dimension through
> a sharing of faith with the members of the
> community ... finally, it is noteworthy that
> the community abides whole-heartedly by the
> principle of personalization in the pastoral
> sense.* (Devestel, 1982)

229

The Fraternity of Cluizel

While the communities mentioned so far have in common their living witness of the true place of the handicapped in religion, it might be asked whether any religious group has taken seriously the prospect that handicapped people including people with mental handicaps might wish to actually join Religious Orders living a life in keeping with the religious vows: chastity, poverty and obedience.

The Fraternity of Cluizel at St-Pierre-la-Balud, Lyon, France, exemplifies movement in this direction. Here, men and women from different religious congregations have come together with people who have mental handicap and they live together a life patterned upon religious discipline. The mentally handicapped adults are asked to understand the meaning of religious life insofar as they can: supported by a Christian attitude and inspiration they may not marry and must live simply and dedicate themselves to the service of God (Devestel, 1982). While these adults with mental handicap live like Brothers, they do not actually formally take religious vows but this novel initiative is a significant step and this young community, founded in 1975, may well represent a particular breakthrough in the recognition of the true place of handicapped people in religion.

CONCLUSION AND IMPLICATIONS

The principal implication of this chapter for religion and those motivated by religion may be stated quite simply. Using a religious phraseology we may say, many of us and many of our brothers and sisters have wounds, physical wounds and mental wounds; we ourselves do not want to be set aside and we do not want to have things done to us or for us; neither should we set aside or do things for or to our own wounded brethren. What we want and what our brothers and sisters want is meaningful relationships in which we can grow and in which our brothers and sisters can grow with us. Any approach which sets us aside and marks us off as objects of pity or as objects suitable to be on the receiving end of *good works* will probably be hurtful and will be unlikely to make any contribution to any important area of rehabilitation.

This principle applies to the approach of the rehabilitation professional as well. Before the rehabilitation professional can prescribe or implement a particular programme with any individual he must first listen to the individual. And this listening must be broad and deep and sensitive. It involves an intimate sharing between client and professional of the desire and hope for growth and for self-fulfilment. Sometimes, because of handicap, the client may not be able to speak or communicate his or her hopes, and this will call for even greater sensitivity on the part of the professional. Dunne (1986b) discusses the implications of this principle for existing mental handicap institutions. Following Reppucci (1973), Dunne argues the importance of developing the philosophy of the institution in conjunction with all of the members of the institution, handicapped as well as staff. A further issue arises: the need for both group and individual advocacy based on the individual's wishes, a role which church authorities and members might well adopt.

It is sometimes argued that people who have severe mental handicaps or mental illness should not be considered eligible to receive the sacraments. A clear implication of this chapter is that every church member is precisely that, a full church member with all of the entitlements and privileges associated with church membership, certainly including the right to receive sacraments. Kelly (1986) states the case particularly well with reference to people who have mental handicap. He says:

> *The reality of the sacraments is the meeting with Christ, the knowledge of Christ. I think that if we can begin to understand the sacraments in terms of relationship and encounter then we can begin to understand why the person with a mental handicap has no great problem both in receiving and living the sacramental life.* (Kelly, 1986)

Finally, the crucial implication of this chapter is that we have as much to learn and to benefit from the person who is in need of rehabilitation as he or she has from us. Jean Vanier states it beautifully:

> *The poor person is a prophet. He challenges*
> *us to change, to adopt a new style of life.*
> *He invites us to live relationship, celebra-*
> *tion, sharing and forgiveness. The rich*
> *person ... may be competent, enlightened,*
> *intelligent; he may have developed his powers*
> *of reasoning and of efficiency, but his heart*
> *is underdeveloped, atrophied. Is he perhaps*
> *afraid of it? This heart to heart relation-*
> *ship is neither sentimentality nor a passing*
> *emotion, neither is it romanticism nor a*
> *sexual experience. It is a deep encounter, a*
> *commitment, a sharing, a real concern for the*
> *other. It consists of gentleness, of*
> *strength, of trust in the other and of*
> *recognition of his gifts.*(Vanier, 1985)

REFERENCES

Allier, H. (1982) 'A Place of Human Growth,' in *The Challenge of L'Arche*, Darton, Longman & Todd, London.

Bach, E. (1981) *Partners in the Family of God*, World Council of Churches, Geneva.

Clarke, B. (1974) *Enough Room for Joy: Jean Vanier's L'Arche: A Message for our Time*, Darton, Longman & Todd, London.

Colston, L. G. (1978) *Pastoral Care with Handicapped Persons*, Fortress Press, Philadelphia.

Devestel, F. (1982) 'A Pastoral Approach to Mentally Handicapped Adults Living in an Institutional Setting,' Unpublished doctoral thesis, The Salesian Pontifical University, Rome.

Donovan, N. M. (1979) *Apostolate of Love: Mary Aikenhead, 1787-1858, Foundress of the Irish Sisters of Charity*, Polding Press, Melbourne.

Dunne, J. (1986a) 'Sense of Community in L'Arche and in the Writings of Jean Vanier,' *Journal of Community Psychology, 14*, 41-54.

Dunne, J. (1986b) 'A Radical Philosophy for Mental Handicap Services,' in P. McGinley (ed.), *Research and Practice in the Service of People with Learning Difficulties*, Woodlands Centre, Galway, Ireland.

Gaylord, R. (1974) *Village Communities for the Handicapped*, Polytechnic, Handicapped Persons Research Unit, Newcastle-upon-Tyne.

Gold, R. A. (1981) 'Judaism and Persons with Handicaps,' *Documencap, 15,* p. 9.

Hauerwas, S. (1974) *Vision and Virtue: Essays in Christian Ethical Reflection,* Fides Publications Inc., Notredame, Indiana.

Heifetz, L. J. & Franklin, D. C. (1982) 'Nature and Sources of the Clergy's Involvement with Mentally Retarded Persons and Their Families,' *American Journal on Mental Deficiency, 87*(1), 56-63.

Jones, A. (1961) *God's Living Word,* Chapman, London.

Jones, A. (ed.) (1966) *The Jerusalem Bible,* Doubleday, Garden City, New York.

Kelly, B. D. (1986) *An Introduction to the Pastoral Care of People with a Mental Handicap - Church, Growth in Faith and Sacraments,* Lisieux Hall, Whittle-le-Woods, Chorley, Lancashire, England.

Kung, H. (1980) *Does God Exist? An Answer for Today,* translated by E. Quinn, Collins, London.

Lant, B. (1981) 'The Jewish Community and Mental Handicap,' *Documencap, 16,* 13-15 (published by St. Joseph's Centre, Diocese of Westminster).

Moede, G. F. (1971) *The Unity of the Church and Handicapped in Society,* World Council of Churches Working Document, SE/17, 7(4), p. 5.

Mosteller, S. (1982) 'Living With,' in *The Challenge of L'Arche,* Darton, Longman & Todd, London.

Myles, L. (1981) 'Some Historical Notes on Religions, Ideologies and the Handicapped,' *Al-Mushir (The Counsellor), 23*(4), 125-134.

Offner, C. B. & Van Straelen, H. (1963) *Modern Japanese Religions with Special Emphasis upon their Doctrines of Healing,* J. Brill, Leiden.

Philippe, T. (1982) 'Communities of the Beatitudes,' in *The Challenge of L'Arche,* Darton, Longman & Todd, London.

Reichgelt, G. J. (1957) *The Brothers of Charity 1: 1807-1880,* Brothers of Charity Central Administration, Rome.

Reppucci, N. D. (1973) 'Social Psychology of Institutional Change: General Principles for Intervention,' *American Journal of Community Psychology, 1,* 330-341.

Sadler, C. (1982) 'Rhythms of Life,' in *The Challenge of L'Arche,* Darton, Longman & Todd, London.

Saint-Macary, A. (1982)   'In Search of New
     Structures,' in *The Challenge of L'Arche*,
     Darton, Longman & Todd, London.
Stubblefield, H. W. (1975)   'The Ministry and
     Mental Retardation,' in J. J. Dempsey (ed.),
     *Community Services for Retarded Children:
     The Consumer Provider Relationship*, Univers-
     ity Park Press, Baltimore.
Vanier, J. (1979)   *Community and Growth*, Darton,
     Longman & Todd, London.
Vanier, J. (1982a)   'Introduction,' in *The
     Challenge of L'Arche*, Darton, Longman & Todd,
     London.
Vanier, J. (1982b)   'A Struggle for Unity,' in *The
     Challenge of L'Arche*, Darton, Longman & Todd,
     London.
Vanier, J. (1985)   'Blessed are the Poor,' *The
     Way*, *25*(2), 112-121.
Wilkie, H. H. (1980)   *Creating the Caring
     Congregation: Guidelines for Ministering
     with the Handicapped*, Abingdon, Nashville,
     USA.
Wilson, D. (1975)   'The Church, the Eucharist and
     the Mentally Handicapped,' *The Clergy Review*,
     60(2), p. 69-84.
Wilson, D. (1983)   'St. Joseph's Centre,'
     Documencap, *15*, p. 1 (published by St.
     Joseph's Centre, Diocese of Westminster).
Wolfensberger, W. (1972)   *Normalization: The
     Principle of Normalization in Human Services*,
     National Institute of Mental Retardation,
     Toronto.

Chapter Eleven

HOW COMPUTER LEARNING TECHNOLOGY CAN ENHANCE QUALITY OF LIFE

Kenneth A. Ryba

INTRODUCTION

Much has been written recently about the new technological advances which have occurred in the education of disabled children and adults. The rapid developments and the immediate effects these have had on people's lives can appropriately be described as a modern day technological and information revolution. Most of what has been written has focused on the technology and how to apply it to overcome the effects of disability (Rostron & Sewell, 1984; Hawkridge, Vincent & Hales, 1985). Rather less has been said about how people can use the technology as an extension of their intelligence and as a means of strengthening human relationships.

In this chapter attention will be given to describing how people can make use of the technology as an extension of themselves to improve the quality of their lives. Examples are given to illustrate the facilitating effects of technology with regard to applications that improve communication and learning. The focus in this chapter is upon both the cognitive and affective development of the person rather than upon the technical hardware and software. Here, the experiences of people with various disabilities are documented in order to illustrate how using computers has enhanced the quality of their lives.

A recurring theme in this chapter is that quality of life is determined by the way in which a society treats its disabled members. Fortunately, over the past few decades there has been a considerable change in outlook toward the human and legal rights of handicapped people. These changes are reflected in the emergence of such concepts as deinstitutionalization, normalization, integration and mainstreaming. Taking account of these trends, it is advanced that technology can be used to translate these humanitarian principles into practical improvements to the quality of people's lives.

Within the special education field in particular, there has been a world-wide movement to meet individual needs. Several countries, notably the United Kingdom, Sweden and the United States, have put legislation into effect which provides for the right of all children to gain access to free and appropriate education. A significant feature of this legislation is the decision to integrate children with special needs into the educational mainstream. However, the ability to integrate these children will require a full range of resources sufficient to identify and meet the individual, educational, personal, cultural and social needs of every child.

New computer technology is highly relevant to the present focus on meeting individual needs. The flexibility and capability of modern microelectronics, along with reasonable cost, are factors which make it possible now to adapt computers and associated devices to meet particular needs. For example, a variety of input switches (e.g. tongue switch, joystick, puff/sip) can be interfaced with microcomputers to enable disabled persons to input information and interact with programmes in the same way as non-disabled persons do. With the proper design, a person can comfortably and efficiently control all of the microcomputer's functions with a simplified switching device. This, in turn, means that learning can become easier and more accessible in the technical mode than would be the case with conventional teaching methods.

With the ever increasing range of computer software now available, there are usually some applications which can meet individual needs without the necessity of writing new programmes. For instance, conventional word processing packages can be modified for use by blind operators using synthetic speech output. Educational programmes designed for helping young children to develop their thinking skills (e.g. LOGO programming and simulations) may be relevant for use with special education students. Business oriented programmes such as databases and spreadsheets have important educational and personal applications for communication and record keeping. The accessibility of computers by disabled persons means that they can have access to all of these new learning tools.

In the first text of this series, the central theme was upon the provision of integrated programmes for handicapped adolescents and adults (Brown, 1984). This stressed that research in the field of rehabilitation education must integrate with other political and social forces if it is to be effectively applied. Following this theme, the view advanced here is that computers and other forms of technology will need to be fully integrated into the lives of handicapped persons. In this regard, the most effective applications will be those that provide individuals with the capability to extend themselves in all areas of vocational, home living, social and leisure pursuits.

The extent to which computers can be integrated into these major life areas will depend upon the development of new software tools. At present, each area usually requires its own separate device and supporting software (e.g. education, communication, control of the environment). More recently, however, new software applications have combined six or more functions into a single integrated software package. The Trace Center in Madison, Wisconsin, is currently conducting a project to adapt an IBM programme called TOPVIEW for use by handicapped persons. Topview is a control programme that permits a set of independent programmes to run simultaneously on an IBM personal computer (Scott, 1986). For example, a physically disabled person could use the same computer programmes to send electronic mail, order library books, turn on lights and heat, and update his business diary! Such developments are a pointer to the integral role that computers will have as a means of enhancing life quality in the future.

Despite these new developments, however, the extent to which computers become integrated into the life of handicapped people will depend to a large extent on prevailing social, political and educational forces. For this reason, it is useful to understand some of the current social trends and philosophical foundations that have guided the application of technology in the rehabilitation education field to this point.

LINKING TECHNOLOGY WITH LIFE QUALITY

Over the past few decades, there have been some important fundamental changes in the social outlook toward handicapped people. It is partly as a result of these positive humanitarian changes that technology has emerged as a powerful tool for developing human potential.

In this section, attention is given to three interrelated concepts, including:

1) the development of rehabilitation education;
2) the humanitarian principle of normalization; and
3) the concept of respect for persons.

The reason for dealing with these three concepts together is that they seem to provide a foundation for integrating computer technology into the lives of handicapped persons. Moreover, they stress the central role of the handicapped person in acquiring skills to participate effectively in community life.

Rehabilitation Education has been previously defined by Brown (1984) as: *'the treatment and training of individuals through the intervention of a variety of social and psychological strategies to improve the learning and performance of handicapped persons'*. There are three important elements of this definition that need to be highlighted here. First, emphasis is placed upon the capability of individuals to effectively maintain themselves in a quality lifestyle within society. Second, intervention is seen as being part of a transdisciplinary process involving knowledge from such disciplines as psychology, education and social work. Third, it implies a noncategorical approach to treatment which is relevant to all levels of handicap and types of handicapping conditions (Brown, 1984). Viewed in this way, rehabilitation education is a positive process which involves the development of adaptive behaviours and skills that will enhance a person's ability to function effectively in society.

The emphasis on life quality and personal effectiveness contained in the rehabilitation education definition is in accord with the concept of normalization first advanced by Nirje (1969) and then by Wolfensberger in 1972. According to this principle, all handicapped persons, regardless of the extent and type of their disability, should be accorded a measure of human and legal rights commensurate with the level and range of rights normally accorded to non-handicapped in any given society. While the philosophical basis for and the implications of this normalization concept might be debated, there is at least one implication that has been implemented. That is, as a humanitarian principle, normalization requires that handicapped persons be accorded respect in their own right. In practice, this latter concept of respect entails that individuals be given access to the learning resources they require to maintain themselves in a quality lifestyle within society.

Respect for persons is indeed fundamental to normalization and to the desire to provide appropriate forms of education for people with special needs. Computer technology presents one powerful way for achieving this respect through the facility it provides for handicapped persons to exercise greater control than is customary over their own learning. If, however, the microcomputer is really to provide handicapped persons with personal control, and presumably opportunities for personal development, then learning must be conceived of as a process in which the learner is able to actively exercise a measure of control over the learning medium, and to make decisions and to take responsibility for their own actions.

My own research with computers has very much been influenced by the work of Seymour Papert (1980), who strongly advocates for the right of learners to gain control over technology. Papert, the creator of the LOGO educational computing language, believes that, by learning to programme the computer, children achieve mastery over modern technology and, in so doing, learn to direct and develop their own thinking processes. He further suggests that care should be taken to avoid over-subscribing to computer assisted programmed instruction as this defeats the ability of the child to control his/her learning. Instead, Papert argues that we should give children the tools they need (word processors, telecommunications) *'to become more like adults, indeed like advanced professionals, in their relationship to their intellectual products and to themselves'* (Papert, 1980).

Such a view of technology is significant in that it reflects a philosophy about the nature of

239

education and the nature of how people learn to become independent thinkers. It focuses on the capabilities of the person rather than on his/her limitations and attempts to illustrate how computers can be integrated into everyday life as an extension of the learner's own intelligence. With handicapped persons in particular, computer technology provides a means of extending and developing themselves in all the major areas of life - educationally, recreationally, vocationally, socially, emotionally. Thus, when used in appropriate ways as an object to think with, computers can have a profound effect upon the style and quality of life that a person enjoys.

In discussing these personal control aspects of technology, it is important to distinguish between the use of computers for instruction and their use for learning. When employed for instruction, the locus of control rests with the computer programme which has been constructed to guide the student through a fixed instructional sequence in some subject area (e.g. telling time, basic arithmetic). In effect, the student is locked into the sequence and has relatively little freedom to make decisions or deviate from the instructional format. Such instruction often depends more on the machine's capabilities than it does on the student's knowledge. On the other hand, with a learning tool application, the locus of control shifts from the machine to the user such that the machine becomes an extension of the user's intelligence.

Both instruction and learning applications exploit the microcomputer as an educational resource. In both cases, however, the use of the microcomputer is educationally defensible only in so far as it leads handicapped persons toward the development of intelligent capacities rather than the mere formation of conditioned responses. The distinction between computer assisted instruction on the one hand and computer learning tools on the other is not simply a technical choice between one approach or another. Rather, as Papert (1980) has noted, it reflects a fundamental difference in views on the nature of childhood and on the nature of the teaching/learning process. Papert has pointed out that care must be taken not to *infantilize* children through the expectation that they are only capable of being instructed by computers. There is ample evidence now to indicate that, when given access to computers and appropriate enabling software, children are able to fully exploit the computer as an educational resource in such areas as word processing, data analysis, programming and telecommunications.

This word of caution needs to be heeded also by rehabilitation workers who may unintentionally *infantilize* handicapped students through the use of childish learning materials (early childhood books and teaching methods). The use of age inappropriate materials can have an adverse effect on a learner's performance and motivation. By way of contrast, some types of educational computing programmes (e.g. adventures and reading games) provide a learning medium that is suitably designed and motivating for older persons. The provision of relevant learning resources such as computer technology is but one way of respecting the personal needs, desires and interests of the user. If, with the aid of technology, handicapped persons are to generally be accorded respect, then they must be seen as having an essential view-point, as being capable of valuation and choice, capable of making decisions and able to partici-pate in determining the ways in which they might employ the available technology to enhance the quality of their lives.

There has now been ample demonstration of how the lives of handicapped persons can be enhanced through providing them with access to a full range of computer learning tools. Now, more than ever before, computer technology has a crucial role to play in liberating handicapped persons from restrictions imposed by their developmental dis-abilities. In the next section of this chapter, attention is given to actual experiences of people who have used the technology in various ways as an extension of themselves. In accordance with the concepts of rehabilitation education, normaliz-ation and respect for persons, emphasis is placed on software tools that can be controlled and employed by the user for personal development.

QUALITY OF LIFE EXPERIENCES

This section describes the experiences various persons have had in using computer technology as a learning and communication tool. In keeping with the theme of individuals being able to control and apply technology as an extension of themselves, the examples here are presented to illustrate how computers can enhance the lifestyle and personal effectiveness of handicapped persons.

LOGO As a Learning Environment

With the arrival of computers in special education and rehabilitation, enthusiasm has been shown for the view that this technology could help to enhance the learning of handicapped persons. For example, Ryba and Chapman (1983) have described how computers can be used to improve learning strategies and personal adjustment of mentally retarded adults. Weir (1981) has illustrated some ways in which computer learning environments provide a versatile tool for diagnostic, instructional and remedial use with children who have a variety of learning handicaps, including dyslexia, cerebral palsy and autism. As Salomon and Gardner (1986) have pointed out, however, it is not the computer medium *per se* which accounts for gains in learning, but rather the methods and materials that are used in conjunction with the medium. While it is true that the interactive nature of a computer can engage a learner's attention, a computer can only support learning within the contexts set for it by educators and rehabilitation practitioners - theirs is the ultimate decision on how it will be used.

The use of LOGO as an enabling tool for handicapped students is a good example of how the context in which a computer is used can significantly affect learning outcomes. Originally designed for learning disabled students, LOGO is a high level procedural language that is extremely easy to master. In the LOGO environment, students learn how to programme the computer by directing the movements of a two-dimensional *turtle* that resides in the centre of the video screen. Through the use of 'turtle graphics' students learn to control the computer at the level of basic turtle commands by drawing shapes and designs, and at a more advanced level by creating geometric, animated pictures. Simplified versions of LOGO have been used successfully with mentally retarded students to help them learn to follow directions and master basic concepts. For example, the highly graphic and animated features of LOGO can be used to provide a realistic and concrete medium for learning directional concepts and basic reading skills. These outcomes can be accomplished by using some simple procedures that allow students to control the movements of the turtle using simplified keyboard commands such as 'F' for forward, 'B' for back and 'R' for turn. With this simple capability present, the learner is free to explore the commands to see if he or she can move the turtle where he or she wants it to go.

FIGURE 1: LOGO Turtle Graphics

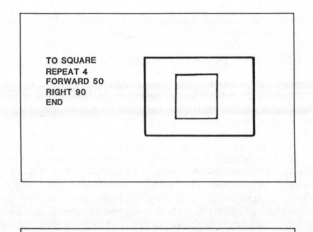

```
TO SQUARE
REPEAT 4
FORWARD 50
RIGHT 90
END
```

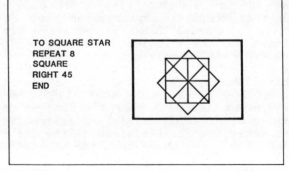

```
TO SQUARE STAR
REPEAT 8
SQUARE
RIGHT 45
END
```

The SQUARE STAR pattern is created by asking the turtle to REPEAT 8 times the commands to draw a SQUARE and turn RIGHT 45 degrees.

Emanuel and Weir (1976) described how the use of LOGO with a seven-year-old autistic child resulted in the onset of spontaneous language and the first active seeking out of social interaction by the child. Working with spastic students, Fung and McDougall (1984) have described how LOGO could be applied to help develop coordination, directional concepts and decision making. Franklin (1985) illustrated how LOGO was applied to systematically assess and develop cognitive and motor skills with a mentally retarded girl who had a limited memory and concentration span. A recurring theme in these examples is that the computer was used successfully as a medium for improving adaptive behaviour in areas of language development, cognitive processing and motor skills.

More recently, Nolan and Ryba (1986a) have developed a model for *Assessing Learning With LOGO*. The aim of this model is to provide educators with a systematic method of assessing and developing specific thinking skills (analysis, planning, self-evaluation, etc.) at each LOGO level. Assessment objectives, tasks and activities and checklists are used to monitor the development of each thinking skill. A study employing the model with junior high school students indicated that a group who were given LOGO learning opportunities outperformed a control group on most cognitive tasks after completion of training (Horton & Ryba, 1986). The suggestion here is that computer applications such as LOGO may provide a useful form of cognitive training for persons who are deficient in skills of logical thinking and problem-solving.

At the Cook Street Training Centre in Palmerston North, New Zealand, a simplified version of LOGO (E-Z LOGO, MECC, 1985) is being used in conjunction with peer tutoring to develop trainees' communication skills and selfconfidence. Adult trainees are first trained in the use of E-Z LOGO and then assigned to 'teach' individual children how to use the computer at a nearby special school. Following a structured sequence of activities, trainees guide the children through tasks that require them to identify the back and front of objects (directional concepts), navigate an obstacle course, and verbalize the movements of an object along a track. A noteworthy feature of the project is that trainees who were previously performing unskilled, repetitive work (assembling nuts and bolts, rolling newspaper) were able to

become competent learners and teachers with a
modest amount of training. Trainees' self reports
indicate that they receive more personal satisfaction from working with computers and tutoring
others than from performing routine vocational
tasks. Here, the computer was used as a vehicle
to facilitate learning and development of adaptive
behaviours. A related point is that, rather than
being instructed and controlled by the computer,
these moderately mentally retarded adults were in
charge of the technology and used it in a purpose-
ful way to increase their social and academic
competence.

Computer Games Aid Adaptive Behaviour

There is evidence now to suggest that self-
directed activities such as computer games, LOGO
and word processing are rather more likely to
promote cognitive development than traditional
classroom applications of computer assisted
instruction. In our own research, for instance,
we have watched with interest as mentally retarded
adults struggle at the outset to understand the
rules of computer games and then advance over a
series of trials to master the programme objectives and achieve scores that would make them the
envy of any game parlour habitue (Ryba & Chapman,
1983). Observations of these trainees' behaviour
indicate the development of a new range of skills,
including planning, anticipating various events,
sequencing left and right, executing combinations
of movements (e.g. moving a cursor and 'shooting'
at targets), shifting attention to different
relevant cues and increasing motor speed and
coordination.

The practical suggestion arising from these
observations of trainees' computer performance is
that games may provide a vehicle for helping them
to develop certain functional skills. A case
study serves to illustrate this point. Mary Anne,
a 25-year-old mentally retarded woman, was unres-
ponsive to psychological testing to the extent
that she was unable to verbalize or follow
instructions as required by the test. Accord-
ingly, she was labelled as severely retarded and
unlikely to benefit from formal training. A few
weeks later, however, we happened to catch a
glimpse of Mary Anne during one of her regular
sessions on the computer and noted her obvious

on-task behaviour. She was playing a space invaders type game and appeared able to understand the requirements of the task. A closer examination revealed that she was able to purposefully interact with the game by moving the cursor left or right to avoid collisions, 'firing' at moving objects, and making judgments concerning the order in which operations should be performed (Ryba & Chapman, 1983).

An important observation from this case study was the apparent incongruence between Mary Anne's performance in the testing situation versus her performance when interacting with the computer. Clearly, some aspects of her abilities might be underestimated on the basis of test results, whereas her actual performance in a real life situation using the computer indicated a much higher functioning level. This raises the point that computer technology may have an important role to play in assessing and training handicapped persons in various cognitive, interpersonal and motor skills.

Other research has demonstrated that performance on the computerized game Simon (Milton Bradley Corporation) is highly associated with established cognitive measures (Ryba & Chapman, 1984). In this study, mentally retarded adults were first taught how to play the game. This required them to reproduce a sequence of colour-sound combinations from memory. Their game skill was then assessed along with performance on memory, coding and motor coordination tasks. Results indicated that ability to play Simon was moderately to highly correlated with IQ estimates derived from the Stanford Binet and Wechsler Scales and motor performance. One practical suggestion arising from this finding is that the highly motivating and interactive nature of such games may be relevant for training in specific cognitive skills in such areas as attending, memory, directional concepts, following instructions, sequencing and motor coordination.

Interest has also been shown in the possibility that simulations and adventure games may be useful for developing students' thinking skills. Several observational studies have confirmed the value of games and adventures as a medium for facilitating reading comprehension, language development, communication skills, problem-solving and creative expression. The decision-making requirement of adventure games encourages learners to verbalize about what ought to be entered into the computer. Here, an environment is provided in which students can learn high-order social-cognitive skills involving resolution, cooperation and consultation. In this regard, Henderson-Lancett and Boesen (1986) have proposed that adventure games provide a framework in which purposive discussion can occur about the task at hand and the content of these discussions encourages metacognition, or thinking about what they are thinking.

The effectiveness of computer games as a form of cognitive therapy for persons recovering from brain injuries has been amply demonstrated by Lynch (1981). Working at the Veteran's Administration Hospital, Palo Alto, California, Lynch has systematically studied the use of various computer games for aiding recovery in several cognitive areas, including spatial orientation, hand-eye coordination, memory and reflexes. Other research by Okoye (cited in Lynch, 1982) has also suggested that sensory integration skills of learning disabled children can be significantly improved through interaction with certain types of video games. Taken together, these studies suggest that the highly structured and interactive nature of computers may be used to help improve information processing strategies. It is interesting then to speculate on what essential features of computers promote learning.

The Microworld Concept

One interesting theoretical explanation for the effectiveness of self-directed learning activities (e.g. LOGO and computer games) is based on the concept of a *microworld*. Essentially, a microworld is an environment where individuals can immerse themselves in a bounded place, with rules to operate by and where exploration takes place. The concept of the microworld was first advanced by Minsky and Papert (1972) to describe the restricted world in which artificial intelligence programmes operate. Subsequently, the concept was extended to explain the characteristics of learning environments in which children with learning difficulties could effectively operate (Adams, 1986). Papert, the inventor of LOGO, has described a microworld as *'a subset of reality... whose structure provides an environment where learner's cognitive mechanisms can operate effectively. The concept leads to the project of inventing microworlds so structured as to allow a human learner to exercise particular powerful ideas or intellectual skills'* (Papert, 1980).

Working with the microworld concept, Sherry Turkle (1985) relates the story of Deborah, an adolescent girl who is described as withdrawn, lacking self-confidence, explosive and overweight, dependent and unhappy. Deborah, who participated in a school LOGO programme when she was 11 years old, was shown how to draw pictures on the screen by giving commands to the turtle. Turkle describes how, at the commencement of the programme, Deborah spent most of her time trying to get the attention of the teacher and making little progress without supervision and support from others. Deborah changed when she restricted the power of her environment by placing an arbitrary rule that would allow her only one turning command, a right turn of 90 degrees.

> *Once she had her rule, Deborah got down to serious work. She drew flowers and rabbits and stars and abstract designs, everything built up from right turns of thirty degrees. 'I really liked my rule. It was neat. It was hard. I had to figure everything out. I thought about it all the time. I was the only one who had a rule.' Suddenly, she found herself, perhaps for the first time, in a situation simple enough for her to control, yet varied enough to allow for creative exploration.* (Turkle, 1985)

A significant feature of Deborah's microworld was that it provided a place where she could take control of the computer and use it to experience success through the achievement of personally valued goals. As Turkle points out, computers are not an essential component of microworlds. Other noncomputer microworlds, like chess, sports, literature and mathematics, are all places which contain boundaries in which a person can operate effectively once he or she learns the rules.

The microworld concept is a significant way of understanding how computers can be applied to enhance the learning and quality of life of handicapped people. Here, the person uses the technology as an extension of themselves to operate effectively within subsets of the real world. The following case study illustrates how this concept can be applied in practice.

> *Joe, a Ph.D. student with quadriplegia, used a word processor to prepare research reports. In the word processing microworld, Joe could write by means of voice input and make full use of the editing and processing features provided. Using the syntax 'rules' he could move and delete text, copy important points to remember onto a note pad, print out drafts on hardcopy, and experiment with different tabulations and margins, etc. until he was satisfied that the final product was of a high standard. The computer also provided Joe with a telecommunications link (StarNet) to the outside world. Here, he was able to send and receive letters from his friends, leave a message on the bulletin board to invite people to join his new teleconference on rehabilitation education, and send a copy of his revised research report to his Ph.D. supervisor. Joe could also access remote databases and other electronic microworlds to check for recent research articles and order abstracts directly via computer from overseas.*

Other examples as well could be provided to illustrate the range of microworlds that are currently available and how these can be integrated into lives of handicapped persons.

The term microworld is not just another way of describing a set of computing tools. Rather, the microworld concept is used here to denote the interaction between intelligent systems (artificial intelligence) and human intelligence. In this regard, microworlds enable handicapped persons to draw upon resources from the surrounding culture and to use these resources as an extension of themselves. The opportunity to learn how to use resources effectively is not only at the very heart of the rehabilitation education process, but in accord with the humanitarian principles of normalization and respect for persons.

In technologically advanced societies, it is increasingly desirable to teach handicapped persons of all ages how to learn and how to access and manage information rather than to focus on the teaching of skills that may rapidly become obsolete. In this regard, microworld learning environments provide a place where functional skills can be learned at each stage of human development. This is possible because the electronic microworlds are themselves adaptive to the requirements of the individual user.

The adaptive nature of microworlds is best illustrated through an examination of their main characteristics. These can be summarized briefly as:

1. A system that is easily accessible and yet extendable according to the requirements of the users. For example, mentally retarded adult tutors developed children's basic concepts (directions, shapes, word reading) use E-Z LOGO turtle graphics. A rehabilitation educator wrote an interactive game in LOGO to help trainees improve their motor speed (shooting at moving targets).
2. An environment that is highly structured but yet able to provide the learner with a chance to freely explore and develop his/her ideas. Deborah, for example, was able to use *her* rule to be creative (drawing pictures of flowers and stars, etc.) by restricting the movement of the turtle.
3. An interactive place that has pathways to various other microworlds that can be accessed as needed by the individual. For instance, the ability to move from a word processor to an electronic mail system is vitally important.
4. A bounded environment in which the individual can effectively operate using a set of absolute rules. Here, the rules are syntactic and conceptual in nature, providing a set of tools for efficient management of resources. For example, a menu driven word processor provides a logical place in which to save and retrieve information. A remote database asks precise questions and seeks precise answers to define the search parameters.
5. A (Piagetian) structure with certain additional properties, including (1) transformation which can be undone so that it is possible to go back to the previous state; and (2) maps (in the precise mathematical sense of the term) to other structures that are representations of concrete actions in the real world. For instance, the LOGO turtle can be controlled by procedures and

then returned to the basic turtle command mode. The procedures can, in turn, be mapped onto the real world by drawing with paper and pencil or by body movement (Groen, 1984).

The interactive and extendable nature of microworlds is particularly well illustrated through the use of robotics as a tool in education. The LEGO Corporation has recently announced the release of technics control kits (linking LEGO blocks, lights, motors and optical-sensor feedback devices with a computer). Using this system, children can create something with LEGO blocks and electronic components and then programme their creation using a variant of the LOGO language (Tatnell, 1986). Physically handicapped children, for example, can work jointly to construct a 'car' and then use a computer to write programmes that control its movements (forward, back, right and left). The advantage of this integrated LEGO-LOGO approach is that children who would otherwise be immobile are able to explore the meaning of such concepts as directions, speed, numbers and geometry. Perhaps more significantly, they have an environment which provides them with a chance to learn high-order social-cognitive skills involving resolution, cooperation and consultation. Through peer collaboration, children have a chance to explore and develop their ideas, to clarify their thoughts and to compare problem solving strategies.

In summary, highly integrated electronic microworlds such as those described above make it possible now to provide intelligent systems which go some considerable distance toward liberating handicapped persons from the limitations imposed by their various disabilities. Using the microworld concept, it is possible to provide places for personal development that are just not possible in the real world. At the same time, it is stressed that the person is experiencing some bounded, simplified part of the real world, rather than an artificial simulated world. The best and most effective microworlds are those that have an interface with real life through such applications as word processing, telecommunications and robotics. The possibilities for further development of microworlds are limitless and it will no doubt emerge as a major area of research in the near future.

FIGURE 2   Robotics as a Learning Tool

A child with cerebral palsy writes a LOGO computer programme to control a LEGO robot.

Productivity Tools

Much has already been said about the desirability of individuals being able to control computers and use them as an extension of themselves. The power of this personal control concept is particularly evident with productivity tool software - e.g. word processors, databases, electronic spreadsheets, and telecommunication systems. While the use of productivity tool software in business is now widespread, rather less attention has been given to personal applications, especially for handicapped persons. Importantly, productivity tools highlight the ways in which computers can be used to make short work of tasks requiring the manipulation of numbers and text. For example, it is doubtful if educators would argue about the value of being able to quickly and easily make substantial revisions in documents without cutting, pasting or erasing. Who would argue about being able to retrieve a desired name and address from a large database in a matter of seconds, or being able to manage one's personal budget or to exchange information with friends and colleagues without having to make physical marks on a physical paper? Some examples help to illustrate the specific benefits of productivity tools.

Vaughan, who has been blind from birth, is currently enrolled in the first year of a B.S.W. degree programme at a New Zealand university. Recently, he was able to obtain the use of a microcomputer to assist with his studies. Using a word processor interfaced with a speech synthesizer, Vaughan is able to write, save and edit text files which are spoken to him by the computer. He can also print out hard copies of the text or convert the text to braille using a special braille printer. For Vaughan, the main benefits of computer use are the privacy and independence it affords. No longer does he need to ask people to read for him when the computer is able to do this perfectly well. He can now take a leading role in tasks that would have been previously difficult or impossible for him. For example, as secretary of the local disabled persons advocacy group, he uses his computer to keep records of members' names and addresses and for sending notices to all members using either conventional text or braille. He can easily check his written work and can submit high quality typed reports that are at least as good as and perhaps better than the majority of those prepared by sighted students.

Andrew Hannah (1985) relates the story of how Tammy, a 9 year-old girl with cerebral palsy (spastic quadriplegia), used a computer as a learning tool.

> *Tammy, a nonverbal student with very poor hand function and moderately good head control, used the computer to develop language skills (reading and writing). She began by copying sentences and creating her own from pages of words previously written. She also used a picture/word matching programme and a spelling checker to strengthen her vocabulary. A 'rocket' programme was used to help develop Tammy's motor coordination and control of the computer. The computer offered Tammy educational opportunities she never had before. She is now able to complete a task by herself. With a simple chin movement, Tammy can select words to convey news and feeling. She is no longer reliant on a teacher to sit and work with her and is*

*able to communicate without the need of a
hand-held communication board.*

Edward and John are fifth form students
(Grade 10) who are using AppleWorks (TM) to
prepare a database on New Zealand birds. Building
the 'birds' database was an interesting decision-
making process. They needed to make decisions
about the kind of information to be collected for
each bird and how this should be represented in
the database. Decisions also had to be made about
the way birds should be chosen for the database,
and how the screen display for a single bird's
information should look. Once the database was
completed, Edward and John presented the project
to their classmates. A brainstorming session
followed and it produced such questions as:

- Do any introduced birds have Maori names?
- Are any native birds brightly coloured?
- Does habitat affect nesting place?
- Do birds that live in the bush all nest in
  trees?
- How does beak shape relate to food?

The ability to pose such questions shows the
students had moved beyond simple data retrieval to
a consideration of the relationships between
classes of data for all the birds in the database.
Here, the computer managed the data storage,
processing and retrieval, while the students were
free to engage in conceptual thinking (based in
part on a class project by Anderson, 1985).
It should be mentioned here that Edward is
one of a small group of deaf students who have
recently been mainstreamed into the regular school
programme. In this school, productivity tools are
used to facilitate integration of deaf students
through collaborative projects such as the one
described above. A significant aspect of this
teamwork is the opportunity it provides for
collaborative learning. Here, hearing and non-
hearing students have a common mission that is
based around interaction in the visual mode. They
have an environment which enables them to develop
and test their ideas.
It is no accident that all of the above
examples are concerned with equity of educational
opportunity. Given the very significant changes
in outlook toward the educational rights of handicapped persons, the search is on for methods and

resources that can be used to aid the integrative process. In this regard, productivity tools can be employed to provide a channel of communication and learning that would otherwise be unavailable. As Tatnell (1986) has noted, however, it is not just the availability of technological tools that is important, but rather how these are applied to allow for self development of the pupil. The provision for self development - opportunities for handicapped persons to improve their learning and performance - is the cornerstone of rehabilitation education.

It should be mentioned here that productivity tools not only enhance the learning of handicapped persons but can increase the effectiveness of educators and rehabilitation practitioners. This is accomplished through improved communication and by the removal of obstacles that previously interfered with the learning/teaching process. For example, the ability to store, process and retrieve information is likely to enhance personal effectiveness at all levels. Special purpose input and output devices (e.g. simplified keyboard, light pen, voice input, synthetic speech, braille print) mean that it is now possible to select preferred communication channels and to convert these from one form to another as required. The effect of all this is that education and training can be conducted in a form that is appropriate for the individual concerned. In this regard, technology has a crucial role to play in making education more accessible to handicapped persons.

With the advent of computer-based telecommunications, a whole new range of productivity tools have recently come available. It is possible now for an individual to shop and bank, attend university, read the latest news reports, check the latest professional journals, order library books, and do their written work on a microcomputer at home. The existence of new electronic information systems such as CompuServe in the United States, Envoy 100 in Canada and StarNet in New Zealand makes it possible for individuals at home to routinely send, receive and store electronic mail, join teleconferences and make use of electronic bulletin boards in their areas of interest. For example, recent experiments by the Correspondence School in Sydney, Australia, have confirmed that electronic mail is an effective way of communicating with home-based students who, because of sickness or isolation, are unable to attend school (McKinnon & Sinclair, 1986).

The Electronic University, developed by TeleLearning Systems, Inc., of San Francisco, has opened a promising new direction in distance education. Nearly 15,000 students are enrolled in classes and seminars on subjects ranging from economics to the subtleties of California wines. More than 1,700 universities now offer credit for courses taken through the Electronic University (Darling, 1985). All it takes to enrol in EU is a suitable microcomputer, a modem and an enrolment package. After registration, students receive an information packet containing study guides, course outlines and perhaps a floppy disk containing a general introduction and series of lessons. Students are required to transmit a progress report to their lecturer via electronic mail and can use this service to communicate directly with their lecturers. Access to administrative and library services is also provided through electronic mail.

Computer-based distance education is especially relevant for handicapped persons who may need to communicate from home. For example, on-line exchanges would make it possible for students to hold electronic forums with other students - a class discussion via computer. Real-time discussions could be held with teaching staff to deal with problems and questions arising from study material. Teleconferencing would enable students to peruse topics of personal interest and to initiate the exchange of information between individuals. In this scenario, Sally in Invercargill could send an essay to Gerry in Whangerei. Or Peter in Hastings could put out a general request on the bulletin board for assistance in locating a particular journal or article.

Telecommunications also provides some tools for special educators and rehabilitation workers. For example, the National Association of State Directors of Special Education (Washington, D.C.) operates SpecialNet, which provides access to databases on educational assessment and programming, electronic mail and bulletin boards which educators can use to communicate with one another or to receive information on computer applications, employment opportunities, in-service courses and conferences, etc. Computerized systems have also been developed for career information and guidance (Jacobson & Grabowski, 1982). Goldenberg (1984) lists a number of electronic resources for special education and rehabilitation.

There is little doubt now that a major shift has occurred away from the use of computers to instruct and control people to the use of productivity tools and other applications which extend the personal effectiveness of the learner. All of the applications described in this chapter have been provided to illustrate how technology can be applied to enhance the productivity and life quality of handicapped people. In fact, given the mission of rehabilitation education to provide interventions to improve the learning and performance of handicapped persons, it is doubtful that the same headway could be made without access to appropriate forms of technology. There are, however, a number of problems and issues that prevent technology from being applied to the extent that it might be as a tool for self development.

QUALITY OF LIFE ISSUES

Recent technological advances such as those described in this chapter represent important new steps in the direction of normalization by enabling handicapped persons to use technology as:

1. Extensions of themselves designed to enhance personal performances either physically, for example, better control over the home environment and ability to attend to personal needs, or intellectually as in using a microcomputer to communicate and participate in distance education.
2. Electronic microworlds through which they can explore and influence the real world.

The application of computers as a tool for self development constitutes a libertarian view of how technology should be employed to enhance the life quality of handicapped persons. There are, however, a number of important issues that must be addressed concerning the present role and future direction of computer learning technology in rehabilitation education.

First, the increasing availability of computers generally has given rise to some serious ethical and social issues concerning the undesirable effects that computers may have on society as a whole. Specifically, concern has been expressed that unequal access to computers may serve to increase the disparity between advantaged and less advantaged groups within society. This equity issue is particularly crucial in the rehabilitation field where people depend upon technology to support their communication and learning. Here, the question is one of giving a learner access to a computer and a chance to use productivity tools alongside both handicapped and non-handicapped peers. It is advanced that this equality of computer access is an important step toward the implementation of the normalization principle that is nowadays gaining increasing acceptance as a major concept underlying the policy and practice of providing public services. The question of access is thus fundamental to the rights of handicapped persons. To deny handicapped persons access to the technology they need to support themselves within the mainstream of the community is to deny their rights to a full measure of participation within a technologically advanced society (Ryba & Nolan, 1985).

Second, there is a need to further develop adaptive devices that provide unrestricted access to computers by handicapped persons. As Vanderheiden (1984) has noted, computers have the potential of creating new barriers and increasing the gap between disabled and able-bodied people rather than assisting the disabled person to overcome these gaps. It is vitally important that handicapped persons have access to standard hardware and software of a kind that can support their communication and learning needs. Goldenberg (1979) has stressed the importance of carefully matching the technology to the needs of individual students. Scott (1986) has provided advice for rehabilitation workers on how to assess the functioning of handicapped persons in order to establish what type of technical aids are best suited for their particular needs. This involves determining what input devices the person can operate and what modifications need to be made to existing hardware and software.

Third, there are a number of issues related to the effective implementation of computer learning technology that need to be considered. The rule here is that, no matter how well developed the computer hardware and productivity tools might be, the entire system can be rendered ineffective by poor implementation strategies. As Sampson (1984) has noted, implementation of computer applications is a dynamic process and requires a continual series of modifications according to the manner in which technology and the needs of the user evolve and interact. It is essential to understand that computers are not fixed purpose machines. Rather, they are transitional tools in the sense that one new development leads to the next. For example, developments in interactive programming led from narrow instructional applications to complex simulations and productivity tools. Special purpose applications such as word processing, data bases and spreadsheets have been linked together through the concept of integrated software packages. The effect of all this is that rehabilitation practitioners need to stay well informed about new developments and to be able to consider how these can be applied to meet the self development needs of handicapped persons. Increasingly, handicapped persons themselves are becoming informed users of technology and are often better placed than non-handicapped people to help with implementation of computer-based programmes.

Resistance to change is one of the greatest impediments to effective implementation of computer applications. There are several related factors that need to be considered here, including:

1) training opportunities for users;
2) amount of opportunity to participate in decision-making;
3) availability of information and opportunities to exchange ideas.

Resistance is, in effect, a state of mind that can be altered by the availability of opportunities to gain information and skills. It is absolutely essential now that all rehabilitation practitioners be given training in computer applications as part of their professional studies. A related point is that handicapped persons themselves should have access to learning opportunities, and an opportunity to participate in decisions about how technology is to be applied. In this regard, it is essential to recognize that technology is only a part of a complete system that has many component parts including user materials, technical support, training, software, hardware - any of which may be inadequate in particular situations and lead to staff or user resistance (McMahon, Burkhead & Sampson, 1985).

Fourth, there are some sound educational and philosophical reasons why computers ought to be used as tools for self development under the control of handicapped persons. The point has already been made that an essential feature of computers is that they function as an extension of the user. If, by controlling the computer as a learning instrument, it were possible to say that a handicapped person's quality of life had changed for the better, then it might be said that they had gained some benefits as persons in their own right. To change for the better might mean that they could now use the technology to do things that were not physically possible before (e.g. shopping, sending mail to friends). It might also mean that they can participate in formal education and gain access to decision making as a direct result of personal computer communications. In all of these examples, the emerging theme is one of liberation from restrictions imposed by other people.

In addition to the intellectual and academic benefits described here, access to computers is important on a more personal, affective level. For example, research by Floor and Rosen (1975) has illustrated that the rigid institutionalized lifestyles to which many handicapped persons are exposed can contribute to compliance and learning helpless responses. As Papert (1981) has pointed out, severely physically handicapped persons are often placed in a passive dependent role as a result of their limitations and have little chance to make an impact on the environment around them. Being able to independently use the same equipment for the same functions as their able-bodied peers can have a positive effect on self image. Papert (1981) noted that severely disabled adolescents using LOGO to perform spatial manipulation and other intellectual tasks not normally possible for them in real life experienced a marked improvement in their sense of self worth. Ryba and Chapman (1983) have described how access to computers can yield psychological benefits including improve-

improvements in self concept and reduction of emotional dependence.

Finally, self development with computers does not occur simply through interaction with computers, but rather through the opportunities that computer-based learning provides to interact with other people. This point was dramatically brought home in a project we carried out with teachers and young offenders at a correctional institution (Nolan & Ryba, 1986b). Here, teachers and inmates learned LOGO, keyboard skills and word processing together as part of the institution's ongoing education programme. The teachers adopted what might be called the enterprise sense of teaching, which incorporates as its main elements both facilitation of learning and teachers learning with their students. In the process of teaching and learning together, a basis was established for the development of more articulate, effective and honest teaching relationships with students (Papert, 1980) than is usually possible either in conventional classrooms or with conventional computer assisted instruction.

The experiences of handicapped persons such as those documented in this chapter indicate that there is a clear causal relationship between having access to appropriate forms of technology and the quality and range of life experiences. There is ample evidence now that computers not only compensate for restrictions imposed by disabilities, but provide new and powerful tools for personal development that were not previously available. Given the rapid technological developments that are occurring within society, every effort must be made to fully exploit the use of computers for enhancing the personal effectiveness of handicapped persons. The rationale for using technology to improve quality of life is firmly based in the process of rehabilitation education and is in accord with humanitarian principles concerning normalization and respect for persons.

SUMMARY

1. While quite a lot of attention has been given to the technical features of computer applications for handicapped persons, relatively little has been said about the ways in which a computer can be used as a tool for self development.

2. Changes in social outlook toward handicapped people have given rise to various humanitarian principles such as normalization, integration and mainstreaming. Computer technology can be used to translate these humanitarian principles into practical improvements to the quality of people's lives.

3. It is essential that computers become integrated into the major life areas of handicapped persons for education, communication, leisure, control of environment and vocational development. However, the extent of integration depends upon prevailing social, political and economic forces.

4. The concept of the computer as a learning tool for developing human potential is centrally related to the main aim of rehabilitation education.

5. Respect for persons and normalization are fundamental principles which can guide the application of computers and information technology generally as a tool for self development.

6. Policies and philosophies governing computer applications are essentially related to views about education and the rights of people generally. Seymour Papert (1980), the creator of LOGO, has strongly advocated for the right of learners to gain control over technology in order to use it in some personally meaningful way.

7. Based on Papert's philosophy of self control and personal development, LOGO provides a set of enabling tools that can be applied to extend the effectiveness of handicapped persons by increasing the interaction they have with their environment.

8. Research evidence is offered to support the application of computer games and simulations as learning tools for the development of adaptive behaviours of mentally retarded people and as cognitive therapy for brain injured patients.

9. The microworld concept is advanced here as a useful theoretical model for understanding and designing electronic learning environments. Examples are provided to illustrate how microworlds enable handicapped persons to draw upon resources from the surrounding

culture and to use these resources as an extension of themselves.

10. Productivity tools such as word processing, databases and telecommunications can enhance the productivity and life quality of handicapped persons. Given the mission of rehabilitation education to improve the learning and performance of handicapped persons, it is doubtful that the same headway could be made without access to appropriate forms of technology.

11. The view is advanced that *'to deny handicapped persons access to appropriate forms of technology is to deny them access to the tools they need to function effectively in a technologically advanced society'*. Issues concerning equity of access and ways of matching technology to individual needs must be given serious consideration.

12. This chapter provides evidence of the cognitive and affective benefits associated with computer access by handicapped persons. However, self development with computers does not simply occur through interaction with computers, but rather through the opportunities that computer-based learning provides for the individual to interact with other people. Computers not only compensate for restrictions imposed by disabilities, but provide some new and powerful tools for personal development.

REFERENCES

Adams, T. (1986) 'Towards a Theory of Microworlds,' in A. D. Salvas & C. Dowling (eds.), *Computers in Education: On the Crest of a Wave*, Australian Computer Education Conference Computer Education Group of Victoria, Balaclava.

Anderson, M. (1985) 'A Database at School,' *Computer Courseware Development Unit Newsletter, 6*, Department of Education, Wellington, 30-33.

Brown, R. I. (1984) *Integrated Programmes for Handicapped Adolescents and Adults*, Croom Helm, London/College-Hill Press, San Diego.

Darling, S. (1985) 'The Electronic University,' *Compute*, September, 30-36.

Emmanuel, R. & Weir, S. (1976) 'Catalysing
    Communication in an Autistic Child in a
    LOGO-like Learning Environment,' in *Proceed-
    ings of Summer Conference on Artificial
    Intelligence and Simulation of Behaviour*,
    Edinburgh, March.
Floor, L. & Rosen, M. (1975) 'Investigating the
    Phenomenon of Helplessness in Mentally
    Retarded Adults,' *American Journal of Mental
    Deficiency, 79*, 565-572.
Franklin, C. (1985) 'The Use of LOGO to Assess
    and Extend the Learning Capabilities of an
    Intellectually Handicapped Child,' Unpub-
    lished Research Report, Massey University,
    Department of Education, Palmerston North.
Fung, C. W. & McDougall, A. (1984) 'Use of LOGO
    for Development of Some Spatial Skills in
    Spastic Students,' in A. Salvas (ed.),
    Computing and Education: 1984 and Beyond,
    Computer Education Group of Victoria,
    Balaclava.
Goldenberg, E. P. (1979) *Special Technology for
    Special Children*, University Park Press,
    Baltimore.
Goldenberg, E. P. (1984) *Computers, Education and
    Special Needs*, Addison Wesley, Reading,
    Massachusetts.
Groen, G. (1984) 'Theories of LOGO,' in R. Sorkin
    (ed.), *LOGO 84*, Proceedings of the National
    LOGO Conference, Massachusetts Institute of
    Technology, Cambridge, Massachusetts.
Hannah, A. (1985) 'Communication and Education
    for the Disabled,' in A. D. Salvas (ed.),
    Communication and Change, Computer Education
    Group of Victoria, Balaclava.
Hawkridge, D., Vincent, T. & Hales, G. (1985) *New
    Information Technology in the Education of
    Disabled Children and Adults*, Croom Helm,
    London/College-Hill Press, San Diego.
Henderson-Lancett, L. & Boesen, J. (1986) 'Dragon
    World 1: Implementing an Adventure Game,' in
    A. D. Salvas & C. Dowling (eds.), *Computers
    in Education: On the Crest of a Wave*,
    Computer Education Group of Victoria,
    Balaclava.
Horton, J. & Ryba, K. (1986) 'Assessing Learning
    with LOGO: A Pilot Study,' *The Computing
    Teacher, 14*(1), 24-28.

Jacobson, M. D. & Grabowski, B. T. (1982) 'Computerized Systems of Career Information and Guidance: A State of the Art,' *Journal of Educational Technology Systems, 10,* 235-255.

Lynch, W. J. (1981) 'TV Games as Therapeutic Interventions,' Paper presented at the American Psychological Society Symposium, Rehabilitation of Post Traumatic Brain-damaged Patients, Los Angeles, August.

Lynch, W. J. (1982) 'Video Games as Therapy: A Modest Success,' *Video Games, 1,* 64-79.

McKinnon, D. H. & Sinclair, K. E. (1986) 'Communications Technology and Distance Education,' *Australian Educational Computing, 1*(1), 53-58.

McMahon, B. T., Burkhead, E. J., & Sampson, J. P. (1985) *Computer Access and Applications to Career Counseling with Vocational Rehabilitation Clients,* Catholic University of America, D:ATA Institute, Washington, D.C.

MECC (1985) *E-Z LOGO.* Minnesota Educational Computing Consortium, St. Paul.

Minsky, M. & Papert, P. (1972) 'Artificial Intelligence,' Memo No. 252, Artificial Intelligence Laboratory, Massachusetts Institute of Technology.

Nirje, B. (1969) 'The Normalization Principle and its Human Management Implications,' in R. Kugel & W. Wolfensberger (eds.), *Changing Patterns in Residential Services for the Mentally Retarded,* President's Committee on Mental Retardation, Washington, D.C.

Nolan, C. J. P. & Ryba, K. A. (1986a) *Assessing Learning with LOGO,* International Council for Computers in Education, Eugene, Oregon.

Nolan, C. J. P. & Ryba, K. A. (1986b) 'Computers in Transition Education: A Case Study with Young Offenders,' in W. Korndorffer (ed.), *Transition: Perspectives on School to Work in New Zealand,* Dunmore, Palmerston North.

Papert, S. (1980) *Mindstorms: Children, Computers and Powerful Ideas,* Harvester, Brighton.

Papert, S. (1981) *Information Prosthetics for the Handicapped,* Massachusetts Institute of Technology, Cambridge, MA.

Rostron, A. & Sewell, D. (1984) *Microtechnology in Special Education,* Croom Helm, London/ Johns Hopkins University Press, Baltimore.

Ryba, K. A. & Chapman, J. W. (1983) 'Toward
    Improving Learning Strategies and Personal
    Adjustment with Computers,' *The Computing
    Teacher*, *11*(1), 48-53.
Ryba, K. A. & Chapman, J. W. (1984) 'Cross-modal
    Memory Coding with a Computerised Game: Some
    Correlational Data with Cognitive Processes,'
    *Journal of Practical Approaches to Develop-
    mental Handicap*, *7*(3), 5-7.
Ryba, K. A. & Nolan, C. J. P. (1985) 'Computer
    Learning Systems for Mentally Retarded
    Persons: Interfacing Theory with Practice,'
    in A. F. Ashman & R. S. Laura (eds.), *The
    Education and Training of the Mentally
    Retarded: Recent Advances*, Croom Helm,
    London/Nichols, New York.
Salomon, G. & Gardner, H. (1986) 'The Computer as
    Educator: Lessons from Television Research,'
    Educational Researcher, January, 13-19.
Sampson, J. P. (1984) 'Maximizing the Effective-
    ness of Computer Applications in Counseling
    and Human Development: The Role of Research
    and Implementation Strategies,' *Journal of
    Counseling and Development*, *63*, 187-191.
Scott, N. G. (1986) *A Manual on Computer Assist-
    ance for Disabled People*, Technical Aid
    Trust, Wellington.
Tatnell, B. (1986) 'Technology: An Aid to
    Integration?' in A. D. Salvas & C. Dowling
    (eds.), *Computers in Education: On the Crest
    of a Wave*, Computer Education Group of
    Victoria, Balaclava.
Turkle, S. (1985) *The Second Self: Computers and
    the Human Spirit*, Simon & Schuster, New York.
Vanderheiden, G. C. (1984) 'Curbcuts and Comput-
    ers: Providing Access to Computers and
    Information Systems for Disabled Individ-
    uals,' in J. E. Roehl (ed.), *Discovery '83:
    Computers for the Disabled*, Materials
    Development Center, Stout Vocational Rehab-
    ilitation Institute, University of Wisconsin,
    Menomonie, WI.
Weir, S. (1981) 'LOGO and the Exceptional Child,'
    Microcomputing, September, 76-84.
Wolfensberger, W. (1972) *The Principle of
    Normalization in Human Services*, National
    Institute on Mental Retardation, Toronto,
    Canada.

Chapter Twelve

REHABILITATION PRACTITIONERS: MAKING A DIFFERENCE
IN THE QUALITY OF LIFE FOR DISABLED PERSONS

Aileen Wight Felske

INTRODUCTION

An individual's quality of life is significantly
affected by his or her self concept. The
perceptions people have of themselves can
determine choices and influence the success or
failure of behaviours. For persons with a
disability and their families, self concept is
influenced by a multitude of daily interactions
with individuals who teach, work, live with and
care for disabled persons (Featherstone, 1980;
Summers, 1986; Hogg & Mittler, 1987). These
individuals are drawn from a range of possibilities: neighbours, volunteers, frontline workers
and specialists from the disciplines in the fields
of rehabilitation education, psychology, social
work and the professions of allied health. Thus
the attitudes, values, approaches and techniques
used by professionals and para-professionals are
important in determining the quality of life for
persons with a disability.

This chapter focuses on the value orientation
and education issues surrounding rehabilitation
practitioners working in rehabilitation settings
such as schools, workshops and residential
settings. Often such employees take their
employment designation from their job functions,
for example, group home trainers, vocational shop
supervisors or special education classroom
assistants. The term rehabilitation practitioner
is used in this chapter to designate a specific
value base and orientation of frontline staff in
employment roles, which focus on giving disabled
persons attitudes, personal interaction skills and

daily living skills needed to improve the quality of life.

Mittler sets the task for the 80s in the field of mental retardation as one of *'helping people in daily contact with the mentally handicapped to update their knowledge and develop their skills'* (1981). The last ten years have seen an explosion in knowledge regarding intervention techniques in teaching delayed learners and in technical aids for physically disabled individuals. The value base and skills developed in this decade for intervention with mentally handicapped individuals have also proven to be transferable as a base to frontline staff working with individuals with physical disabilities, visual and hearing handicaps, and those with more generic social disabilities (Brown, 1984).

Also the attitudes and actions of the average citizen have become an important factor in community living (Donaldson, 1983). The frequency of contacts among disabled and non-disabled people is increasing as disabled persons remain in their places of origin. These interactions will be a base for future positive and supportive relationships, not confrontations.

Mittler's (1981) challenge to the 80s has been met with a complex myriad of conferences, lobby organizations and journals. Dissemination of current information is one of the key functions of parent/advocacy organizations (Wolfensberger, 1973). Yet attempts to get researchers to confront problems of information dissemination have rarely occurred. New information is delayed by book publication deadlines, or appears in academic journals not read by frontline practitioners. Researchers do not necessarily include possible applications of their findings in their academic work. Clarke (1977) expressed concern regarding the slow transfer of information into practice a decade ago. Still, the gap in research to practice transfer has widened. The effect of this on children and adults with a disability is a loss of possibilities in potential, choices and quality of life. The challenge of effective information and skill dissemination in the present has great impact on the quality of life for disabled persons in the next decade.

THE REHABILITATION TEAM AS A CONCEPT

Disabled persons and their family members are joined in 'partnership' with a multitude of various personnel in the rehabilitation process. Specialists from a variety of academic disciplines offer their resources to the disabled individual to increase their quality of life. Such specialists include medical doctors, speech therapists, physiotherapists, occupational therapists, social workers, psychologists, mechanical and electrical engineers, and teachers. The transdisciplinary team which shares its knowledge and goals across disciplines, and the growth of the consumer (disabled person)-focused individual programme plan are exciting developments (Pleiffer, 1981; Caldwell & O'Reilly, 1982; Boberg & Kassirer, 1983; Marlett, 1982). Yet the equality and success of the partnership between professionals and consumers is not yet a clinical reality (Yoshida, 1983).

The following vignettes illustrate some difficulties encountered in effective team participation. They are drawn from the clinical experiences of the author in the past year:

> *A note sent home from school upset a parent for days. Her severely handicapped daughter had not finished her sandwich at lunch. The teacher had decided to discipline her for this refusal by not allowing her to swim that afternoon, although this was part of the girl's therapeutic programme. The teacher's action was viewed as cruel by the parent and symptomatic of the lack of communication. With encouragement, the mother started talking to the teacher rather than yelling at her, and more frequent interactions are starting to create the 'assumed' partnership.*

And in another case:

> *A young quadriplegic man, recently disabled, attended a planning conference at the auxiliary hospital in which he was residing, hoping to plan for a move to independent living. Seven professionals from different medical specialities attended and discussed his condition for two hours. He was never asked for an opinion or his concerns during the conference. At its conclusion the man*

> *stated loudly to his nursing aid that he was never again attending a case conference.*

These conflicts may be generated by the divergent expectations of the disabled person, his family and the various professionals they encounter. The communication failures experienced can be examined in terms of the different worldviews of the individuals on the planning team. Worldview is a concept used to describe the way individuals and groups perceive and define the events they encounter in everyday life (Seligman, 1983). This is based on their experiences and philosophical beliefs regarding intervention with people. The diverseness of worldview for members of the rehabilitation team is shown in Table 1.

TABLE 1: Differing Worldviews of the Rehabilitation Team

Handicapped person and family	Specialist	Practitioner	Bureaucratic Manager
ascription	achievement (high)	achievement (neutral)	achievement (high)
particularism	universalism	particularism	universalism
holistic	functional specificity	holistic (partial)	functional specificity
affectivity (partial)	neutrality	affectivity	neutrality
anomie	dominance	anomie (partial)	dominance

The disabled person and his family are ascribed members of the team. Their role as a receiver or purchaser of rehabilitation services is not chosen, but accidental. In contrast the specialist has entered a professional field after years of study and discipline and expects recognition for his or her skills in a successful career (Mearig, 1982; Knoff, 1983). The expectations for agency bureaucrats is similarly success oriented; however, their business orientation may direct them to see the disabled person as a commodity who may or may not fit their system or be denied access. Rehabilitation practitioners have less career mobility. Although they have deliberately chosen the field, they are often blocked from upward mobility by lack of university level degrees and this may be a factor in the high turnover in personnel entering and leaving practice.

Families enter the rehabilitation partnership solely oriented to their particular family members' needs for services, which they see as unique. The professional, in contrast, has been taught to work using a universal framework as a diagnostic guide. This perspective produces statements such as *'most students like your son'*, or *'we have found in cases like this'*. Families, however, often interpret this generalization as a lack of interest in the individual. This perception is further enhanced by the specialist's tendency toward functional specificity. For example, a speech therapist works only with communication and may label individuals by their speech disorder. Psychologists have historically classified disabled persons using intelligence quotients as a guide. Many disabled persons have made it clear they find IQ and etiology labels offensive. The bureaucratic managers of rehabilitation services are often criticized for their lack of personal caring. Often they do not even know the names of all the clients in the programme.

In contrast again, the family of a disabled person see their member holistically. Further, their commitment to their disabled member is generally lifelong (Anglin, 1981; Suelzle & Keenan, 1981; Brotherson, Backus, Summers, Turnbull, 1986). The practitioner often knows the disabled person as an individual with specific interests, needs and wants. The contrasting typology of affective neutrality is trained in professionals to enable them to work with many different families and their varying needs, without becoming emotionally drained. Overall the rehabilitation team members are marked by varying degrees of dominance and the disabled person and his family.

With such conflicting sets of role expectations and priorities, sides are chosen, and team members are led to define each other in negative ways. The very nature of the team roles, which involve crossing other professionals' or lay

GOVERNORS STATE UNIVERSITY
UNIVERSITY PARK
IL 60466

persons' boundaries, may lead to conflict (Fleming, Fleming, Roach & Oksoman, 1985). Blackavd & Barsh (1982) studied differing perceptions of the handicapped child's effect on the family. Of note is the teacher's assumptions that parents are interested in receiving more information on how their children are taught in school. The parents in this study, however, were uninterested in this information, assigning the educational responsibility to the school.

Other factors which contribute to possible conflict are differing philosophies of personnel, limited resources, rapidly advancing technology and the changing organization patterns of human services. Liebowitz and deMeuse (1982) stress that improving the functioning of individuals and groups within an organization is central to conflict avoidance and resolution. Professional self management and effective team skills are rarely part of the professional's training. Maher and Kruger (1985) directly address such skills in their management system. The resulting success or failure of such approaches to staff training will affect the communication process and, ultimately, the quality of intervention and services that the handicapped person receives. In fact, guidance on effective team functioning has developed theoretically (Bernstein, Ziarnik, Rudrud, & Czaykowski, 1981) and attained legislated status, for example, in the United States (Schwartz, 1984). Despite the strengths of PL 90-142, however, in legislating parental rights in educational planning, very real difficulties remain.

GUIDING IDEOLOGY: NORMALIZATION/SOCIAL ROLE VALORIZATION

A coherent value base, common language structure and approach to intervention are needed to overcome the conflicts of differing worldviews. While certain differences amongst team partners will remain, such as ascription versus achievement, many professionals and practitioners are attempting to be more holistic in their approach to persons with a disability and their families. As well, attempts to give control to the disabled person are clearly reflected in the terminology of *consumers with a disability*.

Accepting the philosophy of normalization (Wolfensberger, 1980, 1981; Wolfensberger & Thomas, 1983) as a framework for the evaluation of services and opportunities for citizens with a disability (discussed in another chapter) creates a need for strong community-based programmes, and for staff trained in programmes of rehabilitation education. A unifying ideology has developed and has been defined as rehabilitation education. A fundamental concept of rehabilitation education is that:

> ...*the treatment and training of individuals [can be best accomplished] through the application of a variety of social and psychological strategies to improve the learning and performance of handicapped persons.* (Brown, 1984)

Rehabilitation education draws from a wide body of knowledge in the disciplines of psychology, social work, medicine and education. Each disciplinary area provides an effective means of support and help as the individual moves in a positive direction to control his/her own life. It can involve technical aids to compensate for a complete or partial loss of function or teaching daily living skills and measures to ease social adjustment or readjustment (WHO, 1980).

This rehabilitation concept clearly reflects the evolving attitudes concerning disabled people, and moves distinctly away from previously accepted approaches. While traditional approaches such as the medical model have made many contributions to persons with a disability (medical treatment and prevention), they have been severely criticized by consumer groups for the perception of the person as a sick or chronic patient (Staub, Psych, & King, 1983). Many service functions that medical hospitals have assumed for disabled people are unnecessarily attached to this structure. This has led to undue labelling and unequal balance between the consumer (disabled person) and service deliverer.

Other service delivery designs based on the charity model have also left disabled persons frustrated. Such persons reject the perception of disability as an insurmountable loss and the professionally dominated solutions that derive from the perception of social service as charity (Enns, 1981). Instead they have approached access

273

to services and opportunities from an equalitarian philosophy demanding first, technological aids to eliminate or alter physical limitations (this includes a barrier free environment) and second, legislative action to mandate equal opportunities in education and work settings (Novak & Heal, 1980). This view was first articulated by De Jong (1979) in his work with people who are physically disabled. It rejects the traditional view of rehabilitation as centered on the individual and restates it as a problem of environment.

PRINCIPLES OF PRACTICE

Rehabilitation education is based on the following assumptions of ethical practice. The rehabilitation practitioner should ask him/herself these questions regarding their practices and attitudes:

1. Do my actions give full recognition to the rights and abilities of disabled persons and their families living in the community?
2. Do my actions assist disabled individuals to maintain themselves effectively in a quality lifestyle in society (Gottlieb, 1983)?
   Can support be offered in terms of:
   a) information on accessing monetary aid (e.g. Assured Income for Severely Handicapped People),
   b) information and support on accessing special conditions of service (e.g. Home Support or respite care),
   c) information and support on accessing, operating and maintaining technical aids which incorporate the full benefits of prosthetics and modern technology (e.g. microcomputer and software such as environmental control or communication programmes),
   d) support and participation in political lobbies to effect legal change (e.g. Obstacles: Report of the Special Committee on the Disabled and Handicapped, 1981).
3. Do I use the most powerful and socially valued intervention techniques available to aid disabled people in learning to live in society? Intervention techniques can be evaluated in terms of these questions:

a)   Is the promotion of physical integration of the disabled person being assisted? For example, do I always attempt to use a generic service setting first, and only allow myself and the individual to access a segregated setting on a temporary (time limited) basis if necessary for specific skill training?

b)   Is the promotion of social integration of the disabled person being assisted? For example, do I help disabled persons to get to know their neighbours in community settings by accompanying them individually to generic settings and activities? Do I remember that groups of disabled individuals are stared at but not approached by other people? Do I question what is to be gained by such group activities?

c)   Do those techniques stress positive image enhancing characteristics and life opportunities for the disabled individual? For example, when teaching a new skill in the community, how do I correct the learner's errors in a way that does not embarrass or imply a lack of ability to achieve? Do I encourage the attainment of socially valued clothes, hair styles and roles?

d)   Do chosen techniques diminish the harmful effect of the disabled person's socially devalued features and personal misfortune? For example, do I encourage the use of valued technical aids, such as calculators and learning techniques in imitation of competent peers?

e)   Do chosen techniques accept and teach disabled persons to make decisions and choose alternatives in their own lives? For example, do I use self management techniques, wherever possible, in intervention plans, so that the learner develops an independent learning style or do I make him teacher dependent by using teacher delivered cues and feedback instead of environmentally controlled feedback?

4.   Are the goals of rehabilitation intervention functionally meaningful in the life of the disabled person and his family? For example, are the goals in individual programme plans

truly reflective of what the disabled person and family have asked be accomplished?

5. Do I function as a good team member, being open with my team members, sharing my ideas and listening to others? Do I manage my time well and keep clear, informative records for my team? For example, a rehabilitation practitioner can make or break a client's chances of achieving a stated goal simply by being supportive or nonattentive when this area is being addressed. If the group home supervisor does not like the client's new job trial setting, the likelihood of successful job placement drops dramatically.

6. Are the goals of the rehabilitation intervention time limited and specified for review? Do I accept that the individual's needs for rehabilitation intervention vary over his/her lifetime (Brown & Hughson, 1987)? For example, ask yourself if you would wish to get up every day to face new tasks that you had never done before, or tasks in which you had earlier failed to meet criteria and must now reattempt? One of the risks of a rigid interpretation of rehabilitation is the creation of a deficit 'umbrella' that the individual spends his life trying to get out from under.

7. Finally, do I accept the disabled individual and his family as my employer, or is it the agency or rehabilitation society? For example, if I believe that an individual will be better served in another agency or different model of rehabilitation, will I tell the person and family, and other members of the team?

INTERNATIONAL COMPARISON OF EDUCATION

In the following section an international comparison of rehabilitation education post-secondary training programmes is presented. The general focus of these descriptions is one of training to work with mentally handicapped children and adults. The educational components, however, provide a useful framework for working with persons with a variety of disabilities. Such applications are being increasingly recognized.

1.   Canada

The last decade in Canada has seen a national move
towards the establishment of training programmes
for individuals interested in careers working with
disabled children and adults. A serious manpower
shortage was created in the 1970s by the closure
of a number of training programmes operated by
institutions to train 'medical' paraprofessionals
to work within the institutions. The positive
effects of services moving to community bases,
however, was being jeopardized by the lack of
appropriately trained support personnel. The
philosophy of normalization and new teaching
technologies rendered old training patterns and
attitudes obsolete. Two groups were in need of
critical education; former institution aides or
health care personnel and those individuals
undertaking a new career (often their first
career) in human services. The educational
challenge of these diverse groups remains today.
      In 1972 the National Institute on Mental
Retardation, Canadian Association of the Mentally
Retarded, produced a report on manpower training
(Roeher, 1978, 1980). They recommended the
formation of a National Manpower Council (NMC) and
community college-based career training programmes
to educate the newly conceived 'personnel'. The
basic premise of the model is that many untrained
frontline staff and volunteers could, with short
term training, do the new functions of teaching
daily living skills. The report commented that
three-quarters of the work force in the area of
disability does not require university level
training. Frontline practitioners could be
trained in community colleges in one or two-year
programmes. Other provincial reports on manpower
training needs at this time made similar recommendations (Kincaide & Brown, 1981). The NIMR
manpower model proposed a four-level system of
training and recognition of personnel in the
field. An important part of the hierarchy is that
workers have clear routes and opportunities for
moving up the ladder, including having their
functions and status within the system clearly
defined.
      The Level I staff members are basic care
workers performing in a technician capacity. They
can aspire to a higher level by obtaining the
required additional education, training and
practical work experience. At Level II, the

individuals are being trained for some leadership abilities. Level III is equivalent to the bachelor's degree, a person trained at a university, with some specialization. The Level IV category of worker includes those in management and administrative capacities, and the various professional disciplines. This calls for an alteration in present Canadian university programmes to develop the essential leadership and management skills in their graduates.

A multitude of community college-based programmes offering one-year certificates and two-year diploma training have arisen independently or as offshoots of the National Model. There are regional differences, largely the result of Advanced Education being provincially controlled. Some provinces are addressing the issues of registering and monitoring the practice of rehabilitation practitioners (Health Disciplines Act of Alberta, 1985). Finally universities are beginning to address the more advanced educational needs of practitioners with courses and programmes becoming interdisciplinary in nature (Brown & Wight-Felske, 1987).

2. <u>Great Britain</u> (written by Barry Gray, King Alfred's College, Winchester)

The following describes what is available in the way of training for staff working with people with mental handicap in day services in Great Britain.

The description is not comprehensive as these restrictions have been observed:

1) A distinction has been made between pre-qualifying, in-house qualifying and post-qualifying training. The bulk of this description is concerned with qualifying training.

2) Day settings in the United Kingdom are varied and might include hospitals, adult training centres/social education centres, colleges of further or higher education, or vocational training centres. These different settings are provided by different agencies each with their own regulations regarding appropriate qualifications. This article is restricted to those settings that are managed by the Local Social Services Department (ATCs/SECs).

Qualifying training may be seen as appropriate in at least two ways: firstly, as a qualification that employers view as relevant to the tasks involved in working in a day setting and, secondly, as necessary for the individual member of staff progressing through a salary scale bar point. The two reasons may not always coincide. For example, employers may view a B.Ed. (Special Educational Needs) as a qualification that equips people with many of the relevant skills required, but, at the time of writing, it would not allow the person to pass through the salary bar. The salary scale and qualification bar is agreed by the employers and the staff unions. Currently three qualifications are accepted as appropriate for progression beyond the salary bar point. These are the Diploma in Training and Further Education of Mentally Handicapped Adults (DTMHA), the Certificate in Social Service (CSS), and the Certificate in Qualified Social Work (CQSW).

The DTMHA, a one-year full-time course, was validated by the now defunct Training Council for Teachers of the Mentally Handicapped and has not been available since 1979. The CSS, a two-year part-time course, was seen by many professionals as an inadequate replacement of the DTMHA and is validated by the Central Council for Education and Training in Social Work (as is CQSW). The CSS schemes vary with regard to the specialist input on mental handicap, but the model of training has many strengths. Students train with other professionals and they have many opportunities to put theory into practice (2 days in college, 3 at own work setting). Within each CSS scheme there are study supervisors who have a major part of their role defined as enabling students to link theory to practice. The CQSW is mainly viewed as the qualification for field social workers and the training is generic in nature. Very few holders of the CQSW work in day settings for people with learning difficulties.

DTMHA used to be offered at colleges of further and higher education. CSS is offered at similar institutions. CQSW is offered at colleges of higher education, polytechnics and universities. There are proposals that by 1991 the CSS and CQSW should be combined as one training. The nature, mode and place of this training qualification has not been decided and much debate continues.

In the category of qualification that employers see as relevant (as evidenced by their employing records) but which are not accepted for progression through the salary scale bar point, it is worth mentioning the Certificate in Further Education and Training of Mentally Handicapped People (CFETMHP). This two-year full-time course was developed some eight years ago in response to the fading out of the DTMHA. It is currently offered at four colleges of higher education and is validated by either the Council for National Academic Awards (CNAA) or a local university.

Still within the day settings for adults with learning difficulties, many staff have no formal qualifications (60% in 1980). There remains a need to provide different options for staff to train (full-time, part-time, sandwich, pre-experience, post-experience, etc.) and this should be in conjunction with a validation process that evaluates the effectiveness of such training.

3. United States (written by Anna Lou Pickett, the Graduate School and University Center of the City University of New York)

In the past, the United States met the needs of children and adults with mental retardation and other developmental disabilities by placing them in institutions. In the late 1960s, a change of attitude began to occur - brought about, primarily, through the initiatives of parents and other advocates concerned with protecting the rights and expanding the entitlements of all people with disabilities. These efforts led to court orders and legislative actions at the federal and state level that created public policies and programmes to enable children and adults to stay at home with their families or to live and work in the community.

While there has been significant progress in providing increased and improved community centered services for people with developmental disabilities over the last two decades, there are a multitude of critical issues and unmet needs that still confront policy makers in administrative agencies and local service delivery systems. Among them are the chronic shortages of qualified professional and paraprofessional personnel. Compounding the shortfalls of trained staff is a lack of viable opportunities for career advancement and other incentives, which in turn leads to high turnover rates in the ranks of entry level personnel.

The move to close institutions and to establish programmes and services in local communities has resulted in large scale shifts in roles and responsibilities for both professionals and paraprofessionals. These changes are grounded in the refocusing of the philosophy of service delivery throughout the human services, and the development of improved, individualized and more precise instructional strategies and techniques for training clients.

Increasingly, the roles of paraprofessionals have become more complex.

Analyses of the responsibilities assigned to entry level workers find that they are becoming technicians who perform administrative and programmatic duties in a wide range of community based settings: they are child care workers in early intervention programmes, instructors in pre-school programmes, and provide training to parents to enhance their skills as primary care givers. These *new technicians* are active participants in all phases of the instructional process in elementary and secondary special education, and they assist in crisis intervention for students and adults with behavioural disorders. They are job coaches and they carry out case management duties that prepare students to move from school and home to independent community living. They are key employees in the multiple levels of residential facilities that are available in most locales. In addition, they augment the work of physical and occupational therapists, health care professionals and rehabilitation specialists.

Despite the fact that paraprofessionals are viewed as major contributors in the delivery of services for infants, youth and adults with mental retardation and other severe and profound disabilities, opportunities for systematic pre- and inservice training, career advancement and other personnel practices that affect their performance on the job have not kept pace.

Although there is a greater awareness of the value of skilled paraprofessionals who are committed to remaining in the field, most service delivery systems have not moved to establish comprehensive career development plans. And therefore training is usually based on narrow parochial needs rather than reflecting the common skills needed by workers in various programmes and settings.

There are at least three factors that contribute to this situation: first, at the present time there are no nationally recognized criteria for employment training or career advancement. Further, throughout the United States there are many government jurisdictions, private sector agencies and funding sources responsible for providing services for children and adults with developmental disabilities, although there are a few fledgling efforts under way to develop employment and training procedures that are transferable across a mix of public and private not-for-profit delivery systems.

The third set of problems deals with opportunities for post-secondary education. There are many community college programmes offering one-year certificates and two-year degree programmes, but, due to the lack of national standards, their curricula were developed independently and reflect local and regional idiosyncrasies. However, a review of the content finds that they are more alike than different. They stress the rights of people with disabilities, the principles of normalization, human growth and the developmental assumption, the roles of paraprofessionals as advocates and effective members of the service delivery team, and behaviour maintenance and management techniques.

The primary problems confronting these programmes in their efforts to recruit and retain students are tied directly to those of the service delivery systems in their community. Unless career development plans are developed and implemented locally that 1) reduce the turnover rates, 2) increase salaries and other benefits, and 3) offer opportunities for career advancement based on education, these programmes do not grow or expand.

4. <u>Australia</u> (written by Trevor Parmenter, <u>Macquarie</u> University, North Ryde, NSW)

In recent years, in those states of Australia which had established large institutions for the care of people with severe and profound intellectual disabilities, there has been a concerted movement towards placing these people in smaller, community-based accommodation. There has also been a concerted move in the majority of states to move the administration of these services from a health to a community services model. With the exception of Victoria, however, ministerial responsibility remains within the health portfolio.

Training provisions for personnel working with people with severe disabilities are slowly reflecting this trend. In all states except Western Australia, the emphasis had been upon mental retardation nursing. For instance in New South Wales, the pattern was for nurses to be trained by the employing authority, the Department of Health. The course, of three years duration, led to the award of a certificate in either mental retardation nursing or psychiatric nursing. The communality of the courses reflected the geographical location of the hospitals which catered for people with severe intellectual or psychiatric disabilities. This association is being slowly broken down.

Despite the trend away from the health model, mental retardation nursing certificate courses continue to be conducted in New South Wales, Victoria and South Australia, where significant numbers of people remain in large institutional accommodation. However, courses with a community integration emphasis are also being conducted in most states, either in Colleges of Advanced Education or in Colleges of Technical and Further Education (TAFE). For instance, it is possible to obtain a Diploma in Residential Care at Brisbane College of Advanced Education, or a Developmental Disabilities Certificate at TAFE Colleges in Victoria. In Western Australia and Tasmania there are courses for social trainers. The change in nomenclature for residential workers reflects the move away from the former health base. For instance, in Queensland these personnel are known as residential care officers.

In New South Wales, one of the last states to address the deinstitutionalization issue, much of the non-nursing training is in-service, consisting of fragmentary courses of a short duration. Plans are well advanced for the establishment of a distance education diploma in a rural College of Advanced Education and a metropolitan College has initiated preliminary planning for a course to be introduced in 1989.

In general terms Australia has been relatively slow in providing relevant training for personnel involved in community-based living and vocational programmes. The above description has been concerned with training for people working in the severe and profound area of disability. However, as in other countries, the largest population of people with intellectual disabilities has always resided in the community, generally at home with parents. Residential and vocational facilities for these people are provided by nongovernment agencies assisted by federal government subsidies. For personnel employed in these programmes there is an almost complete absence of pre-service training. Again there is an undue reliance upon short, uncoordinated in-service programmes. Of some concern, too, is the lack of postgraduate training in the field of rehabilitation in Australia. This situation will further exacerbate the paucity of leadership personnel in this growing field.

In summary, Australia is making some advances towards providing community-based accommodation and vocational training programmes for people with all levels of intellectual disabilities. What are conspicuously absent, however, are comprehensive manpower planning and training policies across the total rehabilitation field. Obviously staff training is not as politically rewarding as the much publicized changes in the structural provisions.

INFORMATION DISSEMINATION IN REHABILITATION EDUCATION

The dissemination of information regarding disabilities is critical to the impact of practitioners on the quality of life for persons with a disability and their families. Historically two separate channels have evolved (Wight Felske & Hughson, 1986). First, researchers in medicine, psychology, social work and, more recently, environmental design and management have published in journals from their academic disciplines. Information held by each of these avenues has often been presented as specific to the etiology of the handicapping condition. Second, information has been disseminated at the grass roots by diability organizations. One of the major problems for practitioners has been the difficulty in accessing new information and integrating it into their clinical practice.

The challenge of effective information dissemination can be met through the use of research and demonstration centres, information clearing houses, and new communication patterns created by widespread public use of microcomputer technology.

Research Centres

Research and demonstration centres affiliated with universities have also attempted to narrow the information dissemination gap. One Canadian example of facilities which focus on change agentry is The Allan Roeher Research Institute (formerly the National Institute on Mental Retardation), funded by the Canadian Association on Independent Living and affiliated with York University (Roeher, 1980). The Allan Roeher Research Institute, which publishes and trains individuals in the use of PASSING (Program Analysis of Service Systems: Implementation of Normalization Goals), is an active proponent of system change and consumer advocacy (Wolfensberger & Thomas, 1983).

A second level of information dissemination occurs through research centres which focus on the implementation of research on clinical intervention into practice in the field. The Vocational and Rehabilitation Research Institute (VRRI), University of Calgary, for example, is a research and demonstration centre which specializes in the needs of mentally handicapped adults. It runs a vocational training programme for mentally handicapped adults and a residential service. This centre has been instrumental in the development of integrated training approaches (Brown & Hughson, 1980). The Mental Handicap in Wales Applied Research Unit, St. David's Hospital, Cardiff, Wales, and the Hester Adrian Research Institute, University of Manchester, have a similar applied focus. Whelan, Speake and Strickland (1984), while at the Hester Adrian Research Institute, gave five basic conditions critical for future success in research to practice:

1) Practitioners should decide and report which problems should be researched.
2) The findings should be communicated clearly.
3) the researchers should demonstrate applications in actual field settings.

4) Practitioners should be given opportunities to try out findings with supervision.
5) Researchers and practitioners should collaborate to ensure applications are built into long-term practice.

Information Clearing-houses

Information clearing-houses are being created in the effort to disseminate research and information as widely and quickly as possible. A powerful example of this new vendor is the Council for Exceptional Children International (Neufeldt, 1984). It has a membership of families, teachers and related professional groups aligned in divisions relating to specialities of interest. The CEC office employs professional support staff to run the organization, offering journals which present recent research and application, and conferences, regionally, nationally and internationally. In addition the CEC has a political lobby in each country, monitoring and lobbying for social change. More examples of such partnerships between disabled persons, families and practitioners are needed to facilitate communication.

Electronic Communication Channels

The impact of microcomputer technology on information dissemination and communication is radical. Tied to microcomputer users with modem capability, it allows people immediate access to information and dialogue. It also alters many traditional roles of professionals as facilitators in information quests.

Three major types of microcomputer communications will be briefly described in terms of their possible role in information dissemination in rehabilitation education.

1.   Electronic Mail

Various electronic mail services are available which allow immediate transfer of information to other people, consumers, programme providers and government agencies. As outlined in the chapter by Ryba in this volume, information sent by electronic mail will be increasingly common in the rehabilitation field.

A recent example of the development of electronic mail as a network linkage is the Walter Dinsdale Disability Information Service Centre of Canada (Marlett, Clark, Keeling, Kieffer & Reed, 1986). Funded by the Secretary of State, Government of Canada, DISC's goal is to increase the computer literacy of disabled people to empower them with the ability to access a national information network. Wight-Felske (1987) is using DISC in college education for rehabilitation education students. Students in a technical aids course are tutored weekly using electronic mail. Their tutors are users of technical aids; disabled themselves, they share a range of experiences, frustrations and knowledge. The tutors live in every province in Canada from Newfoundland to British Columbia. Of note in the messages transmitted is the amount of social support for general life goals exchanged between tutor and student in addition to the structured learning exchange.

2.   Bulletin Boards

An electronic bulletin board is a pot pourri of information bits left by various users who wish to communicate with other people having similar interests. The information exchange may include items for sale, questions regarding the use of computer equipment or any intervention strategy, notes regarding upcoming conferences, and questions/answers regarding consumer searchers for appropriate programmes. In the United States, Special Net has over 25 different national bulletin boards. For example, the board 'Exchange' has special educators request answers to problems and post information of use to others in the field. A more generic board is operated by Compuserve, called Go Disability. The support function of a bulletin board in lobbying for individual or programme change is an interesting phenomenon in information dissemination.

3.   Databases

The traditional avenue of information search has changed from the library to the electronic database. Various disciplines have created databases, annotating their research reports, articles and books so they can be searched electronically by any microcomputer user. Vendors maintain these databases and allow access with payment of financial charges (Behrmann, 1984). Bibliographic Retrieval Services (BRS) and Dialogue are the primary vehicles to access information related to rehabilitation education. Dialogue maintains 159 databases (including ERIC and CEC Clearinghouse on Handicapped and Gifted Children). Some of these publications can be accessed, in their complete form, electronically. Others must be accessed through libraries or ordered from publishing houses.

Overall, it is important to note that the framework for dissemination of information is changing. While forums for the exchange of information such as professional and consumer journals and conferences will continue, the low cost availability of computer technology has changed people's expectations. Computer networks will create a demand for personalized, immediate access to information and stimulate a dialogue among all special interest groups.

CONCLUSION

In summary, quality of life for persons with a disability can be a cycle of poverty, unemployment, limited access to education and transportation and housing concomitant with social isolation. The literature reviewed in this chapter reflects a commitment to the provision of well trained rehabilitation practitioners as a key to changing the quality of life for disabled persons. Several essential components can be identified in training rehabilitation practitioners:

1) the need for a generic and modularized approach to training at a paraprofessional level,
2) a strong functional and practical base for such training,
3) the necessity for such training to link into a career ladder with transfer ability between college training institutions and possibly university programmes,
4) personalized, immediate access to information and dialogue among persons with a disability,

their families and the people who work with them.

Lastly, research on a variety of effective staff development models is just beginning. Mittler (1987) comments that there is *'a growing realisation that courses do not necessarily lead to a change in behaviour of participants, and far less to changes in the clients with whom they work'*. The extent to which rehabilitation practitioners will be a moving force in the creation of valued life experiences for people with disabilities remains a challenge. That challenge must be continually faced if the quality of life for persons with a disability is to undergo significant change.

REFERENCES

Anglin, B. (1981) *They Never Asked for Help,* A Study on the Needs of Elderly Retarded People in Metro Toronto, Belsten, Maple, Ontario.

Behrmann, M. (1984) *Handbook of Microcomputer in Special Education,* College-Hill Press, San Diego.

Bernstein, G., Ziarnik, J., Rudrud, E., & Czaykowski, L. (1981) *Behavioral Habilitation through Proactive Programming,* Paul H. Brookes, Baltimore.

Blackavd, M. & Barsh, E. (1982) 'Parents' and Professionals' Perceptions of the Handicapped Child's Impact on the Family,' *The Association of the Severely Handicapped, 7,* 62-70.

Boberg, E. & Kassirer, E. (1983) *Rehabilitation Teams: Action and Interaction,* National Health and Welfare Canada, Ottawa, Ontario.

Brotherson, M. J., Backus, L., Summers, J. A., & Turnbull, A. (1986) 'Transition to Adulthood,' in J. A. Summers (ed.), *The Right to Grow Up,* Paul H. Brookes, Baltimore.

Brown, R. I. (ed.) (1984) *Integrated Programmes for Handicapped Adolescents and Adults,* Croom Helm, London/Nichols, New York.

Brown, R. I. & Hughson, E. A. (1980) *Training of the Developmentally Handicapped Adult,* C. C. Thomas, Springfield, IL.

Brown, R. I. & Hughson, E. A. (1987) *Behavioural and Social Rehabilitation and Training,* Wiley, Chichester and New York.

Brown, R. I. & Wight-Felske, A. (1987) 'Rehabili-
    tation Education within the Province of
    Alberta,' *Canadian Journal of Special
    Education*, (in press).
Caldwell, D. F. & O'Reilly, C. (1982) 'Boundary
    Spanning and Individual Performance: The
    Impact of Self-monitoring, *Journal of Applied
    Psychology*, *67*, 124-127.
Clarke, A. D. (1977) 'From Research to Practice,'
    in P. J. Mittler (ed.), *Research to Practice
    in Mental Retardation, Vol 1: Care and
    Intervention*, University Park Press,
    Baltimore.
De Jong, G. (1979) 'Independent Living: From
    Social Movement to Analytic Paradigm,'
    *Archives of Physical Medicine and
    Rehabilitation*, *60*, 435-446.
Donaldson, J. (1983) 'Changing Attitudes Toward
    Handicapped Persons: A Review and Analysis
    of Research,' *Exceptional Children*, *46*,
    504-514.
Enns, H. (1981) 'The Historical Development of
    Attitudes Toward the Handicapped. A Frame-
    work for Change,' in D. Freeman & B. Trute
    (eds.), *Treating Families with Special Needs*,
    Canadian Association of Social Workers,
    Ottawa.
Featherstone, H. A. (1980) *A Difference in the
    Family: Living with a Disabled Child*, Basic
    Books, New York.
Fleming, D. C., Fleming, E. R., Roach, K. S., &
    Oksoman, P. F. (1985) 'Conflict Management,'
    in C. S. Maher (ed.), *Professional Self-
    Management, Techniques for Special Services
    Providers*, Paul H. Brookes, Baltimore.
Gottlieb, B. H. (1983) *Social Support Strategies:
    Guidelines for Mental Health Practice*, Sage
    Publications, Beverly Hills, CA.
Health Disciplines Act (1985) Government of the
    Province of Alberta.
Hogg, J. & Mittler, P. (1987) *Staff Training in
    Mental Handicap*, Croom Helm, London & Sydney.
Kincaide, P. & Brown, R. I. (eds.) (1981)
    *Manpower Planning for Serving the Handicapped
    in the 80's*, Conference proceedings, Alberta
    Advanced Education and Manpower.
Knoff, H. S. (1983) 'Investigating Disproportion-
    ate Influence and Status in Multidisciplinary
    Child Study Teams,' *Exceptional Children*, *49*,
    367-370.

Liebowitz, S. J. & deMeuse, K. P. (1982) 'The
    Application of Team Building,' *Human Rela-
    tions, 35*, 1-18.
Maher, C. & Kruger, L. (1985) 'Professional
    Self-Management: Overview of the Process,'
    in C. S. Maher, *Professional Self-Management,
    Techniques for Special Services Providers,*
    Paul H. Brookes, Baltimore.
Marlett, N. J. (1982) 'Individual Service Plans.
    Increasing the Interface Between Research and
    Service Provision,' Paper presented Child
    Welfare League of America Conference
    (published in proceedings, *Journal of Child
    Welfare,* 1985).
Marlett, N. J., Clark, B., Keeling, M., Kieffer,
    R., & Reed, R. (1986) 'Executive Summary of
    Disability Information Systems of Canada,
    Empowering Disabled Canadians through
    Communications,' Report for Department of the
    Secretary of State.
Mearig, J. S. (1982) 'Ethical Complications of
    the Children's Rights Movement for Profes-
    sionals,' *American Journal of Orthopsychiat-
    ry, 52,* 518-529.
Mittler, P. (1981) 'Strategies for Manpower
    Development in the 1980s,' *Journal of
    Practical Approaches to Developmental
    Handicap, 4*(3), 23-26.
Mittler, P. J. (1987) 'Staff Development:
    Changing Needs and Service Contexts in
    Britain,' in J. Hogg & P. Mittler (eds.),
    Staff Training in Mental Handicap, Croom
    Helm, London/Brookline Books, Cambridge, MA.
Neufeldt, A. (1984) 'Advocacy: Evolution to
    Revolution,' in N. J. Marlett, R. Gall, & A.
    Wight-Felske (eds.), *Dialogue on Disability:
    A Canadian Perspective, Vol 1: The Service
    System,* University of Calgary Press, Calgary.
Novak, A. R. & Heal, L. W. (1980) *Integration of
    Developmentally Disabled Individuals Into the
    Community,* Paul H. Brookes, Baltimore.
Pleiffer, S. (1981) 'Facilitating Effective Team
    Decision Making,' in M. P. Gaasholt (ed.),
    Organizing for Change, University of
    Washington, PDAS.
Roeher, A. (1978) 'Models of Staff Training,' in
    H. Spkdich (ed.), *Choices: Proceedings of
    the 7th World Congress on Mental Handicap,*
    International League of Societies for the
    Mentally Handicapped, Lebenshilfe, Vienna.

Roeher, A. (1980) 'Canadian Developments,' in T. Apolloni, J. Cappuccilli, & T. Cooke (eds.), *Achievements in Residential Services for Persons with Disabilities,* University Park Press, Baltimore.

Schwartz, L. (1984) *Exceptional Students in the Mainstream,* Wadsworth, Belmont, California.

Seligman, M. (1983) *The Family with a Handicapped Child. Understanding and Treatment,* Grune & Stratton Inc., New York, New York.

Staub, J. I., Psych, C., & King, A. (1983) 'The Implications of the Consumer Independent Living Movement on Traditional Rehabilitation,' Canadian Congress of Rehabilitation, unpublished paper, Ottawa, Ontario.

Suelzle, M. & Keenan, V. (1981) 'Changes in Family Support Networks Over the Life Cycle of Mentally Retarded Persons,' *American Journal of Mental Deficiency, 86, 267-274.*

Summers, J. A. (1986) *The Right to Grow Up,* Paul H. Brookes, Baltimore.

Whelan, E., Speake, B., & Strickland, T. (1984) 'Action Research: Working with Adult Training Centres in Britain,' in R. I. Brown (ed.), *Integrated Programmes for Handicapped Adolescents and Adults,* Croom Helm, London/ Nichols, New York.

Wight-Felske, A. (1987) 'Electronic Mail as a Medium for College Tutoring of Rehabilitation Education Students by Users of Technical Aides (Disabled Persons),' Mount Royal College, Instructional Development Funding, Unpublished manuscript.

Wight-Felske, A. & Hughson, E. A. (1986) *Disabled People in Canada: A Review of the Literature on Independent Living,* Report for the Social Trends Analysis Directorate Department of the Secretary of State, Federal Government of Canada.

Wolfensberger, W. (1973) *The Third Stage in the Evolution of Voluntary Associations for the Mentally Retarded,* International League of Societies for the Mentally Handicapped, & National Institute on Mental Retardation, 1973. (Expanded opening plenary address to the Congress of the International League of Societies for the Mentally Handicapped, Montreal.)

Wolfensberger, W. (1980) 'The Definition of
    Normalization,' in R. Flynn & K. Nitsch
    (eds.), *Normalization, Social Integration,
    and Community Services,* University Park
    Press, Baltimore.
Wolfensberger, W. (1981) *Training Institute for
    Human Service Planning, Leadership and Change
    Agentry,* The Division of Special Education &
    Rehabilitation of the School of Education,
    Syracuse University.
Wolfensberger, W. & Thomas, S. (1983) *Program
    Analysis of Service Systems' Implementation
    of Normalization Goal* (2nd edn.), National
    Institute on Mental Retardation, Toronto.
World Health Organization (1980) *International
    Classification of Impairment, Disabilities,
    and Handicaps (ICIDH),* WHO, Geneva.
Yoshida, P. K. (1983) 'Are Multidisciplinary
    Teams Worth the Investment?' *The School
    Psychology Review, 121,* 137-143.

modelling 147, 148
money 132, 158
motivation 134, 147, 158
motor coordination 65, 77, 113, 199, 246, 248
music 186, 190

natal care 66, 70
National Institute on Mental Retardation 277, 285
National Theatre Workshop of the Handicapped, The 208
Needs Analysis Scale 114
neighbourhood 3, 22, 28, 112, 267
noise 112, 128
normalization 1, 17, 85, 122, 165, 226, 236, 238, 239, 257, 262, 272-274, 277
nutrition 56, 58, 61, 63, 65, 67-68, 72, 132, 133

objective measures 1, 24, 49, 112
occupational therapists 269

painting 186, 192
paraplegia 216
paraprofessionals 71, 75, 80
parents 4, 5, 56, 63, 69, 72-76, 80, 83, 94, 96-100, 117, 123, 130, 137, 140, 268, 272, 284
PASS 223
peers 208, 251
people monthly placements 122

personal factors 1, 5, 11, 12, 22, 25, 27, 28, 37, 45, 87, 112, 126, 129, 132, 145, 173, 177, 178, 184, 195, 198-201, 211, 216, 238, 239, 246, 248, 264
personnel 5, 209, 276-284
philosophy 5, 63, 112, 116-118, 124, 129, 130, 134, 165
physical health 17, 25, 38, 40, 44, 56, 132, 133, 196, 197
physiotherapists 42, 269
play 63, 74, 95-97, 171, 188
poetry 186
policy planners 20
politics 2, 12, 28, 29, 262, 274
Portage Training 75-77
possessions 45, 96
predictor measures 103
pregnancy 70, 72
pre-school education 56, 63, 65, 68-69, 78
privacy 44, 126, 164, 177
problem solving 147, 148, 150, 151, 250
productivity 19, 20, 252-257
professional activity 2, 3, 12, 17, 40
prosthetics 41-44, 171
psychiatric nursing 283
psychodrama 149
psychologists 42, 238, 267, 269, 271, 273
psychosocial needs 71
Public Law 94-142 13

speech therapists 42, 269
spinal cord injury 19
sponsors 5, 111
standard of living 3
Stanford Binet 246
stereotyping 11, 15
St. Joseph's Centre 224
stress 84, 87, 103, 102-105, 195
Structured Learning Therapy 149
subjective criteria 1, 28, 87, 112, 146
supervision 62, 95, 143
support provisions 28, 41, 43
Swedish Association of Visually Handicapped Artists and Craftsmen 208

teachers 143, 148, 269
technology 235, 238-241, 257, 272, 275
Test of Interpersonal Competence for Employment (TICE) 151
theatres 128
TOPVIEW 237
Training Institute for Human Service Planning 285
transport 19, 20, 39, 85, 128, 159, 170, 194
tuberculosis 203

urban areas 61, 64, 78, 135, 195

Value Priority Scale 114, 116
values 13, 20, 24, 26, 28, 63, 275
verbal instruction 147, 148
videotape modelling 148, 149, 150, 151

Vineland Scale of Social Maturity 86
visual disabilities 10, 11, 88, 253, 257, 268
vocational aspects 111, 117, 121, 123, 129, 130, 135, 137, 141, 146, 164, 267,
Vocational and Rehabilitation Research Institute 285
vocational shop supervisors 267
volunteers 122, 267

walking aids 42
Walter Dinsdale Disability Information Service Centre 287
Weschler Adult Intelligence Scale 113, 246
wheelchairs 42, 194, 222
word processing 250, 259, 263, 267
work behaviour 145
World Council of Churches 229
worldview 270

Yad Voezer 228

305

Russell, J. A. 164, 175, 182
Rutter, M. 86, 103, 104, 109
Ruys, T. 164, 175, 182
Ryba, K. 242, 244, 245, 246, 258, 260, 261, 264, 265, 266

Sadka, N. L. 57, 60, 71, 82
Sadler, C. 227, 234
Saegeit, S. 181
Saggar, K. 76, 81
Sahai, A. 67, 82
Saint-Macary, A. 228, 233
Salomon, G. 242, 266
Sampson, J. P. 259, 260, 265, 266
Sandblom, P. 203, 213
Santana, R. 168, 183
Sarason, S. B. 12, 35
Schalock, R. L. 35
Schechner, R. 189, 191, 200, 213
Scheerenberger, R. C. 15, 16, 35
Schloss, C. N. 149, 161
Schmidt, D. W. 16, 34
Schonell, F. J. 84, 109
Schumaker, J. B. 150, 162
Schuman, M. 213
Schur, E. M. 10, 11, 14, 35
Schwartz, L. 272, 292
Scott, N. G. 237, 258, 266
Scott, R. A. 10, 11, 35
Seligman, M. E. P. 176, 181, 270, 292
Seltzer, G. B. 16, 35
Senior, 193, 213
Senatore, V. 149, 162
Sewell, D. 235, 265
Shaban, N. 204, 213
Sharp, R. 16, 35
Shavelson, R. J. 169, 183

Shaver, P. R. 112, 140
Sheldon, J. 150, 162
Sherman, J. A. 150, 162
Sherrod, D. R. 164, 183
Shoultz, B. 141, 161
Shure, M. 150, 162
Sigelman, C. K. 21, 33
Sigford, B. B. 22, 33
Simeonsson, N. E. 85, 109
Simeonsson, R. J. 85, 109
Simkins, J. 17, 35
Simmons, J. L. 11, 34
Sinclair, K. E. 256, 265
Slater, R. 175, 181
Smith, C. 141, 161
Smith, C. R. 165, 181
Smith, P. M. 16, 34
Sommer, R. 177, 178, 183
Sowers, J. A. 155, 160
Speake, B. 22, 36, 285, 292
Spencer, P. 189, 206, 213
Speno, S. 183
Spivak, G. 150, 162
Sprafkin, R. P. 148, 161
Srinivasan, B. S. 66, 82
Staden, F. 107
Staub, J. I. 273, 292
Stevenson, J. 92, 109
Stoddard, S. 12, 35
Stokes, N. A. 177, 181
Stokes, T. F. 152, 162
Stone, W. L. 149, 162
Strickland, T. 285, 292
Strough, P. R. 178, 183
Stryker, S. 9, 35
Stubblefield, H. W. 220, 221, 234
Suelzle, M. 271, 292
Summers, J. A. 85, 110, 267, 271, 289, 292
Sutton, M. S. 133, 139
Switzky, H. N. 21, 33